PRIUS OR PICKUP?

PRIUS
OR
PICKUP?

How the Answers
to Four Simple Questions Explain
America's Great Divide

MARC HETHERINGTON
& JONATHAN WEILER

Houghton Mifflin Harcourt
Boston   New York   2018

For information about permission to reproduce selections
from this book, write to trade.permissions@hmhco.com or to
Permissions, Houghton Mifflin Harcourt Publishing Company,
3 Park Avenue, 19th Floor, New York, New York 10016.

hmhco.com

Library of Congress Cataloging-in-Publication Data
Names: Hetherington, Marc J., 1968- author. | Weiler, Jonathan, 1965- author.
Title: Prius or pickup? : how the answers to four simple questions explain
America's great divide / Marc Hetherington & Jonathan Weiler.
Description: Boston : Houghton Mifflin Harcourt, 2018. |
Includes bibliographical references and index.
Identifiers: LCCN 2018012316 (print) | LCCN 2018029492 (ebook) |
ISBN 9781328866813 (ebook) | ISBN 9781328866783 (hardback)
Subjects: LCSH: Political culture—United States. | Polarization (Social sciences)—
United States. | Political psychology—United States. | BISAC: POLITICAL SCIENCE /
Political Ideologies / Conservatism & Liberalism. | POLITICAL SCIENCE /
Political Ideologies / Fascism & Totalitarianism. | PSYCHOLOGY / Social Psychology. |
PSYCHOLOGY / Personality.
Classification: LCC JK1726 (ebook) | LCC JK1726 .H47 2018 (print) |
DDC 306.20973—dc23
LC record available at https://lccn.loc.gov/2018012316

Book design by Greta D. Sibley

Graphs and charts by Mapping Specialists, Ltd.

Printed in the United States of America

DOC 10 9 8 7 6 5 4 3 2 1

To our parents — one fixed, one mixed,
two fluid, all wonderful

CONTENTS

INTRODUCTION

IF YOU HAD TO BUY a new car, would you be more likely to choose a Prius or a pickup truck?

When you imagine your favorite meal, does it feature classic American dishes like meatloaf and mashed potatoes? Or do you crave more exotic fare, like chicken curry and vegetable biryani?

When you turn on the radio, do you listen to country music or oldies? Or is your dial set to stations that play hip-hop, reggae, or electronic dance music?

If you've ever had the opportunity to choose a name for a child, have you opted for names beginning with soft-sounding letters, such as Louise or Sean, or hard-sounding ones, like David, Katherine, or Tom?

These might seem like odd questions for two political scientists to be asking. But before we explain, bear with us for one more:

When you think about the values you want children to have, do these qualities include things like respect for elders, obedience, and good manners and behavior? Or would you prefer that children be independent, self-reliant, curious, and considerate?

All of these questions have something in common. They tell us something important about the way you view the world—and also about the way you vote.

To understand why these questions are so revealing, consider an anecdote shared by the MSNBC host Joe Scarborough, a former Republican congressman, in a 2013 television documentary. The subject of the film—the making of *All the President's Men,* the landmark movie about Watergate—gave Scarborough the opportunity to recall his upbringing during the tumultuous 1960s. Back then, protest and violence were being broadcast into Americans' homes on a nightly basis. Republican Richard Nixon was competing with Vice President Hubert Humphrey for the nation's highest office, and the two men had very different ideas about the solutions to all that tumult. Although he was just a small boy at the time, Scarborough knew that the country was divided both culturally and politically, and that people had to choose sides. And the choice was clear. "Did you want to join the side of Jane Fonda or John Wayne?" he asked, rhetorically. "My parents chose John Wayne, which meant they chose Nixon."

Consider those two personalities for a moment. John Wayne was tough, the kind of guy who could keep good people safe and set bad guys straight. He was a throwback to a simpler time when men were men. Everyone knew he was the boss. Jane Fonda, on the other hand, symbolized opposition to the war in Vietnam. She had the gall to question the authority of her leaders and encouraged others to try to understand the war through the eyes of America's enemies in the conflict, the North Vietnamese, earning her the moniker Hanoi Jane from her many detractors.

Not everyone alive today is familiar with the mid-twentieth-century incarnations of John Wayne and Jane Fonda, but the archetypes they represent are still with us, even if the names embodying them have changed with time. The political equivalent of John Wayne is now, perhaps, Clint Eastwood. The likes of, say, Ellen DeGeneres now represent what Jane Fonda embodied in the 1960s.

More than political styles, these icons represent something akin to personality types. One group stands for toughness, the other for empathy and compassion. More basically, each of them stands for a particular outlook on life—or, as we term it, a specific worldview.

The term "worldview" is a catchall for someone's deeply ingrained beliefs about the nature of the world and the priorities of a good society. Worldview can encompass all sorts of cultural considerations, such as ideas about philosophy and morality. It is also, and even more significantly, shaped by psychological influences such as your emotions and the imprint left by past experiences.

Of the many factors that make up your worldview, one is more fundamental than any other in determining which side of the divide you gravitate toward: your perception of how dangerous the world is. Fear is perhaps our most primal instinct, after all, so it's only logical that people's level of fearfulness informs their outlook on life.

If you perceive the world as more dangerous, then John Wayne or Clint Eastwood — strength and fortitude — is the antidote. And if you see the world that way, you're also more likely to prefer to drive a big, sturdy vehicle, have a large, obedient dog for a pet, and vote Republican.

If you see the world as less perilous, you feel freer to embrace your inner Jane Fonda or Ellen DeGeneres, and to work harder to understand the perspectives of people who are different from you. You are also, as it turns out, much more likely to eat Indian food, drive a hybrid car, give your kid a gentle-sounding name, and vote for liberal political candidates.

Don't take it from us. Evidence for the connection between worldview and politics can be readily seen in public opinion data collected during the 2016 US presidential campaign. A random sample of Americans was asked which of the following two statements came closest to their view:

1. Our lives are threatened by terrorists, criminals, and illegal immigrants and our priority should be to protect ourselves.
2. It's a big, beautiful world, mostly full of good people, and we must find a way to embrace each other and not allow ourselves to become isolated.

About half of the survey's respondents chose each option, suggesting that Americans are split roughly evenly between the opposing worldviews represented by Jane Fonda and John Wayne. What is more significant, however, is the *politics* of the people who responded one way or the other. Nearly

80 percent of Donald Trump supporters chose the first statement. Nearly 80 percent of Hillary Clinton supporters agreed with the second.

By any reckoning, this is a huge gap, and it's especially significant when you consider that the question didn't ask people about their ideology — that is, whether respondents were conservative or liberal. Rather, the question was about their outlook on life: something that is deeper and more visceral, but which nevertheless seems to be intimately connected to their political preferences.

People's responses to this simple question about worldview seem to map neatly onto other preferences, as well — preferences that, at first glance, appear to have little to do with physical safety. Those Americans who perceive physical threats as ubiquitous also tend to be more suspicious of people who don't look like them and to believe that threats stemming from cultural change, including mass immigration, lurk around nearly every corner. Similarly, people who perceive their surroundings as a "big, beautiful world" rather than a veritable snake pit are also less likely to think that racial and cultural changes are at all dangerous. Indeed, they're much more likely to believe that the real danger lies in failing to *embrace* such changes.

The preferences associated with higher sensitivity to danger don't end there. Americans who see the world as a threatening place are also more likely to prefer meatloaf to chicken curry. They are more likely to listen to country music than hip-hop. They are more likely to drive a pickup than a Prius. And they are more likely to vote Republican than Democrat.

As it turns out, your worldview reveals a *ton* about you. And while some of these revelations might not seem to be inherently interesting to political scientists like us, you would be surprised at how important they really are. The findings from surveys like the one we just mentioned are shedding new light on some of the most pressing political issues of our time, from America's growing partisan divide to the rise of "fake news" to the dark tide of antidemocratic movements rising around the world.

Researchers interested in learning more about these issues, and the role that your worldview plays in them, can begin to figure out what kind of outlook you have by asking the question we mentioned above — the one about how dangerous or safe you perceive the world to be. But we have found an even more comprehensive way of measuring your outlook on life, and thus your preferences about a whole range of things, political and nonpolitical alike.

Asking you about something as simple as your parenting preferences —specifically, the qualities you believe it's most important for children to have—sharpens researchers' picture of your worldview, and hence your politics, from analog to high-definition. This is because your parenting preferences reveal both how dangerous you perceive the world to be *and* what you think is the best way to cope with those dangers. Indeed, your ideas about desirable qualities in children provide perhaps the clearest window onto your worldview, and the potent combination of political and nonpolitical preferences that arise from it. What's more, the fact that politics is divided along this fault line is central to understanding why polarization is on the rise and feels so intractable these days, among so many other disturbing trends.

This book uses two terms to describe the opposing sides of this divide, two words to sum up what is represented by the personas of John Wayne, Jane Fonda, and their ilk: *fixed* and *fluid.*

The term "fixed" describes people who are warier of social and cultural change and hence more set in their ways, more suspicious of outsiders, and more comfortable with the familiar and predictable. People we call "fluid," on the other hand, support changing social and cultural norms, are excited by things that are new and novel, and are open to, and welcoming of, people who look and sound different.

Of course, the world isn't as neat and tidy as this. Not everyone falls squarely into one of these two camps. Rather, worldview is more like a spectrum, with fixed and fluid outlooks anchoring the ends. People who fall between these two poles, who feel more ambivalent about these fundamental questions of life, we might call *mixed.*

People with mixed worldviews also play an important role in the current political landscape, as we will explain. But the clarity of worldview of the most fixed and the most fluid people among us has helped create a political environment in which most of these mixed types feel that—

much as Joe Scarborough observed about the culture wars of the 1960s — they have to pick a side.

The profound differences in the basic outlooks of these two sides help explain why political conflict today is so unmanageable. That is because the fixed and the fluid have become so dominant in the Republican and Democratic Party bases, respectively. These developments not only further entrench the parties and their staunchest adherents in their respective positions, they also limit the ability of Americans of mixed worldview — those who are less set in their ways and might be more willing to compromise — to envision a different path.

Americans' worldviews and their partisan affiliations are now closely aligned, but they didn't used to be. Joe Scarborough's parents chose law, order, and Nixon in response to the tumult of the 1960s. But the Scarboroughs were Democrats, natives of Kentucky, who lived in Georgia and the Florida Panhandle for many years and attended a Baptist church. At that time, lots of Democrats had fixed worldviews and lots of Republicans did, too. Each side also had its share of people with fluid worldviews. There were still partisans, to be sure — but when people looked across the political aisle, they saw many people with whom they had a shared worldview, a basic sensibility about how to think about the world's dangers and opportunities, even if they didn't identify with the same political party.

During the Great Depression and the decades that followed, Republicans and Democrats were divided primarily by issues that were simply less fundamental than their worldviews. Taxing and spending was the nub of party conflict, not worldview. That style of politics made for what now seem like strange bedfellows. The Democratic Party included large majorities of African Americans *and* segregationist southern whites. Although diametrically opposed on racial issues, the two groups bore the brunt of the worst effects of the Great Depression. Hence both benefited from FDR's Democratic Party, which promised to spend lots of government resources to alleviate their suffering. Republicans wanted government to do less of that. Importantly, Democrats may have argued to spend more and Republicans less, but neither argued not to spend *at all*. Hence both sides were open to negotiating those differences.

The terrain on which the parties fought their major battles began to change with the upheaval of the 1960s and 1970s. With massive protests in the streets, cities on fire, and the Vietnam War raging overseas, the parties redefined who they were and to whom they were appealing. Republicans embraced "traditional" positions on race, including opposition to busing and affirmative action; cultural change, including resistance to evolving ideas about the family and personal relationships; and foreign affairs, namely the role that the American military might play on the world stage.

From Nixon to Reagan to George W. Bush to Trump, the party became more John Wayne, more Clint Eastwood—more *fixed*. As might be expected, this shift alienated the Jane Fondas in the old GOP. Democrats, meanwhile, embraced civil rights, feminism, gays and lesbians, and other mounting challenges to existing traditions. From McGovern to Carter to Obama to Hillary Clinton, the party's persona became more Jane Fonda, more Ellen DeGeneres—more *fluid*.

This remarkable transformation can be seen in patterns of congressional representation, then and now. When the 91st Congress was seated in 1969, after Nixon defeated Humphrey, eighteen of the twenty-two senators from the South—the prototypical John Wayne region of the country—were Democrats. In the states stretching from Maine to the Mason-Dixon Line, Jane Fonda country, twelve of the eighteen senators were Republicans. These proportions are hard to conceive of today. In contrast, at the beginning of the 115th Congress, which began shortly after Donald Trump defeated Hillary Clinton to win the presidency in late 2016, John Wayne's South was represented by nineteen Republicans and only three Democrats; New England and the Middle Atlantic states, meanwhile, had two lonely Republicans among their eighteen senators.

As the major political parties redefined themselves, in short, Americans' worldviews and their party commitments became aligned. Southern and working-class whites who thought John Wayne knew how the world really worked no longer felt at home in the Democratic Party. Many fluid Republicans, for whom seeing the world through the eyes of others was a core value, likewise felt uneasy with the take-no-prisoners brand of politics their party was selling.

One consequence of this transformation is that longtime partisans feel whipsawed by their parties' change in course. For instance, old-time, small-government, free enterprise Republicans have typically been pro-immigrant and pro–free trade. Many of these people are surprised and dismayed by the direction their party has taken in recent years, even though its trajectory has been changing for decades. These old-breed Republicans are partisans, and so have struggled to adjust to those developments, focusing instead on their own political priorities: issues such as corporate taxes and government spending. Yet while they are not entirely comfortable with the party's new agenda, many of these people nevertheless voted Republican in 2016. In a different time, some of these free-enterprise Republicans would have gone a different way, but the fixed/fluid divide has created such a rancorous atmosphere that voting Democratic might have felt to them almost treasonous.

Another result of the recent convergence of politics and worldview is that America's main political parties don't just disagree on how to solve problems, they disagree on what the problems are in the first place. When the two sides clash, partisans don't experience mere intellectual disagreement, but rather something much closer to bewilderment. Their counterparts' viewpoint seems not just different, but dangerous. In a Pew Research Center poll taken in June 2016, near or clear majorities of both Republicans and Democrats reported that the other party made them feel "afraid," "angry," and "frustrated."

One especially stark example illustrates how tightly intertwined Americans' worldviews and their politics have become. This anecdote comes not from Joe Scarborough, but from one of his occasional combatants: Donald Trump.

Among the many images one might conjure of President Trump, performing at a poetry slam probably isn't one of them. And yet, a regular feature of his rallies during the 2016 campaign and then after his election was to read a poem. Trump liked to tease the crowd before reading it, asking the throng whether they *really* wanted to hear it, much like a professional wrestler might cup his ear with his hand to urge the crowd to yell louder. The poem, called "The Snake" and based on one of Aesop's fables, was written by Oscar Brown Jr. in 1963 and popularized in a song by the R & B singer Al Wilson in 1968. It describes a "tender hearted woman" who heeds the call of a snake in distress. She lovingly nurtures him back to health and exclaims how beautiful he is, once revived. And how does he repay her extraordinary loving-kindness? By fatally biting her. As she cries out in horror, asking how he could do such a thing, the snake chastises her.

> *"Oh shut up, silly woman," said the reptile with a grin.*
> *"You knew damned well I was a snake before you took me in."*

The message of this ode to wariness, delivered with the subtlety of a sledge-hammer, is that the world is not safe. People trust strangers at their own peril. Trump used the poem during the campaign to warn of the pitfalls of admitting Syrian refugees, and after his election, he deployed it to sound similar warnings about Mexican immigrants. To listeners with a fixed worldview, this is the kind of commonsense thinking that liberals seem blind to. You can never let down your guard; you can never be too careful. Anyone who disagrees is a threat to the country's security.

Trump's instinctive sense of his followers' particular worldview was critical to his success in 2016—but it also incensed people on the other side of the spectrum. Where people with a fixed worldview hear common-sense wisdom, people with a fluid worldview hear nothing but intolerance. As far as they are concerned, many of the alleged threats to America's national security are dangerously overblown. Syrian refugees and Mexican immigrants aren't snakes; they are human beings in desperate need of help. These huddled, yearning masses are trying to make better lives for themselves and their families, like countless immigrants before them. The poem, as it is deployed by Trump, is not a clarion call to common sense. As far as fluid people are concerned, it's a disgusting incitement of prejudice.

Here, as in so many other domains, the fixed and fluid don't even agree on the problem. For a fixed person listening to Trump's poem, the problem is the outsider—the snake. For a fluid listener, on the other hand, the problem is the willingness of Trump and his supporters to discriminate against the outsider, to condemn them without cause.

Worse, the solution for people on one side of the worldview divide actually _creates_ the problem for people on the other side. For fixed people, the solution to the dilemma posed in "The Snake" is to keep outsiders at arm's length; for the fluid, who value diversity and inclusiveness, that path is tantamount to a declaration of civil war. Similarly, fluid people see tragedies like the global refugee crisis and respond by demanding that we welcome needy immigrants with open arms; for the fixed, this is the equivalent of taking a basketful of snakes into your home and dumping them on your living room floor.

Americans have always had worldviews, and America has always had political parties. But disagreements such as the one epitomized by "The Snake" reveal how intense and emotional our national discourse becomes when worldview and party politics collide. The fixed don't just dislike modern-day Democrats because they disagree with them; they also dislike them because they feel Democrats' refusal to acknowledge the threats staring them in the face is a prelude to catastrophe for the nation as a whole. For the fluid, meanwhile, Republicans' callous disregard for those who are different is an existential threat to the nation's ideals. Because the fluid do not perceive Syrian refugees and Mexican immigrants as "snakes" the way the fixed do, they believe that measures like travel bans and border walls _must_ be motivated by prejudice, not real anxiety about security, and that these efforts must be stopped at all costs.

People on both sides of the worldview/party divide, in short, have come to see their opponents not simply as strangers, but as a collective menace. It is this breakdown, rather than any partisan principles about the proper size and role of government, that may prove to be the real existential threat for a democracy like America's.

• • •

This book explores how our worldviews came to divide us, and how serious the consequences of this shift have been—for America, but also for democracies around the world. It tells a story that has not been told before, but which it will be essential for citizens and policymakers alike to understand if we are to stand a chance of overcoming the challenges confronting our societies today: challenges of which toxic partisanship and political gridlock are only the beginning.

The crisis of worldview politics is so intractable in large part because it is rooted in human psychology. People develop different worldviews because of impulses and orientations that emanate from deep inside them. Startle reflexes and disgust responses, impulses beyond people's conscious control, now map eerily well onto their political beliefs. Those automatic responses, when they act in combination with other learned responses from people's upbringing and life experiences, inform our preferences on a wide array of political opinions about matters ranging from race and gender to immigration and gay rights to gun control and constitutional interpretation, driven by wildly divergent understandings about basic values connected to societal hierarchy, cultural difference, and openness to new ideas. That is one reason why those on opposite sides of the worldview divide struggle so mightily to understand one another when it comes to race, culture, and safety.

Worldviews, and the psychological factors that shape them, also inform people's preferences about a range of issues that are distinct from politics. This is why a handful of questions about desirable qualities in children have proved to be such a useful tool for measuring the gulf between the opposing sides of the worldview divide. Some of our most basic life choices are connected to our worldviews: where we decide to live, what types of jobs we tend to find most satisfying, how long and where we decide to go to school, and whether and where we prefer to worship. Fluid people are drawn to cities, whereas fixed people favor the country. The fixed find strength in prayer, while the fluid are often nonbelievers.

Viewed through this psychological prism, the subtlest differences in personal taste take on new meaning. Whereas these minor choices would have revealed precious little about your politics in a different era, nowadays the TV shows you watch, the coffee shops you frequent, even the brands of beer you drink say a lot about how you vote. As a result, these preferences are now vital to understanding the American political landscape, including why the parties and the people who identify with them seem more like tribal enemies than members of a single national community who disagree about some things.

These dimensions of worldview politics are fascinating—but taken together, they have grim implications. For instance, as politics and worldview have aligned, partisans' dislike of the other party has deepened, increasing the motivation partisans feel to see the world in ways favorable to their side and unfavorable to the other. To be sure, people have always been disposed to see the world the way they want to see it, but this human tendency has intensified dramatically when it comes to politics, thanks to the dovetailing of partisanship and basic human psychology.

Partisan news and social media have extended the reach of this process. People who really care about politics can now marinate in a pool of information that favors their party, and their motivation to do so is stronger now that worldview cleaves one side from the other; the cable news shows that one encounters today, much like one's fellow citizens, are either comforting and relatable, or so different as to seem downright dangerous. Even more importantly, in the new media environment this party-specific information infects people who don't care very much about politics—the large mass of Americans who used to moderate conflict—much like secondhand smoke harms nonsmokers. People do not have to listen to talk radio, or watch Fox News or MSNBC, or visit red or blue websites to be affected by their hyperpartisan content. They simply need to know people who willingly expose themselves to these sources; these primary consumers (the smokers, in our analogy) spread their carcinogens through their social or social media networks.

For these reasons and more, the worldview divide has the potential to imperil American democracy. Scholars in the past have been especially concerned about people with fixed worldviews, believing their wariness about racial and ethnic difference and desire for strong, uncompromising leadership could make possible the rise of a leader who challenges democratic norms. Many commentators, particularly on the left but more than a few on the right as well, have expressed this fear about Donald Trump. The United States has never elected a president who made his sympathy for a more autocratic leadership style clearer during the campaign than Trump did.

Sure enough, Americans with fixed worldviews were central to securing for Trump the Republican nomination in May 2016. But the story is more complicated, and more worrisome, than it may seem at first glance. It was not just people with fixed worldviews who supported Trump, but people whose outlooks on life are a combination of fixed and fluid. Some did it because they were partisans who hated the other side so much they couldn't vote for it; some did it because their preferences are not as different from the fixed as fluid people probably believe is possible. And some did it because they were scared of terrorism and social change and believed a John Wayne–like president could keep them safer than a Jane Fonda–like one.

Electing a leader who challenges democratic norms takes more people than can be found on the fixed end of the spectrum alone. Yet this side of the worldview divide *has* had an outsized influence on the entire US political system, despite the fact that not everyone in America shares fixed people's outlook. For example, when it comes to tolerating difference in race and ethnicity, people with fixed worldviews are more like average Americans—the "mixed"—than are people with fluid worldviews. Thus, rhetoric that might seem deeply intolerant to the fluid might not seem that way to anyone else. In addition, virtually everyone becomes less invested in abstract democratic ideals when deeply frightened, and more open to leadership that promises safety and protection. Opportunistic leaders can gin up fear about a host of issues, making voters think it's better to be safe than sorry—a classically fixed way of thinking, but one that leads to some very dark places.

Americans across the worldview spectrum succumb to their basest survival instincts under such circumstances. So, it seems, do people the world over. Europe, like the United States, recently has seen the rise of

right-wing populist leaders railing against immigration, European integration, and open borders. And sure enough, the same four parenting
questions that reveal so much about Americans' political preferences
also explain a lot about what is happening on the other side of the Atlantic. Worldview was central to the Brexit vote in Britain. It is also central to support for right-wing parties like France's National Front and the
Alternative for Germany (AfD) Party. The same is happening in places as
diverse as Hungary, Poland, Austria, and Denmark. Whether the influx
of immigrants is objectively more like a trickle or a torrent, citizens of all
these places perceive a flood pouring into their countries with the potential to change their culture, a dynamic that heightens the appeal of any
leader who promises to Make (insert country name) Great Again.

In all of these places, people on opposing sides of the worldview
divide have fundamentally different ideas about the problems their countries face, and the solutions that are necessary to address them. But for
fluid types, the way ahead looks especially tough. In Western societies,
at least, the John Wayne–style worldview seems to have certain inherent advantages over the Jane Fonda one. More people appear to have the
former outlook than the latter one. In recent years, moreover, fluid voters
have remained politically competitive thanks to the support of the West's
growing population of racial and ethnic minorities—people who are not
necessarily fluid themselves, but who have been pushed into a political
allegiance with fluid voters by the xenophobia emanating from the opposite side of the spectrum. But these alliances are tenuous, and may not
hold. If they fail, the affected nations will be highly vulnerable to autocratic leaders who could potentially undermine the foundations of liberal
democracy in the very places where it has been the strongest. Preventing
this nightmare from becoming reality is one of the most significant challenges of our time—and one of the ultimate goals of this book.

PRIUS OR PICKUP?

Republicans Are from Mars, Democrats Are from Venus

EVEN IF YOU HAVEN'T READ John Gray's 1992 best seller *Men Are from Mars, Women Are from Venus,* you probably know the punch line: there are fundamental psychological differences between the two sexes. It wouldn't be much of a stretch for someone today to claim the same thing about America's two main political factions: Republicans are from Mars, Democrats are from Venus. That certainly sums up the feeling that many people have today in the United States, where it often seems that our political opponents are not simply from different sides of the aisle, but from different planets altogether.

Of course, partisans are not aliens from faraway worlds. They're not even members of different species (much as people in the opposing party might take comfort in the thought). But that is not to say that they aren't different in a fundamental, even physical way.

Believe it or not, Democrats' and Republicans' bodies and minds do appear to be different. Political scientists have only just begun to figure out how and why, but the realization of this difference emerged from a simple, incandescent fact: people from different political "planets" seem to experience our world in fundamentally different ways.

The emerging field of biopolitics, which studies the intersection between human biology and political beliefs, provides some arresting insights into the bodily factors that help inform our political commitments. Some differences in people's political beliefs appear to have their roots in reactions that occur before conscious thought begins. They seem to be wired in people's physiology, and expressed in their reflexes and in other unconscious ways.

This probably seems like a controversial claim. If people's political beliefs are hardwired, wouldn't it mean that Americans all emerge from the womb as Democrats and Republicans? It doesn't: physiology does not determine how people behave politically. Instead, how a person's physiological differences express themselves depends on that person's environment—the context in which he or she lives. It is the combination of wiring and environment that is important, not solely one or the other.

Most research on ordinary citizens identifies early-childhood socialization, particularly the role of parents in a child's life, as one of the biggest determinants of that child's future political outlook. Other forms of socialization—whether people's parents and those in their communities were Republicans or Democrats, religious or not, rich or poor—are important, too. The genes children inherit from their parents are thus one factor among many. Indeed, physiology and socialization likely reinforce each other—but not always. Moral psychologist Jonathan Haidt puts it well when he observes that we're born with a "first draft of the mind"—a first draft that can be edited, if not completely rewritten, by familial, social, and cultural contexts.

But while people's wiring is certainly not the whole story, it does provide an important window on their politics, because physiological differences and political differences appear to be in sync to a degree that cannot be explained by chance alone. When examined closely, these differences offer a powerful clue about why American voters are so divided today—and why it can be so difficult to see our opponents as human beings rather than the space aliens they so often seem to be. The answer, it seems, is that we can't really agree on what kind of planet we're on in the first place.

• • •

Biopolitics research finds that liberals are different on average from conservatives in the way they react to the world. But the terms "liberal" and "conservative" are more slippery than one might realize. In truth, there are two versions of both categories, one type that is more operational (signifying whether a person values more government taxing and spending, or less of both) and one type that is more symbolic (signifying whether someone values order and tradition, or individual autonomy and the freedom to challenge tradition). The more important of these two versions for most people, the version that defines their political identities, is the second one—the symbolic one. In fact, it is very common for Americans to label themselves symbolically as conservative, but express operational policy preferences that are actually liberal, and vice versa. That is because a staggering percentage of Americans don't understand what it means to be an *operational* conservative or liberal. This is an important point that we will return to later, but the upshot for now is that, if researchers like us want to study people's actual ideologies, we need to be careful, and very specific, about the sorts of questions we ask.

In measuring people's ideology, the biopolitics researchers whose studies we describe here work to unlock the more symbolic component, by using something called the Wilson-Patterson Attitude Inventory. This questionnaire asks people how favorably they feel toward a wide range of things that are now intimately connected to major American parties' policy platforms: issues such as school prayer, pornography, women's equality, the death penalty, illegal immigration, patriotism, and free trade, among others. Conservatives are more favorable toward school prayer, the death penalty, and patriotism, and less favorable toward pornography, women's equality, illegal immigration, and free trade. Liberals are the reverse. Biopolitics researchers use these answers to measure how conservative or liberal people are, for the purposes of their studies. It is important to note that these items do not center on how much government ought to spend on this program or that program. In other words, the inventory taps the more politically potent symbolic form of ideology.

What researchers find, once they carefully pinpoint people's political ideologies and then study their behaviors in the lab, is that the average liberal and the average conservative respond differently to the same experiences. The most important of these differences seems to be how people respond to situations that might be considered dangerous. People on the right are more heavily attuned to danger than those on the left. This makes conservatives erect more barriers—more defense mechanisms—between themselves and their environments. Because danger is less of a concern for liberals, on the other hand, they appear to have fewer boundaries, and thus are freer to pursue less conventional paths and ideas.

In their book *Predisposed,* John Hibbing and his coauthors—among the pioneers of biopolitics research—report an array of findings about physiological differences between liberals and conservatives. In one experiment, subjects received a palette of objects to examine. Some, like tarantulas, were threatening. Others, like beach balls, were not. People were free to cast their gaze on whatever they wished. To allow researchers to observe which objects people looked at, and for how long, subjects wore devices that tracked their eyes and measured the amount of time they focused on the more and less threatening objects.

Both conservatives and liberals dwelled longer on threatening than nonthreatening objects. This is only natural, from an evolutionary perspective; if human beings were not attuned to threats, predators would have gotten us long ago. But while people of all political persuasions were clearly attuned to the threatening objects, some people were much more attuned than others.

Matching the responses from the Wilson-Patterson Inventory with the results of the eye-tracking tests, the researchers revealed that conservatives dwelled *much* longer on the threatening objects than liberals did. Whereas liberals spent less than a half second more time looking at the negative images than the positive images, conservatives spent more than one and a half seconds more looking at the negative than the positive. Given that the exercise lasted a total of eight seconds, the difference is so large that "one vision specialist referred to it as an 'eternity,'" according to Hibbing and his coauthors. This finding demonstrates that conservatives are more sensitive to danger than liberals.

Similarly, researchers have found that people's reflexes — precognitive responses that occur outside the control of people's conscious minds — also match their political beliefs. Two reflexes in particular, startle and gag, are not only strong indications of how sensitive people are to signals of danger in their environment, they are also predictive of the direction they lean politically.

We've all been startled before, like when someone knocks unexpectedly on your door or when a car cuts in front of you on a busy road. These experiences set in motion a number of responses in your body. Your heart rate increases, your blood pressure rises, and your breathing accelerates. More subtly, your body secretes a flood of cortisol, the hormone linked to stress and fear. All these responses put you into fight-or-flight mode.

Everyone startles, but some people react more strongly than others — for instance, by blinking more after being startled. More blinks mean a stronger startle reflex. Thus, by measuring how many times people blink after being startled, researchers can assess whether people are more or less sensitive to danger.

To startle their subjects, researchers outfit them with headphones and, without warning, blow a loud burst of white noise into their ears. A device called a blink-amplitude meter counts how many times people blink in the succeeding seconds. Then the researchers check to see if there is a correlation between the respondents' number of blinks and their answers to the ideology questions in the Wilson-Patterson Inventory.

The correlation is clear: conservatives, on average, blink much more than liberals, yet another indication that they are more attuned to danger. But the researchers also found another, more disturbing correlation: among whites, those with stronger startle reflexes express more resentment toward African Americans than those with weaker startle reflexes.

These results suggest that the tendency to express more negative feelings toward people from different racial and ethnic backgrounds may emanate from deep inside us. How people grow up and are socialized is critical, of course. But the link between startle reflex and racial attitudes indicates that processes deeply ingrained in the body, likely even beyond conscious control, play a big part in these biases, as well.

That is not to say that people aren't responsible for their racial attitudes. They have the capacity to overcome their initial impulses, whether about race or anything else. For example, many people who suffer from anxiety know that their first reaction to an anxiety-provoking situation is to feel, well, anxious, but that hard work and practice can get them past that initial reaction. People who are paralyzed by anxiety have a strong motivation to do that hard work, because they would have a hard time functioning otherwise.

But this analogy also highlights a difference between racial predisposition and many other mental patterns. When it comes to racial attitudes, the motivation to do the work necessary to overcome those initial reactions is unlikely to be very strong. If a white person harbors negative attitudes about people of color, they may not even realize or acknowledge they have such attitudes. Until recently, moreover, racism of this kind was socially acceptable in many white circles. Some would argue that it still is. That makes it all the less likely that more racially biased whites would do the hard work necessary to confront and overcome those biases.

Like the startle reflex, the gag reflex—an indicator of the defense mechanism known as disgust—is an evolutionary adaptation designed to keep humans safe. When people encounter something that might be dangerous if ingested, they gag. Think about what occurs when you encounter a large pile of smelly dog feces or a splatter of vomit on the street, or when you sniff a carton of milk that's a few too many days past its expiration date. You recoil. It feels like you might vomit yourself.

Some people experience this reflex more intensely than others, possibly because of the way we evolved to eat. It is plausible that humans differ in their levels of disgust because we are omnivores. As humans evolved, people developed the ability to find sustenance in a diverse array of nutritional options, making them more open to a wide variety of tastes. But that development also required more sophisticated defense mechanisms to help weed out of our diet any substances that could be harmful.

Properly calibrated disgust, therefore, allowed people to eat more calories than they would be able to consume if they were too easily disgusted, while keeping them safer from harm than they would be if they consumed things indiscriminately.

You have probably already anticipated where this is going: although everyone has a gag reflex, conservatives have stronger ones than liberals. In response to disgusting images like a person eating worms or a soiled toilet, conservatives' hands sweat more than liberals' do, suggesting greater arousal and, with it, a stronger gag reflex. Like the startle reflex, the gag reflex sheds light on attitudes relevant to politics. People whose hands perspire more in response to the image of a person with a mouthful of worms also tend to evaluate homosexuality more negatively and oppose same-sex marriage more than people whose hands perspire less. This provides further evidence that our attitudes and preferences about some particularly divisive political matters have their roots deep down inside us and may be beyond our conscious control.

These tendencies and reflexes can become habits of the mind, with the potential to affect things as fundamental as the shapes of people's brains. Specifically, brain-imaging studies carried out both in the United States and Great Britain demonstrate that the size of the amygdala, which is the part of the brain that governs survival instincts, tends to be larger among conservatives than liberals. Because people's brain structure changes in response to their behavior, it make sense to think that the larger amygdalae in conservatives develop, in part, because of their greater physiological wariness.

These studies might strike you as absolutely crazy. A laboratory setting in which people are being poked, prodded, and imaged by professors in lab coats does not even come close to approximating the real world, after all. And can our reactions to politics *really* involve so little deliberation? These studies have their critics among social scientists, too, because they rely on extremely small sample sizes that are not representative of the population as a whole.

These weaknesses are both a feature and a bug of biopolitics. The materials necessary to conduct experiments like these are expensive and require lab equipment that is usually housed at a university. It would be cost-prohibitive to carry out such studies on a nationally representative sample of Americans. It would be impossible, for example, for survey interviewers to outfit a couple of thousand people with headphones and blink-amplitude meters during visits to their homes. (The interviewees probably would not be thrilled either.) Similarly, brain-imaging machines are not exactly portable.

But there is good reason to believe that these studies reflect larger truths about the American electorate, because other studies that *do* feature large representative samples of Americans provide corroborating evidence that our political beliefs are rooted in our physiology. When researchers simply ask people how grossed out they are by seeing someone vomit, observing maggots on a piece of meat, or smelling spoiled milk, the answers also line up with attitudes that are relevant to politics. For example, people who report being more sensitive to feeling disgust are also more likely to believe that most people aren't "honest and trustworthy."

This makes theoretical sense because one role that disgust plays is to protect people from harm; interacting less with people who are unfamiliar is itself a strategy for reducing harm. In addition, people who report high disgust sensitivity are also more likely to identify themselves as conservative than those with low disgust sensitivity. And those differences in people's disgust sensitivity also reveal differences in their attitudes about specific political issues. Take immigration. People who report, for example, being particularly grossed out by touching a toilet seat in a public bathroom also report more strongly anti-immigrant attitudes than people who are less grossed out by touching a public toilet seat.

These measures of trust, disgust, and perceptions of danger are essentially ways of tracking one simple trait: wariness, the degree of caution and vigilance people employ when engaging with the world around them. Wariness can be beneficial, protecting people from harm. But it can also take a toll, taxing their nervous systems to an unhealthy degree.

People who are especially wary, therefore, must develop shortcuts in order to help them cope with the contingencies of their environment, and the automatic responses that environmental stimuli generate in their bodies and minds. These shortcuts, taken together, provide an important window on our personalities and help illuminate why people's physiological responses would be so helpful in explaining their political beliefs.

For readers who don't feel particularly wary, it might be useful to imagine how a wary nervous system feels to the person who possesses one. Consider what new parents experience during the first several weeks of their firstborn's life. Anyone who has gone through it might remember the ceaseless uncertainty, not to mention the sleep deprivation. The combination has nervous systems working overtime. Given a newborn's physical vulnerability, it feels like just about anything could go wrong. Threats seem ubiquitous. She could drown in the bathtub. The blankets in her crib could suffocate her. She could come home from a quick trip to the grocery store with a terrible virus or horrible bacteria. To cope, new parents make their world smaller. Their circle of trust tightens. Family is probably in it, and maybe—maybe—the closest of friends. Because life feels balanced on a knife's edge, outsiders are, at best, unhelpful. At worst, they're the people who wake the baby up once she has finally gotten to sleep.

Imagine if a person felt that way all the time. If he or she didn't take steps to cope with the sensation that danger lurks around every corner, their life would be deeply unpleasant—and probably fairly short, given what we know about the impact of stress on human longevity.

Personality traits can help wary people manage this bombardment of perceived threats. This is because people's personalities shape their interactions with the world: whether, for example, to be more outgoing or less, or whether to take more risks or fewer. If a person's nervous system is hardwired to make them more wary rather than less, developing an introverted and risk-averse personality can help them to limit the number of stressful situations they have to experience. Those same defense mechanisms, it turns out, will also incline them to think about politics in particular ways.

Some personality traits appear to be more influential in this regard than others. Psychologists who have studied personality have established, based on hundreds of studies that have included many thousands of subjects, that it can be captured along five dimensions. These dimensions are commonly known as the Big Five. Two of them—openness and conscientiousness—are of most relevance for understanding how people approach and steer clear of perceived threats.

These two traits, openness and conscientiousness, are also, importantly, associated with political beliefs. People who are more open to new experiences tend to be more liberal, and those who are more conscientious tend to be more conservative.

To understand the connection between personality and biopolitics, consider the function that these personality traits serve. Openness or its absence might be viewed as an adaptation based on how much danger a person perceives. If danger is everywhere, a trait that minimizes contact with the unfamiliar could prove very useful. Experiences that people have already had and people whom they have already met are inherently safer than novel ones. New experiences could be good, too, but they might also be dangerous, so it makes sense to proceed with caution. People who are more wary want to play it safe, to avoid the unfamiliar, and to react more quickly to potential uncertainty. In contrast, people who score high in openness tend to like things that are different. These people are, as a team of researchers has put it, "curious, creative and arty" types who enjoy "seek[ing] out novel experiences and [who] adopt unconventional beliefs." It is easy to see how differences on this personality dimension might mirror people's biopolitical differences, too.

The second personality characteristic that divides the left and right is conscientiousness. Its implications for our political beliefs are less obvious, but no less important, than those of openness.

As psychologists understand it, conscientiousness is a tendency to value dependability and dutifulness, order and organization. Routines and practices that increase predictability serve an especially important psychological function for anyone who perceives a lot of danger in the world, because they add order to a chaos-riven environment. Perhaps the starkest analogy is life in the military, with its related imperatives for order, tidiness, and hierarchy in the face of persistent threats to physical well-being. As Jack Nicholson's Colonel Jessup memorably intoned in the film *A Few Good Men,* "We follow orders or people die."

Whether military units or residential neighborhoods, tight-knit communities are of central import to people with personalities high in conscientiousness, perhaps because there is safety among trustworthy allies. Arlie Hochschild captures this well in *Strangers in Their Own Land,* a book detailing the views and experiences of working-class white voters in rural Louisiana. Describing one of her subjects, Janice, Hochschild articulates both the woman's values in life and the things that she finds threatening.

> Janice feels proud to have a rooted self, a self based in a busy, dense, stable community of relatives, co-parishioners, and friends. A newer *cosmopolitan* self, one that seemed uprooted, loosely attached to an immediate community, prepared to know a lot of people just a little bit, a mobile, even migratory self—this seemed to be coming into vogue. Such a self took pride in exposure to a diverse set of moral codes, but did a person with that kind of self end up thinking "anything goes"? It was frightening. It was wrong. And Janice was having none of it.

Communities that offer their members protection must themselves be protected. Norms play that role. If you visit the homes of those high in conscientiousness, for example, you are likely to find lawns well kept and flower beds free of weeds. These people mostly go to church, as churches serve as centers of communities and purveyors of traditional values that have stood the test of time. What might seem to those who lack conscientiousness to be small details make the community a better place. Neighbors care what other community members do, in essence policing community standards. If you live in a suburban area, which is likely to be heavily populated by people high in conscientiousness, see what happens if you don't mow your lawn for a couple of weeks or fail to replace a broken mailbox in a timely fashion. Count how many of your neighbors take it upon themselves to comment on your yard and your mailbox.

Among people who are lower in conscientiousness, individual expression, not hewing to community standards, is a badge of honor. People who are low in conscientiousness might take notice of norm violators, just as people who are high in conscientious do—but they might embrace them rather than shun them, as people who are high in conscientiousness might do. More generally, people who are low in conscientiousness are likely to thrive in communities that embrace a broader range of social and cultural practices; these people tend to regard that breadth of acceptable behavior and free expression as a community strength, not a threat. Whereas that might be a great virtue in their eyes, it might seem like chaos to those at the other end of the conscientiousness spectrum.

Of course, lower-conscientious liberals have their own norms and constraints on individual expression, and these can be grating to nonliberals (and to some liberals, too, although they are loath to admit it in this polarized time). For example, they vigorously police language about historically disadvantaged groups, such as African Americans, Hispanics, LGBT people, and religious minorities.

But norms serve a different function for people who are higher and lower in conscientiousness. For more conscientious people, norms distinguish members of one's own group from members of other groups, helping to keep insiders safe by keeping outsiders out. For people who are low in conscientiousness, by contrast, norms are designed in part to *protect* outsiders, to be more inclusive than exclusive.

None of this is to say that one set of norms is inherently better than the other. Both have their purposes. The key is that they are different. One promotes homogeneity, the other heterogeneity.

The personality traits people adopt, in short, help them cope with the uncertainty of the world around them. This has clear ramifications for politics. People who perceive a lot of danger in the world will gravitate toward leaders and policies that mitigate the threat: leaders who project unwavering strength, and policies that emphasize security first. For people who see the world as less dangerous, on the other hand, the real danger is discrimination. Their worldview will point them toward leaders who celebrate diversity and policies that focus on inclusivity.

Biopolitics and the study of personality have a lot to teach us about the way people behave politically. But these things aren't very easy to study. Quite the opposite, in fact. Biopolitics research is difficult and expensive to do. And conducting accurate studies about personality requires researchers to perform extensive batteries of tests on their subjects, which limits the range of their findings. It would be impractical to carry out a full-blown personality test on a political survey, as the questions required to measure personality would outnumber the political ones.

Fortunately, there is another, much simpler way to gauge how people view the world, and how their perceptions are connected to their beliefs.

Four questions about the most important qualities for children to have —a subject that is ostensibly far removed from politics—have become a powerful tool for understanding the outlooks that individual Americans have, and thus the psychological factors that undergird their political beliefs and political identities. Since at least the 1950s, scholars have been using questions about parenting as a window on people's politics, although it is not clear that researchers back then understood exactly why these questions worked. Over time, however, our understanding of these questions' efficacy has sharpened, as has the content and framing of the questions themselves.

The four questions used here are the brainchild of one of political psychology's pioneers, Stanley Feldman. In the 1980s Feldman was especially interested in values, which he thought scholars were thinking about too narrowly. Many researchers were focused on moral values, which— while important—are only the beginning of people's value commitments, Feldman knew. Indeed, moral values might be better thought of as a subset of a broader set of values.

One area Feldman thought especially ripe for inquiry was the degree to which people valued what he described as conformity on the one hand

and freethinking on the other. He saw in Pat Buchanan's fiery culture-war speech at the Republican National Convention in 1992 the essence of his thinking captured on the political stage. Buchanan lambasted Democrats for a range of offenses, such as pursuing "radical feminism," embracing the "amoral idea" of gay rights, and favoring "discriminating against religious schools." To Feldman, what connected these several fronts in the culture war was that they turned on whether people wanted to preserve old traditions (and therefore valued conformity) or challenge them (and therefore valued freethinking). Important political choices seemed to be motivated by where people stood on the freethinking/conformity continuum.

Because he sat on the American National Election Studies (ANES) board, Feldman was able to include on the 1992 ANES survey four questions about parenting, which he believed would prompt people to reveal this critical set of values. Although scholars were slow to incorporate these particular questions about qualities in children into their research, they have embraced them in recent years because of their incredible effectiveness for decoding people's politics in the present era.

These four simple questions do much more than reveal differences in people's preferences for conformity or freethinking, moreover. They are something of a Rosetta stone in understanding contemporary American public opinion.

The questions are typically asked as follows:

Although there are a number of qualities that people feel children should have, every person thinks that some are more important than others. I am going to read you pairs of desirable qualities. Please tell me which one you think is more important for a child to have.

1. Independence versus respect for elders
2. Obedience versus self-reliance
3. Curiosity versus good manners
4. Being considerate versus being well behaved

Most parents would likely say that most or all of the eight qualities listed are important. But the questions make people choose which are more important to them—and the choices they make are extremely revealing.

The answers people give tell us something about their worldviews—their basic outlooks on life. At its root, someone's worldview is a reflection of their primal alertness to the relative safety or danger of their environment. Despite all that humans have in common, after all, some people have always been more inclined to believe that the world is a place to explore and revel in, while others have tended to see it as fraught with danger—and to want, as a result, to make it as predictable as possible. From a caveman perspective, this is intuitive: the more ordered and predictable you can make your environment, the greater your chances of avoiding its pitfalls. On the other hand, when your environment has fewer pitfalls to begin with, you are freer to explore it without having to worry.

The parenting questions reveal this outlook in an indirect way. Taken literally, people's responses to these questions tell us whether they believe children should have lots of room to follow their own path (be independent, be curious) or should instead follow directions and stay on the straight and narrow (be obedient, respect their elders). Which of these paths is best ought to depend on how dangerous people think the world is: whether they think the world is a big, beautiful place to explore, or whether it is a dangerous place that requires them to batten down the hatches.

If the world is dangerous, giving children a lot of leeway might endanger them. Think what always happens to Curious George in the inaptly titled children's book series when he roams around a city with potential perils everywhere. Things rarely end well. On the other hand, if the world is generally a safe place, you can let children explore it on their own without fear of catastrophe. The classic children's book by Dr. Seuss, *Oh, the Places You'll Go!*, channels this mind-set to a tee.

For people who are more concerned about danger, the solution is to make life orderly. This holds true in terms of both their physical and mental environments—the outside world that they experience, and what goes on inside their minds.

These questions about desirable qualities in children help pinpoint people's worldviews, but they don't offer insight into where those worldviews come from in the first place. It's likely, however, that they are shaped by a combination of nature and nurture. For example, someone might have a physiology that disposes them to be more open, more fluid. But early life experiences—being disciplined severely by their parents, or enduring a great tragedy—may cause them to perceive more danger in the world around them. For example, a young American growing up in the 1930s and early 1940s might have written poetry and daydreamed a lot when he was young. Then war came. He joined the Marine Corps and went off to fight in faraway Asia. That intense experience made him much warier of potential dangers, and his worldview came to reflect it. It was not determined at birth.

The parenting questions themselves are so useful because they show *how* people impose order on a dangerous and potentially chaotic world— the steps they take, the devices they use, to make their outer and inner environments more orderly, predictable, and safe. A central theme that runs through these questions is people's orientation toward *hierarchy:* respect for elders, obedience, good manners, and good behavior. Strict parents are more hierarchical, stressing those qualities that reinforce a more hierarchical structure in the home. Strong, unwavering leaders play the same role in the political world. Thus, these people's political preferences tend to mirror their preferences in the social world.

In addition to driving decisions about the external world, deferring to a leader's judgment removes what could be crippling uncertainty in the mind itself. Following directions from established authorities, like presidents, parents, and preachers, can impose order in the mind as well. To borrow a term from psychology, following the lead of those at the top of the hierarchy provides people *cognitive closure:* clear-cut answers to life's many questions.

Not any leader will do. A strict father, embodied by Donald Trump in the political world, is the model for someone who perceives dangers and seeks the orderly. A nurturing one, embodied by Barack Obama, is the antithesis, offering nuanced shades of gray, not simple, clear-cut answers. Moreover, the latter's worldview encourages people to challenge existing hierarchies and traditional pathways. To people who value hierarchy, undermining traditions is dangerous because they are what have kept dangers at bay for millennia.

In that sense, while a candidate's style can reveal whether he or she is the "right kind of leader," his or her approach to existing traditions and conventions is even more important. Because they have been the bulwarks of order and certainty against a dangerous world and have passed the test of history, the proof is in the pudding. Having served society well in the past, those same venerable pathways will serve it well in the future, too.

By their very nature, cultural traditions entrench existing social hierarchies, even if people don't consciously think about them that way. For instance, traditional understandings of family elevate husband over wife, parents over children. Similarly, traditional religious understandings tend to elevate men over women, heterosexuals over homosexuals. The same is true when it comes to race and ethnicity in the United States. Historically, whites have occupied the top of America's racial hierarchy, with other races and ethnicities below them. Sad to say, but white supremacy is an American tradition.

All these things, taken together, explain why these nonpolitical questions about parenting reveal so much about people's politics. It's because they also tell us something deeper: how people view the world in which they live.

These two different ways of viewing the world can be boiled down to basic types: one that we've taken to calling fixed, the other fluid.

People with what we call a fixed worldview are more fearful of potential dangers, and are likely to prefer clear and unwavering rules to help them navigate all the threats. This mind-set leads them to support social structures in which hierarchy and order prevail, the better to ensure people don't stray too far from the straight and narrow.

By contrast, people with what we call a fluid worldview are less likely to perceive the world as dangerous. By extension, they will endorse social structures that allow individuals to find their own way in life. They are more inclined to believe that a society's well-being requires giving people greater latitude to question, to explore, and to discover their authentic selves.

These different ways of viewing the world are encapsulated by different answers to Stanley Feldman's four questions about the qualities people value in children. Fixed people opt for respect for elders, obedience, good manners, and being well behaved. Fluid people choose independence, self-reliance, curiosity, and considerateness.

In the many surveys we've administered over the years, we have found that on average 16 percent of Americans are typically purely fixed, giving the fixed response to all four questions. Another 26 percent are mostly fixed, providing three of four fixed responses. Thirteen percent of Americans typically reveal themselves to be purely fluid, and another 19 percent are mostly fluid. The last quarter of the population typically provides exactly two fixed and two fluid answers.

Based on these findings, we can make some basic generalizations about Americans' worldviews. Worldview is essentially a spectrum, with a purely fixed outlook on one end and a purely fluid outlook on the other end. Most Americans—a bit above two-thirds of the population—sit somewhere in the middle. Across the surveys we fielded, an average of 29 percent of Americans occupy the extreme ends of the spectrum. Yet the fixed side of the spectrum has a marked numerical advantage: 42 percent of Americans fall on that side, whereas only 32 percent fall on the fluid side. The remaining 26 percent are dead center; these Americans are equal parts fixed and fluid.

For simplicity's sake, going forward we will refer to those who select all four qualities designated fluid as "fluid," and those who select all four qualities designated fixed as "fixed." These definitions serve to highlight the contrast between the fixed and the fluid. Anyone who falls in between these two extremes, we'll refer to as "mixed." The mixed are not necessarily as different from the people on the extremes as these simple categories suggest. It will come as a surprise to many that the mixed are often more like the fixed than they are like the fluid.

These simple terms also serve to connect the qualities that researchers have pinpointed in their research using the qualities people value in children with those they have captured in biopolitics studies. And there is reason to believe that both types of research are, at their root, describing the same psychological phenomena. In studies where we have presented people with these parenting questions and also asked them to report how much disgust they feel and how much they trust other people, we have found strong evidence of a correlation between the parenting questions and things like disgust and trust. This suggests that worldview captures the same essence that measures used in biopolitics and personality psychology do, which are similarly revealing about people's political beliefs, but much more challenging for researchers to assess.

For instance, the 2012 Cooperative Campaign Analysis Project (CCAP), which asked people a set of questions about their disgust sensitivity along with the qualities they value in children, found that people with a fixed worldview reacted much more intensely in their disgust. For example, they were twice as likely to say they "strongly agreed" that it made them sick to their stomach to see someone vomit compared with those who had a fluid worldview (33 percent to 16 percent). The fixed and fluid also reacted differently to questions about how disgusted they would be if they were about to drink a glass of milk and smelled that it was spoiled. Forty-seven percent of the fluid described this scenario as very or extremely disgusting, while fully 70 percent of the fixed did. Maybe that is why the fixed reported being more likely to use a hand sanitizer like Purell regularly. Forty-four percent of those with a fixed worldview said they use it at least a few times a week, if not more. Only about 20 percent of the fluid said they do.

Similarly, the 2016 CCAP asked people the desirable qualities in children questions and two questions about how much they trust others. As expected, a majority of the fluid chose the trusting response in both cases: more than half said that "most people can be trusted," and two-thirds think that "most people try to be fair." The fixed respondents, on the other hand, overwhelmingly chose the less trusting responses. Less than half of fixed people, apparently, think people try to be fair. Less than one-third think most people can be trusted.

The questions about desirable qualities in children are also strongly predictive of Americans' symbolic ideology—how they label themselves politically. A significant chunk of both the fixed and fluid label themselves moderate, but there is much doubt among scholars that people have any idea what "moderate" actually means. Rather, people seem to embrace the term, like they embrace "independent," because it sounds good to them, not because they are particularly moderate or independent. So we focus here on the majority of people who label themselves either liberal or conservative. Among the fixed, 84 percent of those who chose one of these two labels chose conservative. Among the fluid, 80 percent of those who chose one of them chose liberal.

Studies like these demonstrate that worldview captures the same essence that concepts in biopolitics and personality psychology do. These studies also support the theory that you can use the parenting questions to predict people's political beliefs. The same people who say that they prefer obedient children who respect their elders also say they experience strong disgust and don't trust others; they also identify as conservative. This suggests that the four questions about parenting provide a powerful lens through which to understand politics.

As fundamental as our worldviews are, however, they do not explain our *operational* ideologies. For example, it's not obvious why worldview ought to guide people's general orientation toward taxation or government spending on schools or infrastructure. These issues simply do not bear on the question of how safe or dangerous the world is.

This apparent disconnect between people's worldviews and preferences about big government is surprising when you consider that a person's worldview really is an extremely good indicator of their political affiliations. Worldview shouldn't tell us so much about people's political choices—yet it does. What is going on here?

The close linkage between worldview and political behavior points to an insidious trend in recent American history. For roughly the last half century, Americans' voting behavior seems to have been shaped less by their operational ideology—which in the United States mostly has to do with one's general orientation toward the size of government—

than by their feelings about racial, cultural, and security-related issues. Symbolic ideology has effectively eclipsed size-of-government considerations, leading to a situation where the American political system is being driven by an electorate that cares about politics precisely because it has become so intimately aligned with worldview. This dynamic has proven to be uniquely polarizing. It has also reshaped the political environment in the United States in ways we are still struggling to understand.

2

"A Hell of a Lot More Abstract"

WORLDVIEWS AREN'T INHERENTLY POLARIZING. In the mid-twentieth century, for example, people with different worldviews did not gravitate so clearly to different political tribes. Even opposition to the Vietnam War was equally split between Democrats and Republicans in the 1960s, evidence that at the time, both parties had their fair share of people of a more-fluid persuasion.

Things are different now. America's two main political parties have provided people on both sides of the worldview divide with ready-made political identities, which lure them toward one party or the other. The policies the major parties trumpet, and the candidates they offer, are increasingly designed to appeal to fixed voters on the one hand, and fluid voters on the other.

This has happened despite the fact that people don't consciously think of themselves as fixed or fluid. Rather, people embrace one party or the other because it represents their core preferences and values—that is, because it caters to their particular worldview. People whose worldview is more mixed are not as well represented by the two major parties in the US party system. They are therefore forced to choose between the two. But because of the centrality of partisanship to people's political belief systems, they'll naturally come to identify more with the components of that party's worldview.

As a result, Americans' worldviews and our party identities are now in alignment as never before. According to the 2016 American National Election Study, the premier academic survey taken each presidential election year, 71 percent of the fluid identified as Democrats and only 21 percent as Republicans. (The other 8 percent called themselves independents.) Put differently, the fluid were more than three times as likely to identify as Democrats than as Republicans. The fixed, in contrast, skewed strongly toward the GOP—60 percent Republican, 25 percent Democrat, and the rest independent. This merging of worldview and partisanship stands in marked contrast to the 1990s, a change captured graphically below. In 1992, the fixed and the fluid were both nearly identical in their party choices.

This marriage between worldview and party weaponizes political partisanship. During the same period that saw this unprecedented convergence, political partisanship in the United States has heated up. In survey after survey, US partisans express more dislike for their opponents

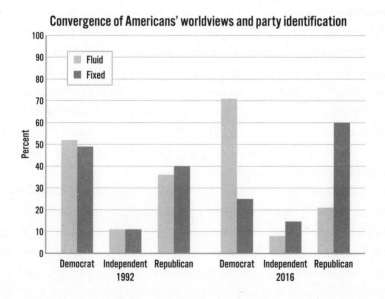

Convergence of Americans' worldviews and party identification

than at any time in the history of public opinion polling. It is not just the other party they've come to hate. The feelings have grown personal. Fully 70 percent of Democrats said Republicans were more "closed-minded," according to a recent survey from the Pew Research Center, and 52 percent of Republicans thought the same about Democrats. Nearly half of Republicans described Democrats as "immoral," "lazy," and "dishonest." And perhaps this is why, when they think about the other party, they see it as not just disagreeable but dangerous. Nearly half of both Republicans and Democrats believe the other "party's policies are so misguided that they threaten the nation's well-being." When fixed and fluid people commingled in both major US political parties, as in the 1960s, for example, you would rarely have heard Americans talking about those from the opposite party in such stark terms. But the times are changing. Partisans today demonstrate more prejudice against members of the other party than they do against people of other races and ethnicities, despite the fact that racial prejudice remains alive and well in America.

This dramatic uptick in partisanship is confounding on one level because Americans in general demonstrate little interest in politics. Faced with the choice of spending an hour familiarizing themselves with candidates for public office or regrouting the bathroom tiles, most Americans are likely to head to Home Depot. Americans' lack of knowledge about politics is truly staggering: it is common for only about 10 percent of Americans to be able to identify the chief justice of the Supreme Court, even when they have been spotted his name. Typically fewer than 50 percent are able to say which party holds the majority of seats in the US House and Senate. Two-thirds of Americans regularly fail to identify the three branches of the federal government. (Brownie points for naming the executive, legislative, and judicial branches.)

If Americans lack even such rudimentary knowledge about politics, it is highly unlikely that their intensifying partisanship results from deeply thought-through *ideological* disagreements. An ideology, after all, is a unified philosophy about how best to govern. It helps people tie together what positions on issues go together with what others. But because most Americans lack interest and hence expertise in politics, they don't have coherent philosophies on governing. Indeed, a lack of ideological coherence has been a feature of American public opinion for as long as there have been political surveys. Since the late 1960s, political scientists have commented on Americans' "ideological innocence" (a term that two scholars defined recently, and memorably, as meaning that Americans are "indifferent to standard ideological concepts, lacking a consistent outlook on public policy, in possession of real opinions on only some issues of the day, and knowing precious little").

Americans are so oblivious to what ideological labels actually mean that they even identify themselves as adhering to ideologies that they fundamentally disagree with in many respects. For instance, many people call themselves conservative and say they believe in small government. But, when asked about whether government ought to spend more or less on specific programs, they consistently answer that they want more. Are people who call themselves conservative actually conservative if they almost always want government to do *more*, not less?

These "conflicted conservatives" label themselves as conservative because that word describes them well in the nonpolitical parts of their lives. They go to church and are generally wary of change. That is not the same thing as having a conservative *political* ideology, especially when one's preferences about specific areas of government involvement are more likely to be liberal than conservative. Yet because of the dual nature of political identity, it is possible to be simultaneously liberal and conservative: symbolically conservative, but operationally liberal.

The one place where this political dualism doesn't hold up, however, is in the voting booth. Come election time, "conflicted conservatives" cast their ballots for Republicans, not Democrats. This suggests that the operational dimension of conservatism is much less important to them than the symbolic one. That makes sense; operational policy preferences are abstract and hard to keep straight, whereas symbolic political identification is much easier to conceptualize and adhere to because it represents people's feelings about a whole range of things both inside and outside of politics.

This is precisely why the word "conservative" is so attractive to many people: it describes them in the *nonpolitical* parts of their lives. It sums up their preference for doing things as they've been done in the past, and embracing traditions that have endured for generations. Being conservative, in this sense, also means believing you can't be too careful when you encounter other people, especially strangers or those with newfangled ideas. If change must happen, it is better if it is incremental.

This understanding of conservatism is no ode to limiting government spending, the virtues of low taxes, or the dynamism of free markets and the free enterprise system. Instead, it sounds an awful lot like a fixed worldview.

Over the span of political history, indeed, something akin to a fixed worldview is what conservatism has most often meant. Only in the last hundred or so years have governments had sufficient resources to offer generous programs and services. Hence only recently has it even been conceivable for the term "conservative" to refer to limiting the size of programs and services government offers.

Before that, "conservative" meant something different — something that people with a fixed worldview would instinctively embrace. Reading scholarship from the beginning and middle of the twentieth century reminds us of that fact. Back then, conservatism saw people as creatures of appetite, "doomed to imperfection . . . governed more by emotion than reason." As a result, they needed to live under institutions and norms that have "survived the ordeal of history" to minimize the damage from humans' "evil impulses." This strain was not necessarily connected to a specific political party in the United States before the New Deal, but it found an outlet in the populist movements that merged forces with the Democratic Party of the late eighteenth and early nineteenth centuries. Conservatism in the pre–New Deal era is obviously different from what most readers grew up with — which, in turn, is very different from conservatism as we know it today.

Whether people realize it or not, "classic" American conservatism — with its emphasis on small government, balanced budgets, free trade, and the innovative firepower of the free enterprise system — has become an anachronism since the rise of Donald Trump as a political force. As he emerged as the leader of the "conservative" party, he advocated enormous increases in government spending, producing huge budget deficits; promised trade protectionism; and worked to close borders to immigrants. What conservatism means today has, in a sense, gone back to the future. William Jennings Bryan—a turn-of-the-twentieth-century Democrat—would be happier than either Barry Goldwater or Ronald Reagan with the sort of agenda now put forward by the Republican Party.

Because this style of conservatism encompasses a host of racial, cultural, and national security matters that appeal to people on the fixed side of the worldview spectrum, it might be more accurately called "fixed-worldview conservatism." It owes its rise to the fact that American voters now gravitate toward one party or the other based less on rational calculations about which party or governing philosophy would better suit their material interests than on unconscious judgments about how dangerous they perceive the world to be. They vote for the party that better reflects their ideas about what is threatening and what should be embraced.

As worldview has moved from the periphery of American politics to the forefront, politics has begun to feel more and more like a matter of life and death. Because, in a psychological sense, it is. Over a period of decades, America's political parties have taken consistently different and clear positions on a range of issues that people experience less logically, more emotionally. American voters' responses to these issues, and hence to the parties' positions on them, hinge less on a philosophy about government intervention than they do on the psychological factors that are central to their worldviews: namely, their attitudes about *hierarchy* and *cognitive closure*. These preferences, in turn, shape people's attitudes about *tradition*, and also—crucially—about *race and ethnicity*, which together have become a dividing line of sorts between the two major political parties in America today.

By looking at how these deep-rooted preferences shape Americans' political choices, it becomes easier to comprehend how this recent, momentous shift in American politics has taken place: how Republican and Democratic leaders, by adjusting their parties' policy platforms, have either knowingly or unwittingly played into the deepest psychological divisions between Americans, giving rise to a political system organized more by worldview than by a philosophy about the proper size and scope of government. In so doing, leaders on both sides have driven an enormous wedge into the heart of the body politic.

The evidence that follows comes from a range of surveys, many of them our own. Over the last decade or so, we have fielded a half-dozen surveys that include the four questions about desirable qualities in children, the first in November 2006 and the last in April 2017. Seeing the change in the issue agenda from economic to worldview issues and the polarization that accompanied it, we sought to capture whether the questions were becoming more central to Americans' political choices. The Cooperative Campaign Analysis Project (CCAP) and the Cooperative Congressional Election Study (CCES), two massive online data collections, have also included the parenting questions in their surveys since 2008. Finally, the American National Election Studies (ANES) have been asking them regularly since 1992. The results from these surveys demonstrate the power of people's basic worldviews in explaining their preferences about the critical matters that divide the parties so sharply today.

The parenting questions that we introduced in the previous chapter are, at their core, measures of people's attitudes about hierarchy and, by extension, their need for cognitive closure. People develop these habits of mental processing in response to their perceptions of danger in the world; these mental shortcuts allow them to cope with the threats and uncertainty they see around them. People of a fixed mind-set, for this reason, prefer to have a strict patriarch at the top of a family's hierarchy. This is a time-tested way of keeping a family safe. Similarly, they prefer political leaders who project an aura of strength, and who therefore seem to belong at the top of the country's hierarchy.

This top-of-the-food-chain style is perhaps best embodied by Donald Trump, but fixed voters had been gravitating toward Republican presidential candidates who represented this kind of leadership long before he came along. Think of the widely circulated image of George W. Bush in a flight suit in May 2003, striding across the deck of an aircraft carrier to announce "Mission Accomplished" in Iraq; now compare that to the widely shared photos of John Kerry windsurfing off the coast of Nantucket during the 2004 presidential campaign. For fixed-worldview voters, the contrast between a decisive leader on the one hand and a New England elitist on the other could not have been clearer. Likewise, conjure in your mind the conflicting images of the reed-thin, arugula-eating Barack Obama and the solidly built, meat-eating Mitt Romney. It's no coincidence that, in 2012, 72 percent of fixed voters chose Romney over Obama. Even in a bad year for Republicans, when John McCain lost by seven percentage points, 71 percent of fixed-worldview voters preferred him to Obama. The same was true when Bush beat Kerry and Al Gore.

Fixed voters' high level of support for any Republican standard-bearer reflects the fact that these voters are, in effect, presented with a binary choice in a general election: a choice between a Republican who represents their fixed worldview, and a Democrat who espouses beliefs that attract fluid-worldview voters.

The strong preference for hierarchy among people with fixed worldviews better reveals itself in Republican primaries when all the candidates competing are Republicans. Each of them knows their audience, so all attempt to convey that they are the true alpha dog, the one who belongs at the top of the ladder. Trump is the archetype of this style. Even in a field full of alpha dogs, his style would have stood out to fixed voters.

Although it is difficult to find political surveys conducted during the primary season that ask the questions about desirable qualities in children, two such surveys, one from 2008 and the other from 2016, enable us to compare the appeal of Trump with previous GOP nominees. The results from 2008 suggest that worldview had no impact on support for either John McCain or Mitt Romney among Republican primary voters. About the same percentage of those with fixed worldviews (26 percent) said they voted for McCain as those with less-fixed worldviews (28 percent). The same was true of support for Mitt Romney. About 27 percent of the fixed said they had voted for him compared with 28 percent of those with less-fixed worldviews.

In 2016, however, Donald Trump was the candidate of choice for those of fixed worldview. Trump commanded the support of a remarkable

In their public personas, Republican and Democratic leaders have increasingly channeled opposing worldviews. President George W. Bush presented an image of strength and resolve while declaring an end to combat in Iraq in 2003. Brooks Kraft LLC / Corbis via Getty Images

50 percent of this group. Only 38 percent of the less fixed said they voted for him. No other candidate attracted a similar pattern of support. For Jeb Bush, Ben Carson, Marco Rubio, and John Kasich, support was the same across the worldview spectrum. Rubio, at the time the survey was taken, was the candidate running second to Trump. Those with less-fixed worldviews provided him with 13 percent of their support, statistically the same as the percentage of the fixed who supported him. Based on the primary voting results, it appears Trump's uber-hierarchical style was especially attractive to those with fixed worldviews.

Senator John Kerry cut a very different figure from President Bush in a widely publicized windsurfing session off the coast of Nantucket in 2004. AP Photo / Laura Rauch

In short, although voters with a fixed worldview beat a path to the GOP long ago, many of them found their ideal candidate in Trump. This is in part because of how hierarchically he operates. But it is also because of the binary view he expressed about the world. He framed issues like this: You are either with us or against us. If you are against us, then we will crush you. Trump seemed to convey this more in personal style than in policy substance. His speech at the Republican convention probably captured it best. Facing "poverty and violence at home" and "war and destruction abroad," Trump said, "I alone can fix it." He didn't suggest it was going to be a team effort. Only he was necessary.

To people more sensitive to danger and chaos, Trump's unambiguous style of communication is attractive because it satisfies a need for cognitive closure. The more someone desires closure, the more they prefer *any* answer to a problem, as long as that answer eliminates ambiguity and uncertainty. In general, people of a fluid disposition are more likely to relish deep conversation for its own sake, to pick over the entrails of philosophical minutiae and to otherwise embrace open-ended discussion about a great many issues. Of course, fluid types can be rigid in their thinking and intolerant of views that differ from their own. But the fixed are typically less open to new ideas and even less eager to want to explore ideas for their own sake.

As evidence, consider responses to some questions in the 2006 CCES. The survey asked Americans whether they agree or disagree with two statements: (1) "Personally, I tend to think that there is a right way and a wrong way to do almost everything," and (2) "Nothing gets accomplished in this world unless you stick to some basic rules." Both statements tap people's preference for psychological tidiness. In general, people either strongly agreed or strongly disagreed with the first statement. Among the latter group, fluids outnumbered fixes by about four to one. Likewise, though most agree with the basic proposition that basic rules are necessary to get anything done, four times as many fluids as fixed disagree with the statement.

This divide between people who see the world as complex and open-ended on the one hand, and those who believe answers to most questions in life are clear and straightforward on the other, is perhaps best captured by the word "nuance." Indeed, President Obama became the focal point of a debate about the utility, or lack thereof, of a nuanced way of thinking about the world. While campaigning for the presidency in 2008, in response to questions about his views on Hamas and the Middle East, then senator Obama told the journalist Jeffrey Goldberg that "we don't do nuance well in politics and especially don't do it well on Middle East policy. We look at things as black and white, and not gray."

Obama's embrace of nuance distinguished him sharply from his GOP antagonists. Back in 2004, President George W. Bush told Senator Joe Biden, "I don't do nuance." Former Louisiana governor Bobby Jindal, a Republican, even blamed Trump's ascendance in 2016 on precisely this penchant of Obama's, writing in the *Wall Street Journal* that, "after seven years of the cool, weak and endlessly nuanced 'no drama Obama,' voters are looking for a strong leader who speaks in short, declarative sentences." His remarks mirror criticisms made several years earlier by Mitt Romney, who accused the then-president of being "tentative, indecisive, timid and nuanced." (The response of one liberal pundit shows the fluid perspective clearly: "Obama is 'nuanced'? Yes, but can someone explain why that's a bad thing? It's a complex, 'turbulent,' and ever-changing world. Having a chief executive who appreciates and is aware of 'nuance' strikes me as positive.")

The nuance wars in American politics didn't begin with Barack Obama. In the spring of 1974, a school committee in Kanawha County, West Virginia, recommended adopting scores of new textbooks with the introduction of a new statewide curriculum. The new curriculum included progressive concepts like multiculturalism. By the fall of 1974 Kanawha County had descended into pitched battle over this new education policy. A school boycott spread, with thousands of children being educated in makeshift classrooms in church basements. Opponents of the new curriculum planted bombs at an elementary school and a school board building, dynamited another elementary school, and attacked school buses. The school superintendent received death threats. Thousands of miners, the Ku Klux Klan, and other groups joined the mounting protests against the new books.

In the midst of that battle, which many consider the birth of the Christian right as a force in modern American politics, *Village Voice* journalist Paul Cowan traveled to Kanawha County to try to make sense of what was happening. He wanted to figure out why the introduction of some new and (to Cowan's mind) fairly uncontroversial classroom materials would have sparked such a ferocious backlash. One activist, driving perhaps to the heart of the matter, told him, "You're making an insidious attempt to replace our periods with your question marks."

This is a perfect example of how people with fixed worldviews crave cognitive closure, but there are other, less extreme examples that share the same themes. For instance, the belief in biblical literalism.

People of fixed worldview, who have more need for cognitive closure, embrace the notion that the Bible is the true word of God, and that God has a plan for all believers. Such views remove the need for interpretation and uncertainty. The fluid, more inclined to want to wrestle with ideas, are less likely to see things this way.

This dramatically different measure of the fixed and fluid need for closure was confirmed by the 2006 CCES survey. It revealed that fewer than 10 percent of people with a fluid worldview believe in the biblical account of creation, which appears in the Book of Genesis, more than evolution. In contrast, 60 percent of those with a fixed worldview believe in creationism more than they believe in evolution.

Biblical literalism appears to be an important cause of this difference. A 2010 survey presented people with five different understandings of the Bible ranging from "The Bible is the authoritative Word of God and without error" at one end of the continuum to "The Bible is just another book about religion and morality" at the other. Among the fluid respondents, only 5 percent believed the Bible is the authoritative word of God without error, while 41 percent believed it is just another book about religion and morality, the fluid's most common answer. In contrast, almost 50 percent of those with a fixed worldview believed the Bible is the authoritative word of God without error. Only 10 percent see it as just another book about religion and morality. In other words, the fixed were ten times as likely as the fluid to believe in biblical literalism.

The fixed's "straightforward" and the fluid's "nuanced" thinking about texts is not confined to the Bible. Another study asked whether judges should "consider the original intent of the authors of the Constitution" or "consider changing times and apply the principles of the Constitution," and 74 percent of the fixed chose what advocates refer to as strict constructionism. Fewer than 20 percent of the fluid favored such a literal interpretation of the Constitution. In this case, the worldview divide checks in at more than fifty-five points.

Another policy area that touches on people's need for closure — as well as their attitudes toward the other crucial factors in worldview, from hierarchy to tradition to race — has to do with how the use of military force fits into conducting foreign affairs. If uncertainty is especially uncomfortable to a person, using force might be an attractive alternative to diplomatic negotiations. Given the military might of the United States, the odds of success are pretty good. American military power overwhelmed opponents in both Iraq and Afghanistan in the short run, and it would be reasonable for people to think the same would happen anywhere.

When it comes to diplomacy, in contrast, outcomes are more uncertain. Diplomacy requires protracted negotiations, a willingness to consider a range of viewpoints and to tolerate ambiguous results. The Iran nuclear deal, signed by President Obama in 2015 with the intent to ensure that Iran would not use its nuclear program to manufacture and deploy nuclear weapons, is a good example. It includes complicated enforcement mechanisms and its goal — to prevent Iran from acquiring nuclear weapons — has no clear-cut delivery date. It's an inherently open-ended arrangement. Maybe it will work, but maybe the other side will take advantage of American diplomats. As such, fixed/fluid differences ought to be relevant in this area as well.

Differing perceptions of the world as a threatening place reveal themselves especially clearly in this realm. Numerous surveys conducted at various times in 2016 show the fixed and fluid differ dramatically in perceiving various countries and outside actors as military threats. These include China, Russia, Iran, ISIS, and terrorists. The fixed consistently rate all as more threatening than the fluid by between twenty-five and thirty percentage points. For example, when asked whether they thought China was a military threat, 54 percent of the fixed said the threat was "major" while only 29 percent of the fluid saw it that way.

It is not just the perception of threat that seems to be driving apart the opinions of fixed and fluid people toward China. The fixed and fluid also differ in what they think the appropriate response to an international threat — any threat — might be. Evidence of the size of this divide can be seen in the graph on page 36. The 2006 CCES asked Americans whether projecting strength or using diplomacy was more effective in foreign affairs. Fully 75 percent of the fluid chose diplomacy over projecting strength, while 60 percent of the fixed chose projecting strength over using diplomacy. The 2016 ANES asked people the degree to which they were willing to use military force to solve international problems. Nearly half of the fluid said they were either "only a little" or "not at all willing"

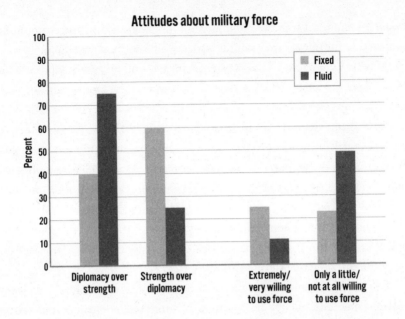

Attitudes about military force

to use force. Less than a quarter of the fixed answered that way. When asked about committing troops to fight ISIS, specifically, the fixed were twice as likely as the fluid to favor military intervention (53 to 25 percent). When it comes to worldview politics, it seems, the need for cognitive closure can express itself in brutal ways.

Differing preferences for hierarchy—the traditional mode of ensuring order and safety—and differing needs for cognitive closure help explain why fixed and fluid people have such different attitudes about *tradition*. And based on what we know about its importance, it should not be surprising that cultural changes that threaten people's traditions about a host of issues—from gender and sexuality to firearm ownership and more—have become flashpoints for worldview politics.

Adopting stable practices can help people cope when they perceive the world as more perilous. Traditions, social conventions, and other customs are tried-and-true folkways for organizing daily life, for reinforcing accepted community values, and for immersing ourselves in the familiar and the comfortable (even if traditions, like sitting in synagogue for three hours on a Saturday morning, can be boring at times, as one of the authors can attest). Virtually all humans like routines, and nearly everyone experiences some fear and uncertainty in the face of new and unfamiliar circumstances. In this, as in other ways we'll discuss, the default mode of the fixed is intuitively appealing.

Without traditions, fixed people sense the possibility that society could quickly become unmoored. The unfamiliar is an inherent danger until it proves otherwise. This makes it easy to understand why the slogan "Make America Great Again" had such resonance among those with a fixed worldview. It harks back to a time when prayer was commonplace in public schools, children respected their elders and unquestioningly pledged allegiance to the flag "under God," and gender roles were strictly defined by traditional norms. The fixed see potential danger in changing norms. A mantra for them might be "If it ain't broke, don't fix it." Departing from tradition injects unnecessary uncertainty, danger, and chaos into the world. The initial reaction to any new wave of social change is likely to be fear and anger about why "we" are being subject to another dangerous social experiment on behalf of "them."

Fluids, by contrast, are more likely to revel in the new, the unconventional, and the nontraditional. Because fluid people do not perceive the same dangers in the world that fixed people do, they call tradition by another, less positive name: conformity. In their view, it carries its own perils. Greatness is unlikely to come from following orders but rather from breaking the mold. In addition, some traditions can do manifest harm to people. It may be true, for example, that legally recognized marriage in the United States has always been between a man and a woman. But that fact alone, in the fluid's reckoning, does not justify the persistence of the belief and legal practice. Maintaining that tradition just because it is a tradition does not make a community safer or better. The only explanation the fluid can conjure for why someone would oppose same-sex marriage is prejudice. And prejudice, as far as even many highly privileged fluid people are concerned, is a threat to everyone's well-being.

Since the 1970s two important fronts in the culture war have also become flashpoints in the fundamental conflict between the worldviews of the fixed and fluid: feminists' challenge to traditional gender roles, and the recognition of rights for nonheterosexuals. Because the fluid, whether they are gay or straight themselves, feel less threatened by social change and are, therefore, less concerned about maintaining traditional arrangements, they have largely embraced proposals that break from the traditional status of women and LGBT people. The fixed, who are more inclined to believe that traditional arrangements are a bulwark against social threats and uncertainty, have generally taken the other side on such matters.

The 2016 CCAP study asked a range of questions about women's role in society. The graph below illustrates some of these results. When asked whether they thought women should "return to their traditional roles," an overwhelming 86 percent of the fluid disagreed, whereas only about half of the fixed did. Fluids were thirty-five points more likely than the fixed to disagree with a statement that women's complaints about harassment caused more problems than they solved.

Similarly, in 2008, the ANES asked what must have seemed to the fluid like a question best posed when *Leave It to Beaver* topped the tele-

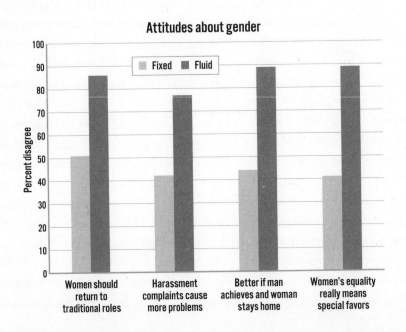

Attitudes about gender

vision ratings in the 1950s: "Is it better if a man achieves and a woman takes care of the home?" Among the fluid, 89 percent disagreed, but (in a disparity that would no doubt shock most fluid people), only 44 percent of the fixed did. Another question asked people whether they supported the proposition that "when women demand equality these days, they are actually seeking special favors." Fully 89 percent of the fluid disagreed, but only 41 percent of the fixed did.

Because the battle for gender equality has been raging for so long, it is somewhat surprising that disagreements remain so deep after all these years. Yet when it comes to attitudes toward gender roles, the difference between the fixed and the fluid remains something of a chasm.

Gaping differences also exist between the fixed and fluid on LGBT issues. Like feminists, the LGBT community demands changes to existing traditions and conventions, something those with fixed worldviews ought to be troubled by but which those with fluid worldviews are likely to embrace. Illustrations of the depth of worldview differences appear in the graph on page 40. In 2006, when gay-rights issues were first becoming a nationwide political battleground, 82 percent of the fluid already supported same-sex couples' right to adopt children, but only one-third of the fixed did. Preferences about same-sex marriage produced similar results — 84 percent of the fluid favored it but only 29 percent of the fixed did. Although the gaps between the fixed and fluid have shrunk on these two questions in the decade since then, they remain very large.

Profound differences also exist across the worldview spectrum on beliefs about the origins of homosexuality. Among the fluid, fully 84 percent believe people are born gay, whereas only 16 percent believe people choose their sexual orientation. Among the fixed, only one-third think people are born gay. When asked about the existence of transgender bathrooms, 57 percent of the fixed describe themselves as "extremely frustrated." Only 12 percent of the fluid label themselves that way.

Of course, feminism and gay rights aren't the only divisive cultural issues these days. Guns and gun control are also a source of deep disagreement between people on opposing sides of the worldview spectrum.

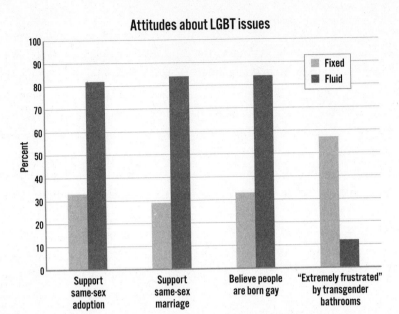

Attitudes about LGBT issues

It is clear why the fixed and fluid might think about this issue differently. People who perceive a lot of danger in the world might also wish to have as much protection as possible against those dangers. This might be especially necessary for the fixed because they are less inclined to trust other people. As such, they're more likely to assume that the bad guys are going to find ways to get guns. Legislative efforts that limit guns' availability to law-abiding citizens are, therefore, only going to make society more vulnerable to those who threaten law-abiding citizens. Unilateral disarmament, in their view, is just plain stupid.

The fluid see the issue differently. Not only are they less likely to perceive crime as pervasive, their more nuanced view of the world ought to make them less inclined than the fixed to think confronting violent people with violence is the best way to proceed. Perhaps because they trust people more, the fluid might also believe laws designed to keep guns out of criminals' hands will actually work.

As one might expect, given these attitudes, there are massive fixed/fluid differences on gun control. In 2016 the ANES asked whether existing gun laws should be made more strict, less strict, or kept the same.

The fluid overwhelmingly prefer stricter gun laws — 67 percent. The fixed don't, with a shade under one-third (32 percent) wanting stricter laws.

The Republican Party attracts fixed voters not just because it emphasizes the value of hierarchy, or trumpets straightforward solutions to political problems, or affirms the importance of tradition. The GOP also appeals to fixed voters because of its stance on issues pertaining to race and ethnicity — especially its pronounced hostility to people who look or behave differently than the members of its base.

Worldview has a strong influence on Americans' opinions about visible differences having to do with race, ethnicity, or religion. Indeed, suspicion of people who belong to different racial, ethnic, and religious groups is one of the hallmarks of a fixed worldview. When people are wired for wariness, trust comes less easily. That is not to say *everyone* is untrustworthy to people who have fixed worldviews; recall that conscientiousness is an adaptation that people develop to cope with a wary physiology, which explains why the same people who believe that most people can't be trusted also have high levels of trust for their families, their neighbors, their coworkers, and other familiar folks. Still, fixed types generally consider most people unworthy of trust until they have earned it.

What's more, people are inclined to trust other people who look like them, and to be suspicious of people who don't. This is likely due to evolutionary processes that shaped the human species eons ago. Evolutionary psychologists believe this tendency evolved to help humans survive in an inhospitable world where resources were scarce and intergroup competition was fierce. Because a couple of hundred thousand years is a mere blip on our evolutionary timeline, humans still have some of this primitive wiring, which manifests itself in doubts — usually harbored by the fixed more than the fluid — about people from other racial, ethnic, and religious groups.

The specific objects of Americans' wariness have varied over the course of the nation's history, but they are often people whose very label of "otherness" reflects the concerns of the country's white, Protestant majority. In the late 1800s, the source of this majority's suspicion was Catholics. That wariness of Catholics provided a lot of the energy behind the temperance movement. For much of the twentieth century, anti-Semitism ran particularly strong in the United States, and some Americans didn't view Jews as being as white as other "traditionally" American groups. In the late twentieth and early twenty-first centuries, Muslims from Arab countries and Latinos have been out of favor with the American religious and racial majority. And, through all of American history, African Americans have been "them," not "us," to the vast majority of their fellow citizens.

But not everyone is resigned to this reality. People with more-fluid worldviews tend to abhor negative racial and ethnic stereotypes. They are less innately fearful of difference, a quality that gives them the leeway to embrace variety. If they hear people speaking different languages, it's likely to put a smile on their face, not annoy them. A picture of a diverse group of people getting along will probably warm their hearts, providing them with a profound sense of comfort and affirming their view that the very differences between people are what makes the world a beautiful place.

That orientation has its limits, to be sure. Principles aside, people with a fluid worldview are not generally clamoring to live next door to people from different racial or ethnic backgrounds. While fluid people find big cities attractive, these socially liberal redoubts remain highly segregated by race and ethnicity, often as a result of exclusionary zoning that fluid voters at least quietly abide. More generally, the process of gentrification is not kind to African Americans in major metropolitan areas, even as it produces spaces that reflect the fluids' diverse cultural tastes. To the fluid, the fixed may seem like racists, but to the fixed, the fluid sure seem like hypocrites.

This dissonance can be explained by the fact that fluid people, like fixed people, do fear racial and ethnic difference sometimes. If a non-Muslim person with a fluid worldview is waiting to board a plane and encounters another passenger at the same gate who is wearing a headscarf, reading the Quran, and praying intensely, might his pulse quicken? Certainly. The difference in this case is that, not only is the fluid person more likely to feel guilty about his wariness toward the "stranger," his reaction at the airport is unlikely to inform his thinking about the general threat that immigrants pose when he is not waiting to board a plane. For the fixed, that sense of potential peril is central to their worldview. As a consequence, they are less likely to revisit that initial instinct in the future. Fluids, by contrast, might reflect on the stereotype they employed, take a second look at their own initial reactions, though not until after their plane has landed safely.

When people view themselves as part of a group, it is only human to bolster their own side and denigrate their opponent. The fluid would rather not consider this tendency to create their own outgroups because part of their ethos is to consider the distinctive value of individuals. But ask someone on the political right what they believe those on the left think of them. One response is almost certain to be that they think liberals believe people like them are a bunch of ignorant, aggressive rubes. Steve Bannon, one of the masterminds behind Trump's 2016 campaign and later his chief White House strategist, put it this way when firing up a crowd of Alabamians the weekend before the Republican primary in 2017 to fill Jeff Sessions's Senate seat: "They think you're a pack of morons."

Anyone who has spent any time around people with fluid worldviews would have to acknowledge that there is more than a kernel of truth to that. When people with a fluid worldview see a pickup truck driven by a person wearing a "Make America Great Again" hat, they are just as willing to put that person in certain boxes as white people with a fixed worldview might be to stereotype a stranger who is African American. Where the fluid differ from the fixed is that, for the fluid, "them" is more likely to be a majority group than a minority group.

Although race and ethnicity divide Americans, the division is not between bigots on one side and nonbigots on the other. No credible social scientific evidence suggests that the percentage of abject racists is particularly high in the United States. For example, a mere 5 percent of whites express a belief that all races aren't equal and only 8 percent express support for the notion of white nationalism. Five percent report they wouldn't vote for a black person for president. And only 16 percent of whites in 2016 said they would oppose a close relative marrying a black person, about half the percentage in 2006. While these numbers are still much higher than many fluid people will be comfortable with, the fact remains that overt racism is mostly a fringe phenomenon in the present day.

But that doesn't mean that race isn't an omnipresent and divisive issue in many Americans' minds. It is so deeply felt that it divides white Americans from white Americans, whites from nonwhites, and nonwhites from each other. It's vexing and complicated. But crucially, it very clearly divides fixed Americans from fluid Americans.

There is perhaps no better example of the profound difference in the racial attitudes of fixed and fluid people than their respective ideas about why some racial minorities are not as well-off as whites. For instance, black Americans suffer from much higher rates of poverty and economic distress than other groups. But white Americans are torn over whether African Americans' economic circumstances are the fault of African Americans themselves or the barriers to their equality are more structural in nature. And this difference of opinion breaks down neatly along the fault line of worldview.

To explore racial attitudes like these, political scientists ask people to think about statements like the following:

1. Over the last few years, blacks have gotten less than they deserve.
2. It's really a matter of some people not trying hard enough; if blacks would only try harder they could be just as well-off as whites.
3. Generations of slavery and discrimination have created conditions that make it difficult for blacks to work their way out of the lower class.

Surveys ask people to indicate whether they agree, disagree, or neither agree nor disagree with each of the statements.

The graph on page 45 displays the worldview differences on answers to these questions when they were posed in the 2016 CCAP study. White respondents with a fixed worldview are significantly more likely to believe that the plight of African Americans is their own problem. Almost 60 percent disagree with the notion that "blacks have gotten less than they deserve." Two-thirds deny that structural racism exists at all, disregarding the legacy of slavery and past discrimination as an explanation for why blacks today are not as well-off as other Americans. Finally, 60 percent believe that blacks simply need to be more industrious in order to be as well-off as whites. (There is reason to suspect that number may, in truth, be a good bit higher, because an unusually high percentage of the fixed—26 percent—say they neither agree nor disagree with the statement, perhaps because they might not want to reveal their true feelings about what they know is a highly charged subject.)

It's worth pausing here for a moment. Roughly 60 percent of people with a fixed worldview—likely well over 60 percent—believe the economic divide between blacks and whites would disappear if only blacks worked harder. For anyone trying to understand how fixed people think about race, this is a pretty good—albeit extreme—indication.

The fluid's opinions differ from the fixeds' dramatically. Only 21 percent agree that African Americans and whites would be economic equals

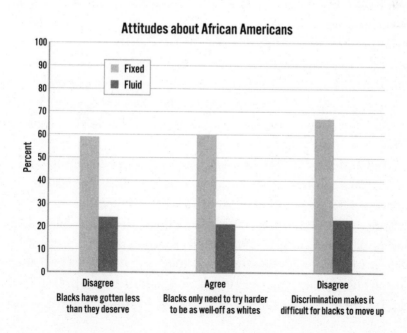

Attitudes about African Americans

if African Americans just worked harder. Only 23 percent think structural racism isn't much of an impediment to blacks. And 24 percent disagree with the statement that blacks have gotten less than they deserve
of late. Across the three questions, the differences between the fixed and
fluid average about forty points.

These differences seem large, but how large are they? A difference
between two groups is usually *statistically* significant when it's five points
or so. That's a pretty low bar. Five points doesn't seem *substantively*
very big.

To understand the magnitude of the difference, it helps to consider
some other examples from the annals of political research. When it
comes to surveys about politics, a massive difference is the gulf between
how minorities and whites vote. Indeed, voting behavior in the United
States has never been as racially polarized as it is today. Racial and
ethnic minorities together cast about three-quarters of their ballots for
Democrats, while only about 40 percent of whites vote Democratic. That
produces a gap of thirty-five points. In most elections, the gender gap is
around fifteen percentage points, less than half the size of the race/eth-
nicity gap but still large enough that everyone pays attention to it. Differences of fifteen points, then, are noteworthy. At thirty-five points or more,
they are stunning.

Statistically speaking, in other words, the differences in racial attitudes between the fixed and fluid are consistently remarkable. All the
more remarkable is the fact that we discern the fixed from the fluid by
asking people about desirable qualities in children, something seemingly
far removed from politics.

The worldview differences also inform fixed and fluid people's reactions to specific contemporary issues related to race. For instance, the
highly publicized killings of unarmed black men by police in numerous
jurisdictions led to the rise of the Black Lives Matter movement. Organizers chose the name to reflect the equal worth of black people's lives
compared to those of whites or people from any other racial background
and to highlight the degree to which, they believe, black lives and bodies have been marginalized and subjected to violence. But the name

became a lightning rod, especially after violence between Black Lives Matter protesters and police flared periodically through 2015 and 2016. Those who opposed Black Lives Matter suggested that Blue Lives (that is, police lives) Matter, too, as, indeed, All Lives Matter. In 2016, the CCAP asked Americans how they felt about the Black Lives Matter movement. Among the fixed, only 19 percent expressed a favorable opinion. Among the fluid, 61 percent did, another jaw-dropping gap of over forty points.

Preferences about government programs that whites believe mostly benefit African Americans also reveal deep differences between the fixed and fluid. In a 2012 survey, 60 percent of those with a fluid worldview supported affirmative action programs, while only about a quarter of those with a fixed worldview did. Similarly, our 2017 survey asked whether people thought spending on welfare—the antipoverty program Americans are most likely to associate with African Americans—should be increased, decreased, or kept the same. Sixty percent of the fixed thought

Demonstrators confront each other at the Unite the Right rally in Charlottesville, Virginia, on August 12, 2017. The two sides generated extremely different reactions from fixed and fluid Americans. Evelyn Hockstein / Washington Post via Getty Images

spending should be cut, but only 19 percent of the fluid did—another dramatic difference.

As with their attitudes about race, people's worldviews deeply divide their opinions on ethnicity. Researchers typically measure this part of people's worldview by asking how they feel about immigration; because Americans are overwhelmingly likely to conjure in their minds a Hispanic face when asked about immigration, attitudes about immigrants and immigration serve as a good approximation of attitudes about ethnicity.

Similarly large differences between the fixed and fluid are evident in this domain, too. Importantly, these differences existed long before Donald Trump came on the scene. A full decade before Trump was elected president, the 2006 CCES asked people whether they thought "immigration was a threat to the US economy." Among the fixed, 67 percent said yes. Among the fluid, fewer than 30 percent did. Ten years before Trump repeatedly promised to build a "big, beautiful wall" on the Mexican border, the same survey asked people whether the United States ought to build a seven-hundred-mile-long fence on its border. Less than one-third of those with a fluid worldview supported the idea, but more than three-quarters of those with a fixed worldview did, a gap of more than forty points. Trump didn't create these opinions among Republicans; rather, he harvested the support of voters who, because of their worldview, wanted to keep immigrants at arm's length.

The fluid, by contrast, find such an approach to immigration counterproductive at best and downright discriminatory at worst, and this difference of opinion about immigration and immigrants has only deepened with time. The graph on page 49 displays several examples drawn from surveys conducted in 2016. A consistent 70 or so percent of the fixed take a negative view of immigrants on all of these questions. When asked whether immigrants threaten traditional American customs, 67 percent of the fixed agree. When asked whether they are bothered when they come into contact with people who speak little or no English, 69 percent say yes, which is about the same percentage (70 percent) that support building Trump's signature border wall.

The fluid's opinions on these three questions are the opposite of the

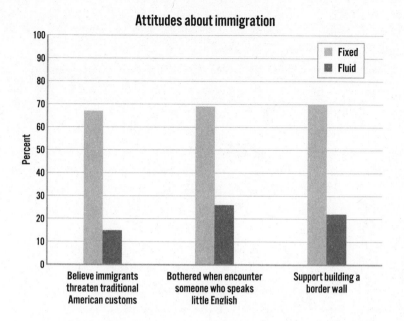

Attitudes about immigration

fixed's. Among the fluid, anti-immigrant sentiment ranges from only 15 to 26 percent on these items. Thus, the fixed/fluid differences on immigration often approach fifty points. The worldview conflict at the heart of party polarization ensures that those on opposite sides of the party divide will see immigration in fundamentally different ways, with a seemingly unbridgeable moat between them.

Although it is true that Americans mostly think about Hispanics when they think about immigrants, it is not the only group that Americans might consider to be outsiders. Before September 11, 2001, most Americans probably didn't think about Muslims very much. Since then, however, Muslims have become a clear flashpoint. Americans have disagreed about whether the religion is inherently violent. They have clashed about whether communities should welcome mosques or fight their construction. Never was the fight more contentious than over the plans to build the so-called Ground Zero Mosque in the early 2000s, not far from where the World Trade Center had been felled by Muslim terrorists. It was not just New York City. Efforts to block the construction of mosques occurred across the nation from Brentwood and Murfreesboro, Tennessee, to Basking Ridge and Bayonne, New Jersey.

Donald Trump made attitudes about Muslims central to the 2016 election when he proposed a temporary travel ban on all Muslims entering the United States until new, supposedly stricter vetting procedures could be implemented. At first, numerous Republican leaders reacted with horror, much like they did after Trump kicked off his campaign in June 2015 by calling Mexican immigrants "rapists" and "drug dealers." After it became clear how popular the Muslim travel ban was with Republican primary voters, however, dissent from Republican leaders mostly disappeared.

The 2016 CCAP survey, which asked about a temporary ban on Muslims entering the country, helps explain why this issue has become so central to the platform of the Republican Party. The results also reveal the same, deep fault line between the fixed and fluid. Seventy-seven percent of the fixed, now central to the base of the Republican Party, favored the ban, but only 25 percent of the fluid did—another fifty-point difference like the ones we saw in the range of questions about immigration.

As they have with African Americans and Hispanics, some Republican strategists have long believed that the growing Muslim population in America might be a ripe target for conservative appeals. If that was ever a possibility, it no longer appears to be. Although American Muslims once held more traditional views on issues like homosexuality and abortion than the American public as a whole, the differences are shrinking rapidly. Not only did the depth of antipathy that Muslims experience at the hands of Republican Party leaders drive them into the arms of the Democratic Party a decade or so ago, their preferences on these social issues have begun to conform more toward those of other Democrats. No wonder polls after the 2016 election indicated that fewer than one in five American Muslims voted for Donald Trump. It was a lesson that, if they looked, Republican strategists would have found in their failed attempts to convert African Americans and Hispanics to their side, as well.

• • •

At this point, many American readers who identify as nonwhite or as part of an ethnic minority might find themselves confused. They are probably Democrats; as we noted a few pages back, about three-quarters of racial and ethnic minorities vote Democratic. This includes a consistent 90 percent or more of African Americans. Yet many communities of color include lots of people who value traditional family hierarchies and top-down authority. In fact, African Americans are the group most likely to have members with fixed worldviews.

Indeed, judging by their worldview alone, it would seem that African Americans should be the most Republican-leaning group in the United States. Instead, it is the least Republican. What is going on?

Like African Americans, Latinos and Asian Americans are often more likely than whites to report fixed answers to the parenting questions. More research will be needed before we can say for sure whether this discrepancy is because these two groups are more fixed in their worldviews. It is possible that they simply have different cultural norms about parenting. But if the worldviews of Latinos and Asian Americans are, like the worldviews of African Americans, more fixed than those of white Americans, this mismatch would reinforce an important truth in politics: when they are under attack, nothing matters more to people than their group identities—not even their worldviews.

Republicans have attacked African Americans for decades, for instance maligning them in an effort to win over white Democrats disenchanted with their party's embrace of liberal racial policies starting in the 1960s. From Richard Nixon's southern strategy to Donald Trump's questioning Barack Obama's country of birth, race has never been far from the surface of GOP campaigns. Although the use of race has often been less than explicit, Republicans' intent has generally been clear. Crime, urban unrest, busing, capital punishment, affirmative action, and welfare have all served as proxies for appeals to white voters' racial biases. Given the way Republicans have run their campaigns and governed over the last fifty years, it would seem a bad bet for African Americans to support them, no matter how their worldviews might better match what the Republican Party has on offer.

Latinos and Asian Americans are in similar positions. Immigrants have more recently been the subject of a steady diet of Republican attacks. Historically, neither group of newer arrivals to the United States has been as reliably Democratic as they are now. Indeed the distinctly anticommunist bent of the Republican Party made it a natural home for refugees fleeing communist regimes in places like Cuba, China, and Vietnam. Furthermore, the Republican approach to immigration was, not long ago, 180 degrees different from what it is now. With a stroke of his pen in 1986, Ronald Reagan provided what today would be called amnesty to more than three million immigrants who were in the country illegally. George H. W. Bush worked with Ted Kennedy, the liberal icon from Massachusetts, to expand immigration, culminating in the Immigration Act of 1990. Among other things, that law introduced the lottery system that President Trump would so adamantly denounce a quarter of a century later. Similarly, George W. Bush supported a pathway to citizenship for many undocumented workers as late as 2007.

Since then, the Republican Party has undergone a sea change, with enormous implications for Latino and Asian American political commitments. Senate Republicans, not Democrats, blocked the younger Bush's efforts at immigration reform during his second term. This turn among Republicans emerged during the period when fixed-worldview whites began to dominate the party's base. Republican officeholders adopted talk of a long border fence instead of comprehensive immigration reform. Increasingly representative of the party's views on immigration, Congressman Steve King, a Republican from Iowa, made a particularly interesting anatomical observation when he said that the typical immigrant possessed "calves the size of cantaloupes because they're hauling 75 pounds of marijuana across the desert." Whether Hispanics have more fixed worldviews or not, it's easy to see why present-day GOP messaging creates inhospitable terrain for those who identify as Latino or Hispanic, and their voting habits make this clear.

The evolution of Asian Americans' political allegiances is especially telling. Republicans haven't attacked immigrants of Asian descent like they have those of Hispanic descent. Indeed, Asian Americans have long been held up as a kind of "model minority" because of their economic success and educational attainment. The group's median income is substantially higher than that of non-Hispanic whites (about $65,000 versus $51,000 in 2017), which is politically significant given that higher-income voters have traditionally supported Republicans. As recently as the 1990s, Asian Americans actually were a strongly Republican constituency. In 1992 only 36 percent cast their ballots for the Democratic presidential candidate. In 2012, despite rising affluence, 73 percent did. Why the change?

Asian Americans feel like foreigners in their own land. One reason is that the group is the frequent target of microaggressions—subtle, indirect, sometimes unintentional discrimination against a racial or ethnic minority. For example, even when their families have lived in the United States for decades, Asian Americans often have to explain where they're from. Although those not of Asian descent may not mean to offend when they ask, "But where are you *really* from?" it is understandable why Asian Americans might take offense. After all, a white person born in Pennsylvania rarely has to answer a question like that, while an Asian American who grew up down the street from that white person might regularly field such questions. Perhaps it ought not be surprising, then, that Americans perceive the porcelain-skinned Kate Winslet as more quintessentially "American" than they do Lucy Liu, despite the fact that Winslet was born in England and Liu was born in New York City.

Such perceptions wouldn't influence party politics if Asian Americans didn't perceive Republicans as being unsympathetic to immigrants. One striking experiment with a group of Asian American subjects shows they apparently do. When subjects arrived for the study but before they answered a political survey, half were treated to a microaggression, such as a white lab assistant asking whether they were actually American citizens. The other half did not have to endure any such encounter. They just answered the surveys. Those who experienced the microaggression identified more strongly as Democrats. They were more likely to see the Republican Party as closed-minded and less likely to see it as representing people like them. They also expressed more-negative feelings toward the Republicans than those who just answered the questions without being questioned about their citizenship. The results suggest that Asian Americans see Republicans as unwelcoming toward immigrants even though their own group has rarely in recent times been the specific object of anti-immigrant rhetoric.

Because racial and ethnic minorities perceive Republicans as attacking their groups, worldview does not explain their party identities the way it does for whites. Fixed worldview or not, these groups can't help but realize that Republicans have targeted their groups to attract white voters. If people believe a party is hostile to their group, their worldviews won't matter much when it comes to choosing sides.

This helps to explain an important omission that you may have discerned already in this chapter: in evaluating the ways in which voters' worldviews shape their politics, we have not included survey respondents who are nonwhite.

That is not to suggest racial and ethnic minorities are not important to present-day politics. They are, in fact, centrally important, and not simply because they comprise a bigger and bigger part of the American electorate, rising from 29 percent in 2012 to 31 percent in 2016. (White eligible voters declined from 71 percent to 69 percent over the same period.) Party politics would not be even remotely competitive if fixed-worldview minorities were not coalition partners with fluid-worldview whites. After all, there are significantly more people with fixed worldviews than fluid ones. Similarly, fixed-worldview whites would not have moved toward the Republican Party had its leaders not disparaged minorities—a dubious distinction, to be sure, but one that only underscores the central role that nonwhite voters play in American politics.

For several reasons, then, racial and ethnic minorities play a crucial role in American politics. Yet they are also different from whites, in that their worldview and their politics do not align in the same way that white voters' do. Instead, minorities' group identities trump their worldviews when picking a side.

This complicates the picture of worldview politics that we have been developing in this chapter and the previous one—but also demonstrates the unique effect that voters' worldviews have had on our nation's political life. After all, if only white voters have experienced an alignment between their worldviews and their politics in recent decades, it stands to reason that America's political parties have reshaped themselves to accommodate only one part of the patchwork quilt that is America's diverse electorate. If demographic trends continue apace, white voters will soon become outnumbered by Americans from other racial and ethnic backgrounds. This could have major implications for the way that worldview and politics relate to each other in the United States—an idea that we will return to in the final pages of this book.

It is important to remember that political elites, not ordinary people, created this divide. By adjusting their policy platforms in the wake of the social upheavals of the 1960s and 1970s and continuing to take opposing positions on those that have followed since, they now appeal to people with one type of worldview over another. As a consequence, the Democratic and Republican parties have unwittingly turned themselves from regular political organizations to supercharged in-groups whose members' loyalty is determined as much by outlook as by politics. And while not everyone in these groups shares their dominant worldview—as is the case, for example, with many black Democrats—the very fact that these mismatched voters have steadfastly clung to their respective groups is a testament to how unwelcoming the racial and ethnic component of the opposing side's worldview has been to them.

The political decisions of many nonwhite Americans are not driven by their worldviews so much as they are determined by the worldviews of those in the tribe they might otherwise have chosen for themselves, simply because that other tribe has come to seem so hostile to them. If political parties are like big tents, no group wants to be stuck under the same one with other groups that in their words and deeds make it clear they don't want yours in the tent with them. Using race and ethnicity to bring fixed-worldview whites into the Republican tent makes it an inhospitable place for racial and ethnic minorities who, when it comes to believing in tradition and hierarchy, might otherwise fit well under it.

This is the strange predicament of any American who, for one reason or another, happens to be on the opposite side of the divide carved by factors like race, hierarchy, and tradition. In fact, the pull of party commitments appears to be so strong that it might change these voters' minds about even the most emotional of issues. For example, in 2012, before Barack Obama endorsed same-sex marriage, only about 40 percent of African Americans expressed support, well below the national average. This was in keeping with the group's more fixed worldview. After Obama's endorsement, however, support from African Americans jumped dramatically. These rapid shifts in political attitudes are a testament to the powerful influence that partisanship has come to have in politics.

Most people like to imagine that the decisions they make about who should represent them, what laws should be enacted, and in what kind of society they want to live are based on reasoned contemplation of choices and their consequences. Instead, the evidence suggests that political differences, at least these days, run far deeper and are, in many ways, inaccessible to our more logical faculties. In that sense, political beliefs on some of the defining issues of the day are unlikely to be based on nuanced understandings or real expertise. Instead, they are based on deeply held, gut-level worldviews or simple identification with a political party.

Moreover, the new relationship between worldview and party has shown the capacity to infect Americans' preferences about a wider range of issues than one might expect. For example, readers might look askance at the claim we've made that size of government is no longer an intense source of political division. Of course it still is! Much of the last decade has been occupied by disagreements about health care, after all, beginning with the introduction of Obamacare, its passage, then years of efforts to repeal it.

Isn't a program that addresses health care, a sector that makes up nearly 20 percent of the American economy, centrally about how much government ought to do? To some degree and to some people, the answer is surely yes. But, because of the worldview divide, voters' disagreements over many issues like this have taken on a symbolic—as opposed to an operational—character.

For example, when the Tea Party emerged as a significant political force in 2009, its primary ostensible concerns were high taxes and government overreach. But a closer look at the participants made clear that racial attitudes and the worldview divide were the real driving force behind the Tea Party's ascendancy. That does not mean everyone who joined a Tea Party group cared only about racial and cultural change; plenty really didn't like government regulation. But what moved the needle was participants' worldview, which is intimately connected to their racial attitudes. According to a 2012 survey, only 15 percent of the fluid supported the Tea Party. Fully 60 percent of the fixed did, another remarkable forty-five-point gap.

On health care and other redistributive issues, support or opposition has become increasingly linked to Americans' feelings about race and ethnicity over time. Size of government plays less of a role these days in explaining attitudes about these programs than whether people perceive program beneficiaries as deserving. Beginning with the war on poverty in the 1960s, so-called welfare programs became racially charged because the dominant image of recipients changed from their being white to their being African American—however much that distorts the reality of who receives government-funded antipoverty benefits.

The same is true for health care. In the 1990s support for Bill Clinton's reform plan had nothing to do with people's racial attitudes, which makes sense. What does race have to do with the provision of health care? Fifteen years later, racial attitudes were highly correlated with support for Obamacare. And it wasn't just African American beneficiaries people were concerned about; ethnicity was important as well. Former South Carolina congressman Joe Wilson infamously violated protocol during Barack Obama's 2009 speech to a joint session of Congress outlining his plans for health care reform, blurting out "You lie!" after the president made the claim that illegal immigrants would not receive Obamacare.

The late Lee Atwater, the legendary Republican strategist who masterminded George H. W. Bush's 1988 presidential bid, explained how this worked while he was a staffer in the Reagan White House. Atwater observed that whereas in the 1950s "you start out saying N-word,

N-word, N-word," by the late 1960s that tactic was no longer politically acceptable. Pivoting to a focus on busing and states' rights, which were more "abstract," gave cover, therefore, and allowed plausible deniability against charges of racism. By 1981, "you're talking about cutting taxes, and all these things you're talking about are totally economic things and a byproduct of them is, blacks get hurt worse than whites . . . 'We want to cut this,' is more abstract than even the busing thing, uh, and a hell of a lot more abstract than 'N-word, N-word.'"

Of course, not everyone who supports tax cuts and opposes Obamacare does so because of racial animus. That's not the point. The focus on hot-button issues like civil rights, feminism, immigration, and terrorism has opened up a worldview-based political divide. And folded into the divide now are bread-and-butter and redistributive issues that, while contentious in a previous era, did not have the same raw, emotional power then as they do today.

Worldviews, in sum, shape people's cultural preferences, their visions for the kinds of lives they want to live, and the political programs they believe are most likely to help themselves and their loved ones realize those dreams. And because the current divide also happens to align with Americans' cultural and partisan inclinations, the conflict it creates has been reinforced and extended into nearly every realm of life.

Today, people on opposite sides of the political divide have come to disagree about both the fundamentals of politics and the fundamentals of life. Worldviews now shape people's political preferences and also their life decisions: where they want to live, what they like to eat and drink, and what they enjoy doing in their free time. City or country, vegetarian or omnivore, dark beer or light, theater or racetrack: unlike politics, these are the things that people really care about in life. And now that they have been grafted on to politics, we have come to experience politics more passionately and viscerally.

One especially disturbing consequence is that partisans on both sides of the political divide find themselves unable to understand their opponents. When people look across the aisle, they don't see people they consider normal. Tough, practical, tradition-minded Americans squint across and see snowflake hipsters who don't understand the importance of protecting the nation or their own families. Brainy, idealistic, modernist Democrats, meanwhile, stare back and see knuckle-dragging racists who don't understand the importance of diversity. This lack of understanding makes each side perceive the other as a clear and present danger to the nation's well-being.

Given how central people's worldviews are to major life decisions, it shouldn't come as a surprise that political beliefs are associated with a wide range of attitudes that have nothing to do with politics. The next two chapters will explore more deeply how people's worldviews shape these nonpolitical tastes. It's impossible to appreciate the full depth and intensity of our political disagreements without understanding how enmeshed they are with much more personal differences—ones rooted in spheres of life far removed from politics. Moreover, differing lifestyles, including places of residence and worship and other cultural habits, have the effect of deepening the profound gulf between Republicans and Democrats— and limiting the everyday contact between those on opposite sides of the political spectrum. This has created a new cultural divide that is only worsening America's fractured politics. Political parties have leveraged this explosive combination for their own gain—but at great cost to our democracy.

3

Worlds Apart

THE BODY POLITIC and the human body have this in common—cells need to communicate with one another to remain healthy. Serious problems arise when they don't. When cells in the pancreas, which are charged with producing insulin, fail to receive signals from cells elsewhere in the body, they don't perform their critical task. The result is diabetes. When the tissue that protects nerve cells in the brain and spinal cord deteriorates and can no longer transmit signals to cells in other areas of the brain, the result is multiple sclerosis. Cell communication is essential for the human body to thrive.

Communication between different parts of the body politic is similarly essential to maintaining a healthy democracy. When Democrats and Republicans stop talking to each other, a *political* sclerosis develops. That is what is happening today, and the disease is getting worse.

Worldview politics is like a virus that short-circuits communication between "red" and "blue" cells, working in subtle, indirect ways. It is clear that many people with fixed and fluid worldviews see the political world so differently because their basic orientations to safety and well-being are so markedly divergent. Those differences, however, explain much more than people's attitudes toward immigration, feminism, the military's role in foreign affairs, and race.

Many of the decisions Americans make in their everyday lives — where to live, what kind of work to pursue, where to go to school, where to worship, what to watch on television, where to eat, what to drink — are influenced by the same worldview that informs their political opinions. Typically, Democrats live in the city, while Republicans live in the suburbs and small towns. Republicans tend to spend their Sunday mornings in church, while Democrats are more likely to spend it at brunch. Democrats watch *Mad Men.* Republicans watch *The Amazing Race.* When they eat out, Republicans are more likely to go to tried-and-true chain restaurants that serve American food. Democrats go to holes-in-the-wall that serve ethnic cuisine.

Americans make these decisions not because they are Democrats or Republicans but because the same worldview that influences their political views also shapes their lifestyle choices. Yet while these choices are not explicitly political in nature, they ironically have had the effect of making party conflict more intense — and more intractable.

When politics was centrally about the size of government and how much to tax, the resulting disagreements were about the fundamentals of governing, which, frankly, most Americans care little about. How hot can disagreements get when the details are complicated and people have little motivation to learn them?

But partisanship isn't just about politics anymore. Political disagreements these days are more about the fundamentals of life, which all Americans have a stake in. People care much more about race, culture, and how to best ensure physical security — for the country and for themselves — than they do about taxing and spending. Because political parties have reorganized themselves around these worldview-related preferences, Americans end up in parties pitted against people who are as unrecognizable to them personally as they are politically.

Democrats and Republicans now look at each other and see little in common. Their counterparts aren't just on the wrong side of political issues. They make everyday choices that are simply incomprehensible to many people on the other side. These little decisions can make it seem like our political opponents are not simply from another party, but from another planet.

This chapter and the next will show that the same worldview that informs Americans' partisanship also informs a range of nonpolitical preferences. As a result, those on the left and the right are increasingly unlikely to find themselves communicating with each other. They live apart, work apart, go to school apart, and spend their leisure time apart. If, by happenstance, they go to the same Little League baseball games or volunteer at the same food bank, they'll have little to talk about because they tend to enjoy different things and lack common experiences.

This lack of contact breeds mistrust and prejudice. Political opponents stop seeing one another as regular people who might disagree with them about a few specific issues. Without contact to counteract the stereotypes they harbor about the other tribe, they tend to view these opponents as caricatures who lack morals and values, making them a danger to the nation's future. Isolated in their partisan enclaves, red and blue cells have stopped communicating, and the condition of the body politic is deteriorating.

This chapter will focus on the ways in which this breakdown in communication has been caused by some of the most consequential personal decisions that people make: where to live, where to work, where to go to school, and which religious or spiritual beliefs to hold dear. Chapter 4 will explore the more idiosyncratic, day-to-day personal consumer tastes that have contributed to our partisan dysfunction. Whether these personal preferences are great or small, however, the key point is that all of them reinforce one another. Personal life choices now bear the hallmarks of readily identifiable political differences, and vice versa. Americans can read these cues in other people, effortlessly deducing political preferences from the simplest consumer choices. Each of these subconscious signals that Americans send and receive further divides the left from the right, and the fixed from the fluid.

Much of the evidence we bring to bear in this chapter and the next will show connections between either party or ideology on the one hand and various life decisions on the other. When it comes to specific residential decisions and occupation choices, it is simply not possible to link them directly to worldview. That is because the four parenting questions don't appear on many political surveys, and people don't publicly register themselves as fixed or fluid. But because people's identification with a party and an ideology today is so strongly driven by their worldview, we can safely assume that people's worldviews are pointing them toward certain life decisions, even if it is not possible to link findings directly to them.

This seems pretty uncontroversial. When you think about it, there is no reason to think people's partisan affiliations or their ideological leanings would cause them to differ in their nonpolitical interests and preferences. It's not like politics is central to many people's lives. Instead, it's likely that whether people are fixed or fluid influences both their political beliefs *and* their residential, occupational, educational, religious, and consumer choices. Worldview, in other words, underpins both political and nonpolitical preferences.

It is important to note that, when we observe connections between partisanship and nonpolitical decisions, we are talking about correlation, not causation. To use a social science term, political ideas are just *associated* with shopping preferences; Democrats do not favor Target over Walmart because they wish to make a partisan statement or enjoy wandering the aisles in solidarity with fellow Democrats. Rather, those with a fluid worldview prefer both Democrats to Republicans *and* Target to Walmart; the fixed prefer the reverse.

But regardless of what causes this relationship between political and nonpolitical behavior, the outcome is the same. Because people with fixed and fluid worldviews have different tastes and occupy different places, they have little contact with people on the opposite side of the political divide, and therefore struggle to understand them. And there is perhaps no starker demonstration of this divide between fixed and fluid than the vastly different sorts of neighborhoods they inhabit.

In the fall of 2004, a friend of ours named Suzanne moved with her family to an upper-middle-class suburban community in the South, a heterodox

decision for a liberal Democrat college professor. Despite the fact that she
knew an overwhelming percentage of her new neighbors were Republicans,
she still made it a priority to find the county Democratic Party headquarters soon after the family was settled. The reason was simple: she wanted to
pick up a Kerry-Edwards yard sign.

When her husband came home from work and found the sign planted
in the front yard, he was apoplectic. All a person had to do is drive the
mile and a half from their house to the highway to know this was Bush-
Cheney country. Their lawn signs outnumbered the Kerry-Edwards ones
by nine to one. Suzanne's husband fretted that the people in the neighborhood wouldn't give them the time of day after they saw the Kerry-
Edwards sign planted in the front yard. The religiously conservative
enclave would, in his fevered mind, conclude that they probably carried
out abortions in the living room.

Undeterred, Suzanne kept the sign up until Election Day. And as it
turned out, her husband was wrong to think that their neighbors would
shun them because of their politics. In fact, Suzanne's family developed
friendships with their neighbors on all sides, though it was probably smart
that they kept politics an unspoken difference between them. Indeed, the
political world would be much to the better if there were more people like
Suzanne and her neighbors.

One curious thing did happen, however—something that speaks to
the insidious way that worldview politics divides Americans. One day in
October, Suzanne found an anonymous note in their mailbox. It wasn't
some threatening screed from an unhappy conservative forced to share
the neighborhood with a liberal. Rather the note said, "I am so glad to see
another Democrat lives on this street."

Talk about distrust! A Democrat in a heavily Republican neighborhood didn't feel comfortable to out himself or herself—even to a fellow
Democrat!—lest the Republicans in the area find out.

America's increasingly partisan-based residential divisions help
to explain why some partisans might be afraid of expressing their politics in their own neighborhood. Political commentators often talk about
red states and blue states, but that is misleading. In blue states, huge

expanses of red usually exist across their rural counties. And, in red states, a few pockets of blue pop up where cities are located. Political consultant James Carville aptly captured this dynamic when he described Pennsylvania as "Philadelphia and Pittsburgh with Alabama in between." Cities, no matter where they are, have more in common with other cities. The same is true of rural areas. In that sense, central Pennsylvania is more like most of Alabama than it is like Philadelphia. Similarly, Atlanta is more like Philadelphia than it is like the rest of Georgia, a mostly rural state.

When viewed at the state level, voting patterns obscure more than they illuminate; what really matters is population density within states. The more densely populated an area is, the more Democratic it will tend to vote. New York is a blue state because its urban population is larger than its rural population. Ohio is the quintessential purple state—one that swings back and forth—because none of its major cities—Cleveland, Columbus, and Cincinnati—are especially large, so it lacks the urban population base for Democrats to win regularly. Tennessee is red because its cities—Nashville and Memphis—are relatively small, and the rest of the state is rural. None of the bottom five states in population density (Alaska, Wyoming, Montana, North Dakota, and South Dakota) have voted for a Democratic presidential candidate since 1992, and, even that year, only Montana went for Clinton, and by a small margin. By contrast, none of the top five states with the highest population density (New Jersey, Rhode Island, Massachusetts, Connecticut, and Maryland) have voted for a Republican presidential candidate since 1988.

Just as worldview is related to partisanship, preferences about hierarchy and cognitive closure, and beliefs about race, culture, and security, it also explains people's residential choices. It is only natural that people who have more fluid worldviews favor cities, where they find themselves among a wide array of diverse people, languages, and cultural options, complete with all the noise and chaotic energy that big cities embody. It is also natural that these urban qualities are not as attractive to fixed people, who are not as open to new experiences. Similarly, people who are high in conscientiousness—more fixed in worldview—favor tradition-minded suburban and rural areas that are predictable and safe, where preserving accepted ways of doing business, literally and figuratively, is a central value. People who are fluid in worldview naturally find such environments much less attractive.

Arlie Hochschild observed the impact of this particular form of residential segregation when she exchanged her urban liberal enclave of Berkeley, California, for the rural pockets of Louisiana where she was carrying out her research.

> Certain absences also reminded me I was not at home: no *New York Times* at the newsstand, almost no organic produce in grocery stores or farmers' markets, no foreign films in movie houses, few small cars, fewer petite sizes in clothing stores, fewer pedestrians speaking foreign languages into cell phones — indeed fewer pedestrians. There were fewer yellow Labradors, and more pit bulls and bulldogs. Forget bicycle lanes, color coded recycling bins, or solar panels on roofs. In some cafes, virtually everything on the menu was fried. There were no questions before meals about gluten-free entrees, and dinner generally began with prayer.

Among the factors that most distinguish people across the urban/rural divide is space — how much they have and how much they value it. In cities, residents only have a little. Outside metropolitan areas, people can get much more. And that is just how people seem to like it. As evidence, a Pew Research Center survey, conducted in 2014, gave Americans two options about the places they would choose to reside if they had a choice. They could live in communities with larger houses, but in which schools, stores, and restaurants were miles away. Or they could live in smaller houses, but in neighborhoods in which schools, stores, and restaurants were within walking distance. By a staggering 77 to 21 percent margin, the people Pew defined as "consistent liberals" preferred the latter set of arrangements. By an equally stark 75 to 22 margin, "consistent conservatives," as identified by Pew, preferred the former.

Worldview, not politics, motivates residential decisions; there's only an association between residential choice and party preference because worldview influences both. Because people who are more fluid in worldview are both more likely to prefer cities *and* be Democrats, a lot of Democrats will end up in cities. Because people who are more fixed in worldview are both more inclined to like suburban and rural areas *and* be Republicans, a lot of Republicans will end up in such places. The effect is residential sorting by worldview and, as a result, by party.

For most of the twentieth century, Democrats and Republicans more commonly lived in the same communities than they do today, although residential sorting by party began to pick up steam late in the century. As worldview became the dominant fault line in party politics in the early 2000s, residential political sorting accelerated even more dramatically. This has had a profound impact on the country's electoral landscape. In particular, counties in the United States are much more politically homogeneous than they once were.

There are about 3,000 counties in the United States, and they vary greatly by size. Some, like Kings County (Brooklyn), are huge — population 2.6 million. Others are tiny, like Loving County, Texas, population 82. Over time, the big ones, with high population densities, have trended Democratic, while the small ones, with low population densities, have trended Republican. That is why, in 1988, Democrat Michael Dukakis won 819 counties of the nation's nearly 3,000, yet lost the presidential election to George H. W. Bush in a near landslide, while Barack Obama won just 690 counties in 2008, 129 fewer than Dukakis, but *won* in a near landslide. The size of the counties that Obama won and the margin by which he won them were, on average, much larger than those that went for Dukakis. These numbers also make clear that Dukakis won a lot more small counties than Obama did. That trajectory illustrates the growing pace of residential sorting by worldview. Urban areas are now so densely populated by Democrats that Democratic candidates do not need to do very well outside of big metro areas to win elections, which is fortunate for them because they are increasingly unpopular in outlying areas.

That hasn't always been so. In 1976, less than a quarter of Americans lived in so-called landslide counties, places where one presidential can-

didate won 60 percent of the vote or more. By 2012, over half lived in
such counties. The change over time has been especially stark in rural
and suburban areas. In 1976, 39 percent of counties that cast 25,000
or fewer votes for president were won by more than twenty percentage
points, and Democrat Jimmy Carter won many of those. In 2012, the percentage nearly doubled to 70 percent, almost all of which were won by
Republican Mitt Romney. Over the same period, the percentage of landslide urban counties more than doubled from 22 percent to nearly 50.

In the most populous counties, the ones encompassing larger cities,
the one-sidedness of political affiliation is staggering. In Manhattan, San
Francisco, and Washington, Mitt Romney won less than 20 percent of the
vote in 2012. Whereas Republican platforms used to talk about the need
to appeal to urban residents and to promote policies aimed at expanding
economic opportunity in urban cores, Republican platforms today invoke
cities primarily to rail against their use as sanctuaries for undocumented
immigrants or, as Donald Trump frequently did in 2016, to call places
like Chicago—a favorite punching bag of his, perhaps because it was
Obama's adopted hometown—unmitigated "disasters."

Clearly, Americans generally tend to choose residences near people
with whom they feel most comfortable, either because of shared ethnicity
or other affinities that make their communities feel like home. And what
attracts Americans to particular communities says a lot about the worldview divide and its consequences.

Consider Reading, Pennsylvania. This small city in Berks County,
Pennsylvania, is a microcosm of larger changes afoot in America. Reading is now 60 percent Hispanic, up from 35 percent at the turn of the
new century and barely double digits just fifteen years before that. The
city has become a magnet for Puerto Rican and Mexican in-migration
because of the shared sense of identity created as these groups reached a
critical mass in the area. The larger county in which Reading sits, however, is mostly white, and whites have been fleeing Reading as fast as
Hispanics have been moving in.

But not all whites have been leaving Reading. Some are staying,
or even flocking to it. Kevin Murphy, the white president of the Berks

County Community Foundation, likes all that has happened in Reading. Although the city still has one of the highest poverty rates in the nation, nearly 40 percent, Murphy peers optimistically into the future. He sees potential economic dynamism and a flowering of diversity that he naturally associates with strong, thriving communities. He touts the transformation of southeastern Pennsylvania more broadly, fueled by a boom in high tech and medical technology and fertilized by growing diversity and openness.

It's this vision—of educated professionals of all creeds working in high tech and other professions in coalition with less-well-off communities of color—that led political experts John Judis and Ruy Teixeira to famously predict, at the turn of the twenty-first century, that an "emerging Democratic majority" would soon come to dominate American politics. Cities and dense metropolitan areas are becoming increasingly dynamic economic engines, even as they continue to suffer from significant pockets of poverty and inequality. That dynamism is a magnet drawing more people to them.

But that magnetic pull is only attracting a self-selected group—racial and ethnic minorities on the one hand and white professionals who tend to be fluid in their thinking on the other. People with a fixed worldview are repelled. They see places like Reading becoming off-limits redoubts of crime and "foreignness." They want to build distance between themselves and such places, so they choose more homogenous suburban and rural areas away from the city.

As a result of this push and pull, Berks County is increasingly balkanized. Each school district is its own distinct pocket of worldviews, as if there are physical border posts marking the boundaries between the fixed and the fluid, community by community.

Of course, not all small towns have witnessed the demographic transformation and influx of professionals that might eventually help Reading rebound from being among the poorest cities in America. One such example is Winchester, Virginia. When the journalist Joe Bageant returned home there in the early 2000s, he was struck by the economic stagnation and sinking morale of those he called "his people," lifelong inhabitants of a once-bucolic enclave about seventy-five miles west of the nation's capital. Members of this working-class community of mostly Scotch-Irish descent had become more conservative, more demoralized, and more resentful of the big city than he remembered it was when he left decades before. Bageant noted that, in towns like Winchester, big employers like the Rubbermaid plant reinforce the urban/rural divide. When supervisors express their (invariably) conservative opinions, workers "suck up reflexively," echoing their bosses' political beliefs regardless of whether they would have independently espoused them; in a way, this is inevitable, given the precariousness of work and life. Right-wing talk radio provides the ambient background music for workers. All this makes people in towns like Winchester "Republicans by default."

More and more nonurban American communities look, feel, and sound like Winchester, once a Democratic-leaning area that is now deep red. This trend is self-reinforcing. As the suburbs and countryside become more and more Republican, the environment for Democrats, particularly those who are more fluid, feels less hospitable. As a result, if they can, they're increasingly likely to move to places that better suit their sensibilities and to communities where they won't have to resort to leaving their neighbors anonymous letters when they want to express their political beliefs.

In sum, Democrats and liberals are flowing in ever larger numbers to urban areas, concentrating themselves in big, noisy, polyglot places that fit their worldview. Republicans and conservatives are leaving those areas, which don't fit theirs. And people who have stuck around in the smaller, rural communities beyond the suburbs, people who are more likely to be fixed in outlook, see increasingly little they might have in common with urbanites.

The combination of migration and stasis are helping to make Americans more residentially sorted by party than before. Their physical segregation compounds the profound cultural differences between these fellow citizens, and diminishes opportunities for them to bridge their differences. It also persuades politicians that there's simply no point in making a campaign stop in areas they're likely to view as enemy territory. Now that worldview divides one party from the other and one neighborhood from another, Democratic candidates see few benefits to getting to out-of-the-way rural communities. Such trips are time-intensive and unlikely to attract more Democratic votes. This ensures that residential segregation gets built into our very electoral landscape, perhaps for generations to come.

Residential polarization is only one of the many ways in which people's worldviews shape their biggest life decisions, and thereby cleave the fixed from the fluid. Occupational polarization is another.

When fixed and fluid people leave home in the morning, they are unlikely to be headed to work in the same places. This is, in part, a consequence of residential choice. Not many loggers, farmers, and oil workers—three of the most overwhelmingly Republican professions—will live in cities. That's understandable, because forests, farms, and oil rigs simply don't exist in urban areas. Similarly, taxi drivers, comedians, and chefs, three of the most Democratic occupations, will have far more opportunities in cities than in outlying areas, because cities have more restaurants and comedy clubs, and a bigger market for taxicabs. One set of choices reinforces the others, strengthening the great worldview-political divide.

Intriguingly, however, occupational differences between fixed and fluid people appear to go far deeper than differences in where they choose to live. This was demonstrated in research by Verdant Labs, which used campaign-contribution data collected by the Federal Election Commission (FEC) to classify various professions by party. The researchers were able to correlate donors' political affiliations with their jobs because the FEC receives information on the profession of the donor when a campaign reports who its contributors are. Based on the party of the candidate receiving the contribution and the data on the profession of the contributor logged by the FEC, Verdant Labs identified fifty occupations that lean decidedly left or right. If you are a midwife, a yoga instructor, a bookseller, a gardener, or an architect, you are likely to be a Democrat. Conversely, beer wholesalers, car salespeople, home builders, exterminators, and insurance agents are disproportionately Republicans.

These professional differences don't necessarily mean that Democrats and Republicans have no professional contact with each other, of course. Sometimes left- and right-leaning professions will bring people together in the same work space; for example, pilots are mostly Republicans while flight attendants are usually Democrats. In other cases, the kind of work that people on opposites sides of the political divide perform is sufficiently similar that they should be able to find common ground easily; for example, Episcopal priests tend to be Democrats whereas Catholic priests tend to be Republicans. But such examples are the exception, not the rule.

Someone's level of education goes a long way toward explaining the linkage between their occupation and their party preference. And there is a linkage — a very clear connection between how much schooling people have and how they vote. Indeed, the divide between working-class whites, defined as those with less than a college degree, and better-educated whites has been growing increasingly stark. In 2016, Donald Trump was trounced by nearly twenty points among whites who had postgraduate degrees, while winning by nearly forty points among whites who had not graduated from college. And just as education level is tied to voting behavior, it is also related to job choice. An advanced degree is not necessary to work on an oil rig or work construction. It is, however, a requirement for architects and professors. This suggests that the relationship between people's jobs and their party affiliation is shaped, in part, by their education.

To be sure, plenty of college-educated people are Republicans. Both sides have lots of white-collar supporters. But not all white collars, it turns out, are created equal.

John Judis and Ruy Teixeira identified a useful distinction between members of this seemingly homogenous demographic — a distinction that can help to explain why two white-collar Americans might vote in opposite ways. They suggested that a group they call "professionals" tend toward the Democratic side. These professionals are typically white-collar workers with college or advanced degrees. They include "academics, architects, engineers, scientists, computer analysts, lawyers, physicians, registered nurses, teachers, social workers, therapists, fashion designers, interior decorators, graphic artists, writers, editors, and actors." In the 1950s, according to Judis and Teixeira, such professionals represented only 7 percent of the workforce. Today, after a decades-long transition from a blue-collar, industrial economy to one where the engine of growth is ideas and services, they represent more than 15 percent of American workers.

These so-called professionals stand in stark contrast to more traditional managers and corporate executives who remain on the political right. Professionals and managers differ in one big aspect of their work: managers judge outcomes by profit and loss calculations, a bottom-line, black-and-white metric; on the other hand, professionals judge outcomes by the quality and aesthetics of the products and ideas they produce — a much more nuanced, shades-of-gray metric. For instance, consider two people with different jobs in the film industry: one manages the books and the other does costume design. If the film nets $100 million, the manager is thrilled regardless of esoteric things like how the characters looked in their costumes. In contrast, the costume designer might not care how much money the film made, but he or she would care a lot about whether the film won an Academy Award nomination for costume design.

The most scientifically complete research on party leanings and professions has focused on the medical field. Medicine is a particularly interesting example, moreover, because people who enter this general field have to make a lot of choices about what specialty they will pursue. This allows researchers to see how very fine-grain professional differences are reflected in people's political leanings.

One such study matched a list of all the doctors in the United States with voter registration data in the twenty-nine states that ask voters to declare a party. The researchers could then see whether doctors in specific professions — they surveyed twenty-four different medical fields — were more likely to register to vote as Republicans or Democrats. The study found, for example, that surgery attracts mostly Republicans, while Democrats gravitated more toward psychiatry and infectious-disease prevention.

Compensation appears to be part of the explanation for why people with particular political beliefs might gravitate toward the fields of medicine they do. Both orthopedics and anesthesiology attract lots of Republicans and come with especially high salaries. Pediatrics and internal medicine are two of the least well-paying fields, and Republicans are much less interested in them than Democrats are. But compensation doesn't tell nearly the whole story. Cardiology, for example, is among the most highly compensated areas and yet it is equally split between Republicans and Democrats.

Worldview offers a clearer lens onto the decisions that soon-to-be doctors make about their specialties. Areas that are not particularly cut-and-dried, such as psychiatry, or that involve what might be considered higher-risk work, such as infectious disease, may attract people with more fluid worldviews and repel those whose worldviews are more fixed. This makes sense, considering what we know about fixed people's need for cognitive closure. And given that fixed people seem to have a higher propensity for disgust, infectious disease, in particular, can't be very appealing to them. By contrast, the type of medicine that an orthopedist or an anesthesiologist practices tends to be more formulaic. It is not that all knee surgeries are the same; they are not. But the blueprint for treating someone with a torn ACL is much more straightforward than for treating someone with chronic depression. In the case of psychiatry, the constant slog through messy emotions might be much less appealing to people for whom cognitive closure is a priority. Conversely, it would intuitively seem to appeal much more to those for whom the formulaic field of orthopedics might seem boring.

The takeaway from all this is that occupational choices, whether between professions or within them, appear to have taken on a partisan character—and it's plausible that worldview is at the core of many of those decisions. Worldview likely helps people decide whether they are going to be happier being a logger or an environmentalist, working on an oil rig or behind a desk as a software engineer. Even within white-collar occupations, worldview appears central to whether someone becomes a manager, with a focus on the bottom line, or a professional, with an interest in the aesthetic.

This sort of professional segregation is yet another reason that people on opposite sides of the political divide encounter each other less than they did before the rise of worldview politics. And when conversations around the watercooler and at company holiday parties no longer foster contact between "red" and "blue" cells of the body politic, that is sure to take a toll on our nation's health.

The choices we make about where to live and what kind of work to perform reflect fundamental differences in our worldviews. Fixed people tend to prefer predictable routines whether at home or at work. Those tendencies also extend to educational decisions—not simply the level of education that people choose to attain, but also where they seek to attain it.

In fact, the amount of time people attend school is one of the life choices most strongly associated with worldview. In the 2016 CCAP, more than half (51 percent) of respondents with a fixed worldview reported having either a high school education or less. In contrast, only a quarter of the fluid reported not attending at least some college. Among the fixed, only 12 percent completed a college degree while an additional 6 percent earned a postgraduate degree. That means 18 percent of the fixed had a bachelor's degree or more, which is about equal to the percentage of those with a fluid worldview who earned postgraduate degrees (17 percent) alone. Another 25 percent of the fluid earned bachelor's degrees, so 42 percent of all fluids earned at least a four-year degree, easily more than double the rate for those with a fixed worldview.

The relatively higher level of education of fluid people compared to fixed people is striking. It probably helps to explain why, in 2012, when President Obama suggested that all Americans should have the opportunity to complete at least one year of college, community or otherwise, former senator and GOP presidential candidate Rick Santorum exclaimed, "What a snob!" It also probably helps to explain why attitudes about college are so remarkably different between Republicans and Democrats these days.

In July 2017 the Pew Research Center asked Americans how they felt about a wide range of institutions and whether each was having a positive or negative impact on the country. Not surprisingly, Republicans were high on religious institutions, with 73 percent saying their effect is positive and only 14 percent saying it is negative. (Democrats, too, came out as more positive than negative toward religious institutions, but only by a 50 to 36 percent margin.) At the same time, Republicans were down on the national news media; only 10 percent of them viewed the media positively, and fully 85 percent saw it as a negative force, whereas Democrats were split roughly evenly on the media's impact.

But perhaps the most bracing partisan differences to have emerged from this study involve colleges and universities. Seventy-two percent of Democrats regarded the impact of these institutions as positive, while only 36 percent of Republicans felt the same—a striking gap in support for what has historically been a pillar of the American dream for so many people. The difference between Democratic and Republican support for institutions of higher education is especially notable because, until just a few years ago, Republicans also viewed them quite positively. But today, college—like seemingly everything else—has become another point of contention in the worldview-party nexus.

It's likely that the image of certain types of schools prompts Republicans' negative general assessment of higher education. Nearly half of the Americans who voted Republican in 2016 did go to college, after all. But they seem increasingly wary of some of the most elite schools, especially those with ivy on the walls. As far as Republicans are concerned, these institutions are increasingly infested with intolerant liberalism.

The result is that, today, the worldview divide appears to be influencing where high school graduates decide to matriculate. College handbooks, like the *Princeton Review,* now provide information to prospective college students and their parents about the observed ideological leanings of colleges. Because of the perceived dominance of liberalism at most elite colleges and universities, conservatives are increasingly attuned to the political biases they might face if they attend one of these institutions. So it would be natural for them to decide that they might be more comfortable enrolling in a school where more of the student body shares their worldview. Institutions like Baylor, the Baptist school in Waco, Texas; Brigham Young, the flagship Mormon university in Salt Lake City, Utah; and Texas A&M, the behemoth public university in College Station, Texas, all provide such an ideological safe haven for conservative, fixed students.

The political divide at college is evident in informal surveys that colleagues took at Vanderbilt University in Tennessee and Auburn University in Alabama during the 2016 presidential campaign. At Vanderbilt, an introductory American politics class of one hundred students revealed in a confidential survey that it preferred Clinton to Trump by a margin of 70 to 20, with the Libertarian Party's Gary Johnson receiving the remaining 10 votes. At Auburn, by contrast, the vote was a whopping 95 to 5 for Trump.

Battles over so-called political correctness and its dominance on college campuses have been raging off and on for many years. These have only intensified since the 2016 election. A few months after the election, a reporter from *USA Today* called one of us to ask whether we were teaching college students differently in the age of Trump. Indeed we were. One change included a new assignment that asked students to seek out a member of the opposing party to interview. The purpose of the assignment was to provide students an opportunity to assess whether those on the other side were as different from them as they thought. The reporter, who had been a student at the University of Pennsylvania, said that such an assignment would have posed a practical dilemma at her Ivy League school because finding Republican students to interview would have been hard.

The flight of conservative students from the Ivy League and fancy northeastern liberal arts colleges is not entirely new. The right has persistently leveled charges of elitism against the left for decades. Highly educated cosmopolitans seem to more tradition-minded conservatives to be America's biggest critics — and least trustworthy leaders. In 1963 conservative activist William F. Buckley famously said, "I would rather be governed by the first two thousand people in the Boston telephone directory than by the two thousand people on the faculty of Harvard University." The following year, Ronald Reagan's nomination speech on behalf of Barry Goldwater suggested the choice in 1964 boiled down to "whether we believe in our capacity for self-government or whether we abandon the American revolution and confess that a little intellectual elite in a far-distant capital can plan our lives for us better than we can plan them ourselves."

Now that less educated whites have evolved from being a solidly Democratic constituency to a central part of the Republican coalition, it is a rite of passage for GOP office seekers to target what they see as the excesses of elitism. Rick Santorum put it this way in 2012: "There are good, decent men and women who go out and work hard every day and put their skills to the test that aren't taught by some liberal college professor trying to indoctrinate them." After a generation of GOP candidates bashing liberal college professors, it is a given in the minds of Republicans who do not live on the coasts that liberals today are a bunch of elitists with fancy degrees from places like Harvard, Princeton, and Yale who think they are better than the rest of America.

Of course, the last three Republican presidents — George H. W. Bush, George W. Bush, and Donald J. Trump — all had Ivy League pedigrees. But particularly in recent years, the venom conservatives have directed against "political correctness" and the dominance of demonstrative liberalism on college campuses has made higher education one of the higher-profile battlegrounds in the worldview conflict. Indeed, no major party candidate spent more time hammering political correctness than Trump did in 2016. As a result, whether people went to college or not, and regardless of where, their perceptions of what professors were teaching students on college campuses and for what purposes would certainly be colored by their worldview.

• • •

As striking as these residential, occupational, and educational differences are, the religious differences between people with opposing worldviews run even deeper.

There is an old saw that Sunday-morning church time is the most segregated hour in America. Typically this has referred to the way that religious and racial identities go hand in hand, but commentators and scholars have also long noted a deepening religious schism between Republicans and Democrats. This religious-political divide dates back to the 1980 election, when Ronald Reagan's campaign openly courted the support of deeply faithful religious conservatives. (While it is almost impossible to imagine now, before that point, religious conservatives had different party cues to follow; in the 1976 presidential election, they had to pick between a pro-choice Republican, Gerald Ford, and a pro-life Democrat, Jimmy Carter.)

Around the same time that Reagan was elected to the presidency, denominational differences between Democrats and Republicans began to evolve, with white Catholics (formerly a solidly Democratic group) drifting toward the GOP, and mainline Protestants finding more in common with the Democrats. Yet another subset of Protestants was skewing even more quickly to the right than Catholics were, and that sect was also growing in numbers. The Supreme Court's decisions on school prayer and abortion woke evangelical Protestantism from a decades-long political slumber. With Ronald Reagan promising to fight these decisions, evangelicals became the backbone of the new Republican Party.

The ties between evangelicals and Republicanism is so strong today that, in 2016, even an irreligious Republican, Donald Trump, could best a devout Methodist, Hillary Clinton, by fifteen points among Protestants as a whole. That was because whites who called themselves either "evangelical" or "born again" cast 80 percent of their ballots for Trump and only 16 percent for Clinton.

It is comical to think evangelicals were centrally attracted to Trump because of his traditional, moral character, a point we return to in chapter 5. More plausibly, the fixed-worldview values that he projected appealed to them. After all, evangelicals are more likely to possess fixed worldviews than any nonminority group. It's not coincidental that evangelicals are among the most likely to subscribe to biblical literalism—just the sort of straightforward, unnuanced approach to the world that should suit people with a fixed worldview.

This kind of fundamentalist versus interpretive division exists not just among Christians. Among Jews, as well, a clear schism has emerged between secular, Reform, and Conservative Jews on the one hand and Orthodox Jews on the other. Of all groups about whom enough evidence exists to make such a claim, Jews are the most likely to be fluid. As such, they are among the most resolute Democratic voters in the country. But that is only true among secular, Reform, and Conservative Jews. Orthodox Jews have, as a group, become increasingly politically conservative over the past two decades. Although the group is numerically too small to measure its attitudes using survey research, it is hard not to think its members, with their focus on texts and traditions, wouldn't be highly fixed in their worldview. The result is that, as the commentator Peter Beinart has put it, there is no longer a "Jewish vote" in the United States. As among Protestants, there is a worldview divide among Jews.

A second, nondenominational religious divide also began to develop in America in the decade prior to Reagan's election in 1980. As the country began to grow more secular starting in the 1970s, the frequency with which people went to church started to reflect the choices they made in the voting booth. Today, religious attendance is one of the big factors distinguishing Republicans from Democrats. Trump won by about fifteen points among the one-third of Americans who report going to religious services at least weekly, but lost by about thirty points among the one-fifth of voters who report never going. The latter group, now commonly referred to as the "nones" has emerged as a significant new bloc in Democratic politics. Other research has shown that Democrats do reasonably well among the mainline Protestants and Catholics who report going to church only irregularly, but Republicans prevail by a large margin among the churched who actually go to church.

In some ways, these data obscure the extent to which the religious divide that now exists between the parties is also a worldview divide. The religious differences between the parties would be even greater if not for the fact that racial and ethnic minorities, stalwart Democratic groups, are among the most religious groups in American life. Indeed African Americans and Hispanics both attend religious services at much higher rates than whites do. But because racial and ethnic minorities choose their party based on their group identities, their strong religious leanings simply do not factor into their political decisions as much as those of white voters do.

Indeed, leaving nonwhites out of the equation, the religious preferences between fixed and fluid *whites* are extraordinarily large. To measure just how big, our April 2017 survey—the most recent of the half-dozen we have conducted since November 2006—included questions that the Pew Research Center has used for years to tap religious commitments, and which made it possible for us to see precisely how different the fixed and fluid are in this respect. The results were stunning. One survey question asked people to evaluate whether religion in their own lives was "very important," "somewhat important," "not too important," or "not at all important." Religion mattered a lot to the fixed, with more than three-quarters answering either very (51 percent) or somewhat (26 percent) important. The fluid were a near mirror image, with only 12 percent answering very important and another 19 percent answering somewhat important. The most common response by far among the fluid was "not important at all," with fully 49 percent choosing that option.

Given the gulf between these responses from fixed and fluid people, it is not surprising to see a similarly yawning gap between the two groups when it comes to religious attendance. Among the fluid, fewer than 10 percent report going to religious services at least once a week, and fully 47 percent say they never go. In contrast, 35 percent of the fixed attend services at least once a week, with fewer than one-quarter reporting that they never go.

Of course, people don't necessarily have to attend services to have a relationship with God—or, as the fluid might prefer, to engage with "a higher power" or to be "spiritual." People can and do pray privately. But when they do, the fixed pray much more than the fluid. More than half

say they pray at least once a day, with 37 percent praying several times
a day and another 16 percent at least once a day. Only 12 percent of the
fixed report never praying. Among the fluid the most common category
for them is "never," at 41 percent. Another 22 percent place themselves
in the "seldom pray" category. Only 12 percent of the fluid say they pray
several times a day and another 10 percent that they do so once a day.

Asked about denomination on our April 2017 survey, the fixed were
most likely to report they were Protestant or Roman Catholic. Among
the fluid, in contrast, the most common response was "nothing in particular." In fact, the combination of atheist and agnostic outpolled the combination of Protestant and Catholic for those with a fluid worldview. Talk
about being worlds apart!

The style of worship that fixed and fluid people reported following
only deepens this massive divide between them. Researchers have also
asked people whether they consider themselves "born again." Although
the term is widely misunderstood even by those who go to church regularly (for example, lots of faithful Catholics report they are born again,
even though the Catholic Church explicitly recognizes only "one baptism
for the forgiveness of sins," which regular churchgoers repeat weekly in
their profession of faith), researchers believe the label captures a tendency toward a more evangelical style of worship. Not surprisingly, fewer
than 10 percent of the fluid describe themselves as born again, compared
with 45 percent of the fixed.

These differences all but ensure that the fixed and fluid are not going
to run into each other at the church social or on bingo night, and their
kids are not going to spend time bonding with each other at weekend
retreats. But religious differences go even deeper than this, not only limiting contact between the fixed and fluid, but also shaping their outlook in
even more subtle and unusual ways.

In addition to all the other questions in our April 2017 survey, we
asked people to do something a little off-the-wall. We wanted them to
rate how they felt about certain words — thirteen, to be exact — on a scale
from 0 to 100 degrees. If they liked the word, they were to rate it above
50, with scores closer to 100 indicating more-positive (warmer) feelings.

If they disliked the word, they were to score it below 50, with scores closer to 0 suggesting more-negative (colder) feelings. If they felt neutrally about the word, they were to answer 50 exactly.

One of the words we asked them to rate was particularly relevant to our goal of understanding people's differing orientations toward religion: "faith."

You would expect people on both sides of the divide to have reasonably positive feelings about the word "faith." Instead, it turned out to be an especially telling symptom of the worldview divide. The spread between the fixed and fluid in their assessment of it was dramatic. The average score that the fixed gave it was 81 degrees, which is around the same average that they gave to most of the terms. The average among the fluid was only 44 degrees, a bit lower than the neutral point and considerably lower than their feelings toward all the other words. This is a difference of 37 degrees — about the same as the difference between the responses of fixed and fluid respondents to the controversial questions about race on the 2016 CCAP survey.

This result is especially striking because religious faith is not the only type of faith in modern-day vernacular. It is impossible to find a self-help book that doesn't trumpet the importance of having faith in oneself. In singing about a romantic relationship, John Hiatt, the great singer-songwriter, beseeches his partner to "have a little faith in me." Eric Clapton revealed in the 1980s that he was "Running on Faith." Jon Bon Jovi implored us to "Keep the Faith" in the following decade. George Michael won a Grammy with an album titled *Faith*. None of these characters fit the definition of Christian rocker in any way, shape, or form, and they used the word freely. And yet, somehow, this simple term has become part of the deep and wide fault line between the fixed and the fluid. This is a striking testament to the divisiveness of religion in America today.

Fixed and fluid people not only have different outlooks on life; they also seem to live in different worlds. This is true in a very literal sense: The fixed prefer to live in wide-open spaces while the fluid like densely populated areas. But it also is true in the sense that these two groups inhabit different spheres in all of the most important areas of their lives, which limits the opportunities for people in one group to encounter people in the other.

In sum, as people enter adulthood, their worlds are increasingly populated by those with a similar worldview, because of decisions they've made about whether and where to go to college, where to work, where to live, and where to pray. This lack of contact between the fixed and fluid has profound implications. When the parts of the body politic fail to communicate, the whole becomes endangered. This political sclerosis engenders other types of scleroses—namely, social diseases such as discrimination and prejudice.

Prejudice often results when people who are different encounter each other only rarely. Faced with an unknown and mysterious "other," people rely on stereotypes. Consider racial prejudice. Whites once overwhelmingly perceived African Americans as subhuman rather than as people who might actually have things in common with them. Only with the forcible end of racial segregation has America made strides to combat these awful misperceptions—and all it takes is a glance at the headlines to see that the country still has a long, long way to go on this front.

Contact is necessary for people to see each other as people. Communication between whites and blacks, straights and gays, Christians and Muslims, or people with any other sort of difference between them has the capacity to build understanding, which, in turn, can help overcome prejudice.

Scores of studies detail how increased contact between people belonging to different racial groups or those with different sexual orientations cause them to be more tolerant of the group to which they do not belong. For example, the first instinct of people with a fixed worldview might be to dislike gays and lesbians, whom they perceive as violating existing social conventions and religious traditions. However, someone with a fixed worldview who nevertheless has contact with the LGBT community might see the group more positively. Former vice president Dick Cheney, the proud father of a lesbian daughter, springs to mind as real-world evidence. Rob Portman, Republican senator from Ohio, had a similar "conversion" on the issue after one of his sons came out.

Contact does not have to be personal for it to have a salutary effect; it can come in the form of information. Using door-to-door canvassing, one innovative study found that information that explained why some people experience a disconnect between their sex at birth and their gender identity could reduce the negative feelings that gender-normative Americans tend to have about transgender people. Researchers had fifty-six canvassers meet with about five hundred voters in South Florida and Southern California. Canvassers asked voters whom they met on doorsteps to engage in a "perspective taking" task. They asked the voters to tell them about a time in their own lives when they believed others had viewed them in a negative light for being different in some way, just like transgender people might be made to feel different all the time. They then asked a number of questions, including how the voters felt about transgender people. To create a group to compare them to, researchers also identified different people in the same two communities with the same characteristics as the five hundred people who received the transgender treatment. They sent canvassers to their homes, too. Instead of giving these people information about transgender people, however, the canvassers provided them with information about recycling.

To see what effect the information about transgender people had on those who received it, the researchers compared the feelings expressed about transgender people by those who received the transgender treatment, with the feelings about transgender people expressed by those who received information about recycling. Given the design of their study, it might not be particularly surprising that people who got "information contact" with transgender people expressed warmer feelings toward the group. More surprising is the size of the effect and how long it persisted.

The average feeling thermometer score (like the measure used to gauge people's feelings about the word "faith") for transgender people was ten points higher for those who got the transgender information than those who got the recycling information. This effect is huge by survey

research standards. By way of comparison, the average feeling thermometer score for "gays and lesbians," which is reported every four years by
the ANES, increased by only 8.5 degrees between 1988 and 2012. Not
only that, the increase in positive feelings generated by the transgender
treatment persisted three months later, when the scholars did a follow-up
study with those who received it.

Even mediated contact has the potential to change attitudes. A major
turning point in straight Americans' attitudes about homosexuality
occurred when the number of gay characters on television and movies increased in the 1990s. Before that, LGBT people rarely appeared in shows
other than as two-dimensional caricatures. The late-1970s/early-'80s sitcom *Three's Company*, which starred John Ritter as a young chef who lives
with two women and pretends to be gay to mollify a conservative landlord,
tended to play up gay stereotypes for comic effect. *Ellen* changed that
in 1997, when the title character, played by Ellen DeGeneres, came out
as a lesbian in the series' fourth season. DeGeneres played an appealing three-dimensional character, shorn of the stereotypes that had typi-
fied gay characters on television before that. Hollywood's use of more gay
characters surely reflects warmer public attitudes, but recent research
makes clear that more gay-friendly popular culture increases tolerance
and support for the LGBT community, too.

But in order to achieve this sort of understanding, people need to have
contact with each other, or at least possess information about each other.
That is not what is happening in America today. Quite the opposite, in
fact.

As politically polarized Americans also isolate themselves residentially, professionally, educationally, and religiously, opportunities for
contact narrow. Among the people with whom they share these enclaves,
they will of course find they have plenty in common. Their shared choices
bring them together — to the extent that Americans actually still do things
together these days. Indeed, the decline in social interaction generally is
another recent development that is driving the fragmentation of America
into different tribes.

In his masterwork *Bowling Alone*, political scientist Robert Putnam points to a precipitous drop in what he calls social capital. By social capital, he means the assets accrued by people belonging to social organizations like bowling leagues, churches, fraternal organizations, and the PTA. In the post–World War II years, such organizations flourished. They are not as popular today. As Putnam notes, more Americans than ever bowl, but fewer bowl in leagues. Instead Americans bowl alone, at great cost to social trust, the oil that lubricates the engine of civil society.

When social capital was at its peak in the postwar years, social organizations brought Democrats and Republicans together. Partisans of both stripes joined the Elks, the Knights of Columbus, bridge clubs, and knitting circles. More informally, they used to eat at each other's houses and drink at the same neighborhood bars.

These interactions produced, to use Putnam's term, "bridging" social capital. They built bridges between people who might not naturally fit together. The act of being together with people who might not be similar politically or otherwise produced shared understanding. This is the kind of social interaction that could help to overcome prejudice, and help Americans see each other's common humanity despite their differences.

But instead of having social contact with people in other groups, Americans now have the majority of their interactions with people who are part of their own group. When already like-minded people belong to the same formal and informal social organizations, it builds a less useful form of social capital—"bonding" social capital. It simply deepens bonds that already exist. It fails to increase people's understanding of those who differ from them. More time spent among those who already see the world the same way serves to reinforce what people already believe.

Because Americans on the left and right are increasingly living in different worlds, the most common type of social capital today runs the risk of being of the bonding, not the bridging, variety. And because Americans also inhabit different media environments—a topic we will return to in later chapters—they are not getting the sort of information that would help them to comprehend people on the opposite side. And so the country's fractured politics has begun to ossify.

But the differences that Americans experience in these major spheres of life are only half of the story. Even on the most quotidian level, the life patterns and preferences of the fixed and the fluid—their coffee and beer tastes, the music they like to listen to and the television shows they watch —leave less and less room for points of mutual interest and engagement. It might not seem obvious that your preferences about entertainment, food and drink, or the qualities you value in children are connected to your outlook on life, or the way you vote. But this is exactly what research has demonstrated—and it shows just how deeply divided America's warring tribes have become.

4

A Day in the Life

SHORTLY AFTER HE BECAME vice president—elect of the United States in November 2016, Mike Pence attended a performance of the Broadway musical *Hamilton*. Created and composed by Lin-Manuel Miranda, an artist of Puerto Rican descent, and with an openly gay, HIV-positive actor as Miranda's alternate for the role of Alexander Hamilton, the musical is the embodiment of the American dream, fluid-style. It rewrites the founding of American history as a racially complex, multicultural tale. Its meter is rap music. It's about a New Yorker, by a New Yorker, and, of course, became a worldwide sensation in New York. So when the audience booed the culturally conservative former governor of red Indiana after his presence in the theater was acknowledged, it was as perfect a storm as one could conjure in the age of the worldview divide.

Indeed, Mike Pence at a Manhattan theater is a lot like Michelle Obama attending a NASCAR event in the Deep South. That actually happened in 2011. When the track announcer recognized her and Jill Biden at a race they attended to honor veterans, the crowd showered them with boos, too.

Such is the chasm that exists between these two most clichéd manifestations of the worldview divide — elitist theater snobs on one side and uncultured hicks on the other. These reactions, however, are symptomatic of a more general pattern in American politics.

How Americans identify politically is now inseparable from their tastes and preferences about a dizzying array of both the most personal and mundane matters. Many of the choices that make up the guts and marrow of Americans' day-to-day lives are remarkably different depending on which side of the party divide they sit. This is critical to understanding the raw feelings that partisans have about each other. And it is central to the story of how the convergence of Americans' worldviews and their political identities not only drove a wedge between ordinary citizens, but also has helped to keep them apart.

When worldview didn't divide Democrats from Republicans, they used to be more inclined to live among each other. They were more likely to work together, to go to school together, and to worship side by side. Worldview-sorted parties make all those things less likely. But they have also made it much less likely that Americans' other, much simpler—and in some ways more elemental—preferences will overlap, too.

Today, Americans are divided by choices that seem much more trivial than where they live, work, and worship. Which beer they like to drink, how they feel about Cracker Barrel and Chick-fil-A, and the relative virtues of Whole Foods Market: while these day-to-day preferences say less about their convictions and values than do choices about occupation, residence, and religion, they nevertheless reflect how Americans think about the world more broadly. They're now "tells"—signs of larger beliefs about the world, and about their political commitments.

Of course, people's party identification does not cause them to have certain tastes. Their worldview affects both their personal tastes *and* their political orientations. If something other than worldview directed people toward one party or the other, such as how high taxes ought to be or how much government ought to spend on infrastructure, then their politics would not line up with their personal preferences as they do today. In that case, worldview would still affect people's personal tastes but not their politics.

Because party politics is animated by clashes about race, culture, and debates about how best to protect the United States, however, these things are all interconnected. As a consequence, people can (and do) make some pretty good guesses about others' politics based on where they shop, what they wear, what they drink, what they watch on television, and how they spend their free time. There are deeper, more ominous implications, too. In the course of their day-to-day lives, Americans are bombarded with a cascade of evidence that people on the other side of the political divide are not like them. And when people feel they have nothing in common with their fellow citizens, the very fabric of American democracy begins to fray.

To illustrate the cultural chasm that has now intersected with America's political divide, imagine two families — one fixed and one fluid — with similar incomes. They both decide to move to the Nashville, Tennessee, metropolitan area. Who wouldn't want to live in such a booming metropolis? Sure, it is hot in the summer, but it is *the* place to be. Construction cranes dominate the downtown, adding larger and larger buildings to the city's skyline with each passing month. The rate of new construction is similarly brisk in the suburbs that ring the city. Nashville has been growing fast, its population having doubled to more than 1.5 million in the past twenty years. Although many Americans surely have a stereotyped view of the city as fueled mostly by country music and honky-tonks, it possesses in reality a varied and vibrant economy. Music is a big part of it, but so is health care, higher education, book publishing, and more. Among the biggest recent additions to Nashville's business landscape is the Bridgestone tire company headquarters, located in Cool Springs, about fifteen miles south of downtown. Opportunities abound in the entire metro area.

Consider the decisions these two families are likely to make as they relocate. The fixed-worldview family, the Redds, prefer the suburbs. Just south of town sits the most affluent of them, Brentwood. Growing at a pace similar to the city of Nashville itself, Brentwood offers public schools that are the best in Tennessee. Although signs of development are everywhere, it still feels traditional, with its well-kept brick homes sitting on zoning-mandated one-acre lots. Enormous churches representing just about every Christian denomination cut a high profile in town. A few years before the Redds arrived, citizens rose up against plans to build a mosque not far from the Catholic church. The town council blocked the project. The demographics of Brentwood are about what one would expect in an affluent southern suburb, especially one that was incorporated right after busing came to Nashville in the 1970s — 89 percent white, and only a combined 4 percent African American and Hispanic.

The Redd family breadwinner, James, works at the Nissan headquarters. Having received his BA from a major public university, James works in middle management. He makes a very good living, allowing his wife, Mary, to stay at home to focus her energies on running the household and raising their children. In addition to being satisfied with work, the couple is happy that a vibrant church community welcomed them upon their arrival. Indeed, a neighbor brought by a meal shortly after the moving truck pulled out of the driveway, and generously invited the Redds to join them for services at their church that weekend. It just so happened that both families are Southern Baptists, which allowed the Redds to find their religious home at Brentwood Baptist quickly.

The fluid family, the Bleus, made different decisions when they moved to Nashville. Both Finn and Phoebe earned PhDs and are professors at Vanderbilt University. They chose a home in the hip Belmont section of town. On a chilly day, it is a long walk or a short bike ride from work. It costs about the same to buy a house in Belmont as it does in Brentwood, but the houses and the yards are much smaller in the former. Belmont compensates with its other advantages. It is always hopping, with myriad cool bars, restaurants, and boutiques. Foot traffic and car traffic are plentiful, creating a bustling atmosphere. Although Nashville is not an especially diverse city, this part of town is. In fact, the Islamic Center of Nashville sits right in the middle of Twelfth Avenue South, sandwiched between two very popular independent coffee shops. The Bleus don't go to church, but they worship at the coffee shops every Sunday morning.

These major disparities are just the tip of the iceberg, however — only the beginning of the differences that exist between our hypothetical fixed and fluid families. To show just how divergent the tastes and preferences of these two groups are, we'll not only come up with a backstory for the Redds and the Bleus; we'll also imagine a day in the life of each family, to show how the littlest differences add up to a nearly insurmountable barrier between them.

We should pause here to issue a disclaimer of sorts. This idealized example is meant to demonstrate that the fixed and fluid don't have much in common, but it is also designed to present an extreme case. Not everyone with a fixed or fluid worldview will possess all these tastes and preferences. Our aim is simply to produce the kind of caricatures that partisans carry in their heads about people who identify with the other party. Nonpolitical differences seem to be central to why Republicans and Democrats see their counterparts as so alien. These admittedly potted exemplars also illustrate how, in everyday decisions big and small, the two Americas are growing farther and farther apart—even when their inhabitants live in relatively close proximity and share the same race and class. These commonalities used to provide common ground for Americans from all points along the worldview spectrum. Now, they have been buried under an avalanche of small but significant differences that are reinforced from the moment we wake up each morning to the time we go to sleep each night.

Our hypothetical "day in the life" of a prototypical fixed-worldview family and a typically fluid one begins with both households getting ready for work and school. Out in Brentwood, James and Mary Redd have three kids, two of whom are in elementary school and one not yet school-age. In the city, Finn and Phoebe Bleu have only one child. This simplest of differences reflects a marked fertility gap between conservatives and liberals.

A recent estimate suggests that conservatives have over 40 percent more children than liberals do. That number actually *underestimates* the difference in fertility between fixed and fluid whites, because liberal African Americans and Hispanics have higher birthrates than whites. It's possible that this fertility gap is due to the fact that tradition-minded conservatives tend to marry younger than liberals do, which increases the number of years that they are married during peak fertility years. Less tradition-minded, more liberal women are likelier to remain single longer and live with their romantic partners before marriage, perhaps so that they can pursue career opportunities with fewer constraints. Their partners don't seem to be in any rush to marry, either, which is consistent with a worldview that places more emphasis on women's equality than maintaining traditional gender roles.

The connection between birthrates and politics is arresting. In 2012 each of the ten states with the highest fertility rates voted for Mitt Romney. The top five were the mostly rural states of Utah, Alaska, South Dakota, North Dakota, and Idaho. None are remotely politically competitive at the presidential level. In contrast, all eleven states with birthrates below sixty births per thousand women of childbearing age went to Barack Obama, with Rhode Island, Vermont, New Hampshire, Maine, and Connecticut making up the bottom five in fertility. Among them, only New Hampshire is competitive in presidential elections.

Not only will conservatives have more children; they will also give them more-traditional names. Sure, plenty of liberals, also, name their boys Michael, David, James, and John. But the data show (yes, there are data for this sort of thing!) that liberal parents, at least those who are well educated, are much more likely to choose more-obscure names than conservatives. Liberals also favor names that begin with softer, more feminine-sounding letters, such as L and S. If you run into a little boy named Liam at the playground, you can be pretty sure whom his parents voted for in the last election. In contrast, conservative parents tend to favor names that begin with harder, more masculine-sounding letters like K, B, and D. So James and Mary named their kids David, Kathryn, and Ben. The Bleus' daughter is Esme.

Both the Redds and Bleus have pets, since Americans of all political stripes love animals. But it turns out there is a dog/cat divide that breaks down along partisan lines. Euromonitor has tracked pet ownership in the United States and around the world. Its state-by-state map of dog versus cat preferences doesn't look much different from the electoral college map. Cats outnumber dogs in the Northeast, Upper Midwest, and the Pacific Coast. The South and Southwest are dog country. Including the District of Columbia, of the ten states with the largest cat-to-dog ratios, nine regularly vote Democratic for president — Massachusetts, Maryland, Maine, Vermont, Connecticut, DC, New Hampshire, Pennsylvania, and New York. Only Ohio fails to fit the pattern. Of the ten states with the largest dog-to-cat ratios, eight regularly vote Republican — Arkansas, Texas, Oklahoma, Louisiana, Mississippi, Arizona, Tennessee, and Missouri. New Mexico is the outlier here. Other studies have also revealed a relationship between ideology and pet preferences, with conservatives more dog-friendly and liberals more cat-friendly.

Since they're in dog country, both the Redds and the Bleus have dogs. But they do own different types. The fixed family chose their dog based on its size and its capacity to be trained. Big dogs with a loud bark are well suited to scare off would-be thieves. Even though Brentwood has a vanishingly low crime rate, people who see the world as a dangerous place can't be too careful. (Those differences in wariness help explain, incidentally, why the Redds keep a gun in a lockbox, while the Bleus find the idea of a gun in the home to be anathema.) For owners with a fixed worldview, large and untrained is a bad combination, however, so obedience is an important characteristic in dogs. When they are out for a walk, the Redds' dog, Rex, follows close at James's heels. When he's inside, Rex knows where he doesn't belong, namely on the furniture. Man's best friend gets a smack on the nose when he tries to get up on the couch. The notion of him sleeping in the same bed as James and Mary is a nonstarter.

Finn and Phoebe's dog is a lot different. She is small and adorable. Soon after the Bleus adopted Mocha from the shelter, she achieved equal status with Esme, their human daughter. When she goes on a walk, Mocha, not the humans, chooses the path, sniffing every fire hydrant and mailbox along the way. The "parents" follow behind her. Sometimes a kindly older neighbor will walk by and say hello. But he always makes the same joking remark, which is starting to annoy them — "Sure looks like your dog is walking you, not the other way around," he'll chuckle. Finn and Phoebe have started to mutter under their breath to each other that he probably voted for Trump. Sometimes they lament that they didn't train their dog better—she jumps on visitors when they come to the house and tries to sniff all the other dogs' butts when they pass. It's embarrassing, but that is just how it has to be. They lack the heart to do anything that might break Mocha's warm, positive spirit. When it comes to being inside, the pooch has the run of the place. The Bleus can't help but be tickled when Mocha jumps up on the couch and nuzzles their faces and licks them. That's something the more germ-averse Redds find disgusting. And there was probably a time when Finn and Phoebe tried to keep Mocha from sleeping in bed with them, but they gave up on that long ago.

After the dogs are walked, it is time to get the kids to school. When Finn and Phoebe moved to the city, they thought the schools were a little spotty. Although they express their strong support for public schools in principle, they found it hard in practice to send their daughter to a school that is not the best available. Hence, the Bleus chose private school for young Esme. If the public schools improve, they tell themselves, they will move Esme there. They chose the school where the educational elite send their kids, University School of Nashville. The educational philosophy is open-minded, providing children with significant ownership of their educational decisions. A high percentage of USN grads go on to Ivy League–type schools.

While little Ben has his bottle with his mother, Mary Redd, before his morning nap, James loads David and Kathryn into the car for the trip to the local public school. One of the main reasons they chose Brentwood was because the schools are so strong. The classes are bigger than at private schools, and there is not much racial or class diversity. But the bottom line is how well the kids do, and the kids who matriculate through Brentwood schools chalk up the best test scores in the state. In fact, many students score as high as the kids who go to private schools that cost more than $20,000 a year.

Not that the Redds' kids are likely to end up at the same colleges as Esme Bleu after they graduate. While the Bleus eye the Ivies for their daughter, the Redds don't appreciate the liberal indoctrination their kids might receive at a place like Yale or Princeton. Moreover, in considering the bottom line, they wonder if it is really worth paying a couple hundred thousand dollars for their kids to go to an Ivy, when they can graduate debt-free from the University of Georgia or Ohio State and get an excellent education that will prepare them to compete in the world of business or engineering. When the Bleus imagine Esme going off to college, they're picturing perhaps a small liberal arts college in the Northeast, like the one that the Bleus themselves met at when they were in school. And when they talk with friends about what their kids might do for a living one day, the most common refrain is "whatever makes them happy," although they secretly hope she'll consider being a professor like they are, or maybe an artist or book editor.

The Redds and the Bleus both drive their kids to school—but when they do, they get into different types of cars. The Redds own two big, hulking SUVs, a Chevy Suburban and a GMC Yukon XL. People who are wired for wariness will make car-buying decisions in no small part based on what might go wrong on the road. A smart hedge is to be ensconced in a few thousand pounds of solid steel. The Suburban and Yukon are particularly good choices, because the Redds like buying American. GM runs in the family. Their parents drove General Motors cars, and so did their grandparents. Tradition dictates that James and Mary do the same.

The Bleus, naturally, drive a Prius: the ultimate liberal driving machine. Because they don't experience the same wariness the Redds do, other values, namely protecting the planet, guide their decision. Reducing their carbon footprint, not surviving an accident, is their central concern. The Bleus don't give much thought to the fact that Toyota is a Japanese company. To the extent they do, they can at least tell their friends that the car was assembled in the United States. Better still, they seem to remember hearing about a study that recognized Toyota for its equal-opportunity hiring practices. If its corporate profits go to Japan, so be it.

The automotive decisions of the Redds and Bleus track the findings of a study by the online car-repair service YourMechanic. YourMechanic maintains relationships with mechanics all around the country and sends one of its certified repair technicians to people's home or place of work

to fix their cars. When people use the service, they provide the company
with their state and zip code along with their car's make and model. This
allows YourMechanic to examine whether people who live in red districts
or states and those who live in blue districts or states drive different types
of cars.

The answer is yes. Automobile preference, it seems, follows a pattern
similar to baby names. Just as Michael and David are popular names with
all types of people, so, too, are Honda Accords, Ford Focuses, and Toyota
Camrys. Indeed, the top five cars that YourMechanic services are exactly
the same in both blue and red states and districts.

But interesting differences appear beyond consensus top sellers.
YourMechanic identified cars in each state and congressional district
that were "unusually popular"—that is, which were overrepresented
compared with the national average. So, for example, a Volkswagen Jetta
is not a particularly popular car nationally, but in certain states and districts there are a lot of them.

The red/blue divide manifests itself clearly when it comes to unusually popular vehicles. In the twenty-four states won by Mitt Romney in
2012, the most unusually popular car was American-made in three-quarters of them. Of the twenty-six states that Barack Obama won that year,
the most unusually popular car was foreign-made more than two-thirds of
the time. The Jetta is big in New Hampshire, for example. Two different
Subarus, the Japanese automaker with the especially gay-friendly repu-
tation, are unusually popular in Maine, Oregon, and Colorado. In contrast, the Chevrolet Silverado is the most unusually popular vehicle in
Louisiana and Arkansas, with the Chevrolet Impala being particularly
prevalent in Alabama, Tennessee, and South Carolina.

Because a place's population density is a better indicator of its politics than the state it is in, breaking the data down by congressional district allows for a better test. For instance, when we look at congressional
districts held by Democrats in 2012, the most unusually popular car was
—you guessed it—the Toyota Prius. This particular car sends a loud and
clear message. As the conservative blogger Dan Pera articulated exqui-
sitely about the Prius: "We all know it's *the* car of choice of liberals eve-

rywhere. They are as much a political statement as anything. By driving one of these cars, these folks are saying 'I care more about everything than you, and you hate the environment and support torture.'" The other nine vehicles that fill out the top ten list of most popular cars in Democratic congressional districts are, like the Prius, all foreign-made; none are pickups or SUVs.

Congressional districts represented by Republicans reflect car preferences that are the exact opposite of those in districts held by Democrats. All ten of the unusually popular vehicles in those parts of the country are pickups or SUVs, led by the Dodge Ram 1500. With the exception of two, all are American-made.

Our 2017 survey delved deeper into Americans' car preferences. In addition to answering the questions about desirable qualities in children, which determined whether they were classified as fixed or fluid, a random sample of Americans indicated what type of vehicle they most often drove. The results complement those from YourMechanic. Cars like the Honda Accord and Ford Focus were relatively popular among both the fixed and fluid. But there were more differences than similarities. Among the fixed, domestic cars outnumbered foreign cars by 64 percent to 36 percent. In contrast, 60 percent of the fluid drove foreign cars, compared with 40 percent who drove American cars. Also consistent with the YourMechanic study, the fluid were more likely to drive a small sedan (in car-rental terms, an economy, compact, or mini) than the fixed, while the fixed were more likely to drive an SUV. Finally, barely a soul among the fixed copped to driving a hybrid or electric car, while about 10 percent of fluid drivers said they drove these most-fuel-efficient of models. Like their choice of schools, then, the Redds' and Bleus' means of transportation divide them, rather than giving them something in common.

A few hours after James Redd and the spouses Bleu make it to work, they'll take a break for coffee. Here, as at other points during the day, their worldviews will guide them toward different choices.

Coffee is more polarizing than most products, apparently. In 2012 a consumer research firm called Buyology conducted a survey to assess brand loyalty among four thousand Americans. Starbucks is among the companies that Republicans and Democrats feel most differently about. Democrats love it; Republicans don't. Republicans do like coffee, but when they go out for it, their brand of choice is Dunkin' Donuts, not Starbucks.

The difference between these two alternatives couldn't be starker. At Starbucks, the drink sizes are Italian words, not English ones. The array of coffee concoctions that one can choose from takes up multiple boards above the barista's preparation station. There is, by contrast, no "barista" at Dunkin' Donuts. Until recently, there weren't an awful lot of choices at Dunkin', either. Small, medium, or large. Cream, sugar, or both. (James usually goes with a medium coffee with sugar. It is practical and costs about two bucks. It gets the job done efficiently.)

You're unlikely to walk out of Starbucks with a two-dollar cup of coffee. But that's not what the Bleus are looking for. Starbucks offers a kaleidoscope of options, many of them daringly offbeat, and the company's ethos clearly aligns with the priorities of fluid people—even if it occasionally stumbles, as with its #RaceTogether campaign, which was intended to foster conversations about race among its customers, but which drew a harsh and speedy backlash from across the political spectrum. But that hasn't stopped the Bleus from frequenting the chain. Indeed, the fluid's love of nuance, the less traditional, and the pursuit of individual fulfillment is on full display at Starbucks (or any of the other cutting-edge coffee shops in the Bleus' neighborhood, which are full of people expressing their individuality with lots of tattoos and piercings).

For someone who, like James Redd, prefers the simplicity and straightforwardness of Dunkin' Donuts coffee, a trip to Starbucks is like a journey into another dimension. In much the same way, one-size-fits-all coffee does not cut it for the Bleus. Phoebe's favorite order is the "grande two-pump skinny vanilla latte." Finn almost always gets a "grande skim latte with mocha and peppermint, 4.5 pumps, nonfat, no water, no foam, with extra hot chai." Although people with fluid worldviews talk about these drinks among their friends fully believing that everyone knows what they mean, the Redds would probably need a translator to learn that

vidal!!!!!!!!!!
@vidalwuu

Follow

y'all realize there are no coloured hands in the press photos right @Starbucks #RaceTogether

12:21 AM - 17 Mar 2015

1,959 Retweets **1,653** Likes

195   2.0K   1.7K

Starbucks is a favorite of fluid Americans, although occasionally its efforts at progressivism fall short of its standards, as in the ill-fated #RaceTogether marketing campaign of 2015.

Phoebe has ordered a large skim-milk latte with a half shot of sugar-free vanilla syrup, while Finn has asked for a medium nonfat latte with four and a half pumps of chai syrup, no water added, the foam taken off the top, and the cup filled with extra-hot steamed milk.

If the Redds and the Bleus can't find common ground on coffee, surely they'll have better luck over a beer at happy hour after work. Fat chance. A 2012 study of the purchasing patterns of 200,000-plus consumers revealed strong micro versus macro, foreign versus domestic, and light versus dark divides between Democrats and Republicans in beer prefer-

ences. Microbrews, taken as a class of beers, skew strongly Democratic.
Those on the political left are, in general, much more open to new products on the market than those on the political right. It makes sense, then,
that the fixed might not be as open to microbreweries, as they are often
upstart companies lacking established national reputations. The only
craft brew that does not fit the overall pattern is Samuel Adams, which
skews Republican. It is hard to determine exactly why, but it is probably
worth noting that it has a longer history than most craft breweries.

Curiously, the data also suggests there is a divide between light
beer and regular beer, with Republicans leaning toward the former—
the lighter the color and fewer the calories, the greater the Republican
skew. The famously watery Coors products stand out for disproportionate Republican consumption, both the full-calorie and low-calorie alternatives. The same is true of Miller Lite, Michelob Light, Michelob Ultra,
Amstel Light, and Corona Light. Yet the data also shows that light-in-color
but full-calorie American macrobrews, such as Budweiser and Miller, are
slightly more popular on the left, even though these are long-standing
brands, which would suggest they'd be more popular on the right.

While it seems unlikely that Republicans are more calorie-conscious
—in the next section, we will describe their yen for mozzarella sticks
—perhaps the light beer versus regular beer schism has to do with the
strength of the beverages' flavor. In addition to having a third less calories, light beer also tends to have about a third less taste. An explanation
that centers on the sharpness of the taste would also be consistent with
the strong Democratic skew toward hoppy microbrews and leafy green
vegetables like arugula and kale, the latter of which is something only
liberals love.

But the left's love of microbrews is not just a function of the boldness
of their flavors or newness of the companies that produce them. Microbrews allow fluid people to revel in the aesthetic detail of the beers and
to make a personal statement. Microbreweries don't just make a regular and lower-calorie option, like traditional breweries. They usually feature over a half-dozen varieties. Pilsners, lagers, pale ales, session ales,
IPAs, Trappists, Hefeweizens, porters, stouts. Some are made from wheat,

some aren't. Some have a lot of hops. Some have less. There are so many details, so many options. For the less well initiated, approaching the bar at a craft brew establishment (or even talking with the beer guy at Whole Foods) can be as intimidating as approaching the barista at Starbucks. But the Bleus are well versed in the vernacular of microbrews, because they love the choices and the remarkable craftsmanship in these smaller-batch products.

For the Redds, all of those options and extraneous ingredients only muddy the waters. An ingredient that goes in a pie does not belong in a beer. They don't want blueberry beer, or a sour that includes peach extract. They prefer the recognizable, the tried-and-true. They can find macrobrews anywhere, after all, and when they order one, they know exactly what they are going to get.

There may be another reason Bleus love all these coffee and beer choices—they're more likely to be neurotic. In personality psychology, being more neurotic includes a greater propensity to experience worry and anxiety. As a result, neurotic people tend to dwell more on the negative aspects of life than the positive. The same research that suggests liberals are more open to experience and conservatives are more conscientious also shows those on the left scoring higher in neuroticism than those on the right. Although the relationship between ideology and neuroticism is less well established, it might go a long way toward explaining why liberals appear fussier, more particular, and more likely to engage in hand-wringing and second-guessing about their choices. Expansive options might satisfy both their general desire to ruminate and their anxiety about getting things just right. As for politics itself, neuroticism seems a characteristic of liberals, who never seem satisfied with their side's best efforts. Complaints about President Obama securing *only* $800 billion in stimulus spending after the financial crash and settling for a hybrid health care system rather than fighting for single-payer were common among liberals during his first term in office, despite the overwhelming practical obstacles to achieving more.

The bottom line is this: if the Redds and the Bleus found themselves together for happy hour, they wouldn't be able to talk about how nice it is that Michelob Ultra tastes great even without all the carbs. Indeed, the Redds would have a hard time even beginning to understand why the Bleus are willing to spend ten dollars for a pint of some high-gravity brew that no one has ever heard of when you can get three Bud Lights for that money. Similarly, the Bleus would wonder why the Redds fail to appreciate the remarkable advances in beer making that have occurred in the last twenty years, especially given the well-established fact that Bud Light tastes like swill.

If alcohol fails to bring people together, food probably won't either. To some degree, of course, the same differences in taste that guide the couples' coffee and beer choices also inform their decisions about what to eat. For instance, evidence suggests that palates differ between people at opposite ends of the political spectrum. Some people have a taste receptor that others do not have. For those who have it, certain green vegetables (and, one assumes, ultrahoppy or sour beers) will have a sharp, unpleasant flavor. For those without it, these vegetables taste just fine. People who take conservative positions on a range of different issues are more likely to possess this taste receptor.

Discussion of vegetables and politics is rare, but maybe it shouldn't be. Whole Foods, the stereotypical grocery store of choice for lifestyle liberals with money to spend, carries more types of lettuce and other produce than all but the most committed veggie eaters could identify. All these varieties have a stronger flavor than iceberg, which is the most popular type of salad green by far in the United States. So it should not be surprising that kale has become an embodiment of what the liberal diet looks like to conservatives.

Grocery shopping is one of the myriad domestic tasks that Mary Redd accomplishes each week. Being organized is the only way to survive, with three young kids and a husband with ambitions at work. She doesn't have the luxury of going to the grocery store every day. Although two boutique groceries are within driving distance of Brentwood, they don't make much sense for the Redds. Kroger and Super Walmart have so much more stuff and for a better price, and both are close to the elementary school where Mary volunteers at the welcome desk most days. Mary chooses which of the two big groceries to go to based on what items they have on sale that week. One or the other always seems to have a thirty-pack of Miller Lite for a couple of dollars off. After deciding on Kroger for this week, Mary dons her Lululemon crops, loads baby Ben into the Yukon, and hits the road.

The differences between the Redds' and Bleus' tastes in coffee and beer pale next to their divergent choices at the dinner table, whether or not the meal occurs at home. Home is where the Redds eat. All five gather nightly at six thirty in the dining room, except on a special occasion when they might go out to Olive Garden as a family. If it's a date night, Mary and James might splurge on Ruth's Chris before a trip to the twenty-screen multiplex in Franklin. The family says grace every night and, once the meal begins, the older kids are expected to finish what is on their plates. On this particular night, Mary has whipped up one of her specialties—meatloaf with mashed potatoes. James Redd likes a nice salad with dinner as well. Only iceberg lettuce will do, with a couple of tomato wedges and a few strips of carrot on top. Kraft's ranch dressing or its Thousand Island equivalent makes a good accompaniment in his mind. A meat, a starch, and a vegetable—a perfectly balanced meal.

Things are often a little chaotic at the Bleu house at the dinner hour. Actually, who knows when the dinner hour will be? It depends on what is going on that night. Finn and Phoebe spend a lot of time fussing over Esme's diet, worrying about the latest studies about gluten—they're concerned she has an allergy, though no obvious signs are yet manifest. On this particular evening, they pick up Esme from afterschool at five thirty in the Prius. It's a bit too late to plan a nice dinner at home. In general that takes a lot of advance planning, not the Bleus' strong suit. (Of course, Finn and Phoebe tried the meal-kit delivery services Blue Apron and Hello Fresh, but they still had to find the time to prep and cook the food, so these "life hacks" never completely took.) Still, to the Bleus, being organized isn't as important as being creative, and their dinner choices reflect that.

Trader Joe's is right around the corner from the house, and its frozen Mexican offerings are pretty good. Better still, Nashville is full of great ethnic joints known for their takeout. A couple of them, in particular, are really exciting to the Bleus. One is a terrific vegetarian Indian place off Interstate 440, not far from home. It has the best malai kofta and palak paneer that Finn and Phoebe have ever had, including the time when they did that backpacking trip in the Himalayas during their gap year. It is going to be either there or the new Thai place on Eighth. They read about it on Yelp a couple of weeks ago, and the reviews make it sound great—like a quick trip to Bangkok, minus the airfare. Unlike the glorified stir-fry places, this restaurant is the real deal, superauthentic, and it even features gluten-free options. The Bleus also like the idea of trying someplace new.

They think takeout is the best way to go because, as good as the food is at Thai and Indian restaurants in town, the wine lists often leave a lot to be desired. They only seem to offer pedestrian options from the biggest mass producers around. Chateau Ste. Michelle and Columbia Crest just won't do it for Finn, especially. Worse still, these places' pairing options are always off. The wine lists will feature four different overly oaked California Chardonnays, when everyone knows that a crisp Alsatian Pinot Gris is the only wine that can really stand up to the kind of heat you'll find in an authentic vindaloo or tom yum. Finn and Phoebe would rather have the option of opening a properly chilled Riesling or perhaps a rosé from Provence when they get home. Bonus: they get to drink it out of their elegant Riedel stemware.

Food preferences also differ markedly across the worldview divide. In 2016 *Time* magazine used data from Grubhub—the online portal through which its more than seven million active users can order carryout from local restaurants—to paint a picture of the Republican and Democratic diet. Grubhub does not ask people whether they are Republicans or Democrats when they order, but it does log customers' addresses. To understand ordering patterns, *Time* examined what was more and less popular in the nearly two hundred congressional districts where Grubhub does enough business to allow for meaningful analysis. *Time* found that, of 175 popular items ordered on the website, three-quarters were associated with the partisanship of those congressional districts. In more concrete terms, the more Republicans there were in a congressional district, the more orders were placed for mozzarella sticks. Similarly, Democratic-leaning districts could only mean one thing—a surge in orders for veggie burgers.

Based on these data, *Time* invited readers to estimate how Republican or Democratic their own diet was by asking them to choose between ten different two-dish alternatives. The ten choices included several of the following:

veggie burger	hamburger
chicken tikka masala	sweet-and-sour chicken
muffin	brownie
avocado salad	Caesar salad
lentil soup	wonton soup
BLT	buffalo chicken wrap
margherita pizza	barbecue chicken pizza
guacamole	mozzarella sticks

The items in the left column are all more likely to appear on orders from Democratic-leaning districts. Those in the right column are common orders from Republican ones. (In the interest of full disclosure, the authors of this book both logged a Democratic-leaning diet, although Hetherington far prefers a hamburger to a [frankly pathetic] veggie burger and Weiler has eyed meat eaters' food options covetously for years.)

After finishing up their respective dinners, the Redds and Bleus unwind by doing the same kinds of activities, distinguished by a qualitative difference in tone and style.

Our April 2017 survey asked the fixed and fluid what they like to do in their free time. For both, the three most commonly cited first choices were reading, watching television, and listening to music. But the specific things they like to read, watch, and listen to demonstrate little to no overlap.

Take reading. Goodreads, an online ratings portal for readers, queried its users during the 2012 campaign about which candidate they intended to vote for. Although our survey found the fixed and fluid differ in whether or not they read for pleasure, the Goodreads survey found that, among those who do read, Obama and Romney supporters both logged the same number of books on average over the course of the year. However, Obama supporters were more critical in their ratings — not terribly shocking, given the particularity of liberals' tastes in a range of other products, from coffee to beer to food.

Goodreads also found that liberals and conservatives flocked to fundamentally different types of books. Obama supporters outnumbered Romney supporters by three to one in reading books written by Jonathan Franzen, the critically acclaimed fiction author. Romney voters, by contrast, read David McCullough at a rate of two to one compared with Obama voters. McCullough, too, is highly acclaimed, having been awarded two Pulitzers during his decades-long career — but he writes popular historical nonfiction, a genre more in line with a practical-minded, fixed worldview and very different from Franzen's style.

The popular book that featured the largest gap between Obama and Romney supporters was *Heaven Is for Real: A Little Boy's Astounding Story of His Trip to Heaven and Back*, by Todd Burpo and Lynn Vincent. Presumably because fixed people have much stronger religious leanings, Republicans were four times more likely than Democrats to have read this account of how a child's near-death experience gave him a glimpse of the afterlife. In a similar vein, the fluid are probably almost completely unaware of Tim LaHaye's Left Behind series, which includes sixteen books about the biblical end times. Actually, the fluid may not even know what the end times are. These books have sold over sixty-five million copies and spawned four movies. The books' religious themes, and their clear distinction between good and evil, are sure to appeal to anyone who places high importance on cognitive closure, a key characteristic of those with fixed worldviews. On the other hand, given the hostility of fluid people toward organized religion and biblical literalism, it's easy to see why they make up such a small portion of the readership of the Left Behind series.

Could television provide more of a bridge between the left and right? Perhaps it could, if only the programming options today were as limited as they were in 1975. But the explosion of options has fractured television audiences dramatically, driving yet another wedge between fixed and fluid Americans.

In today's fragmented market, microtargeting data suggest Democrats and Republicans tend to watch different television shows. In keeping with their penchant for microbrews, the shows Democrats favor over Republicans tend to appear on cable or streaming services like Netflix, Hulu, and Amazon. Excepting partisan news programs, two of the shows with especially large Democratic skews over the last decade are *Mad Men* and *Dexter*. *Mad Men,* a show about the excesses and sexism in the advertising industry of the 1960s, features few, if any, characters that people would care to identify with personally. They are not paragons of virtue. Don Draper, the main character, is both charismatic and complicated, a heavy drinker and womanizer with a penchant for self-destructive behavior. The protagonist in *Dexter,* a long-running show on Showtime, is a serial killer who murders other serial killers. He is complicated, too (leaving aside his tried-and-true method of killing people). Another long-running show that Democrats disproportionately like is the sitcom *30 Rock,* starring Tina Fey as a neurotic TV executive who frequently cannot get out of her own way. These kinds of quirky, complex characters (if you can call being a serial killer "quirky") are apparently not the types of people that Republicans want to spend their evenings with. Democrats, on the other hand, can't get enough of them.

In a sense, fixed viewers have been left behind by recent trends in the world of TV. Many observers have dubbed the two-decade period beginning at the turn of the new century the new golden age of television, kicked off by *The Sopranos* and *The Wire*, and including *Breaking Bad*, *Game of Thrones*, *Orange Is the New Black*, *Girls*, *The Americans*, *Transparent*, and others. These shows have been deemed pathbreaking by critics, and have become dominant cultural touchstones, receiving the vast majority of coverage and attention from high-profile and prestige media.

What's notable about the new golden age is what these more recent shows have in common: their audiences skew liberal in a more niche television environment than existed forty years ago. Conservatives have long decried Hollywood as a liberal bastion. The legendary Saturday-night CBS television lineup of the 1970s, for example, featuring *All in the Family*, *Maude*, *M*A*S*H*, and *The Mary Tyler Moore Show*, all reflected liberal sensibilities. But those shows were also watched by most of the country. The more recent spate of highly regarded, culturally dominant shows, in contrast, are more narrowly targeted than their 1970s predecessors. This is because the media landscape has changed so profoundly, especially the explosion in viewers' choices.

One outgrowth of this new golden age has been an avalanche of highbrow commentary about the shows and their many meanings. This day-after analysis is part of a nearly exclusively liberal cultural enclave. It tends to feature long-form storytelling (even the word "long-form" is part of a liberal discourse likely alien to many Americans who sit outside that particular bubble), highlighting deeply flawed and complex characters and moral ambiguity, which is perhaps the coin of the realm for fluid cultural consumption. There is also an ironic mode that appears to be distinctively liberal. TV shows like *30 Rock*, *Parks and Recreation*, and *Modern Family* typically portray neurotic liberal characters (with the occasional conservative foil thrown in for contrast).

They also tend to be highly self-referential, poking fun at their own liberal tastes. One good example is Leslie Knope, the main character portrayed by Amy Poehler in *Parks and Recreation*. In one episode, Knope appears on the local public radio station for an interview, hosted by one Derry Murbles, to promote a book she's just written. Murbles has all the caricatured affectations one might conjure for an NPR host—the self-serious tone, the constant attempt to achieve, in every question posed, a deeper philosophical truth. As the excruciatingly pretentious segment winds down, Murbles asks Knope to introduce the group whose music closes the show. With ironic resignation, she presents listeners with a "lesbian, Afro-Norwegian funk duo, Nefertiti's Fjord."

For liberals, that self-effacing, self-aware, "smart" sensibility is precisely what is so attractive about these shows. But for many Americans on the other side of the divide, the "smug style" of this entertainment is anything but appealing. Take a television show like the early 2000s Aaron Sorkin blockbuster *The West Wing*, which portrayed a liberal's fantasy version of a White House whose chief executive was a brilliant economics professor turned progressive sage. Martin Sheen's Jed Bartlet was surrounded by hyperverbal, witty, neurotic, Ivy League–educated advisers who wanted only to do what was best for the country, liberal-style. That world, and Sorkin's brilliant writing, tickled the fancy of many liberals. But the show's smarter-and-holier-than-thou affect also made it nauseating to many conservatives. A few years later Keith Olbermann, and later still Rachel Maddow and Chris Hayes on MSNBC and Jon Stewart and Stephen Colbert on Comedy Central, exemplifies a superbrainy and sardonic approach to political commentary that exemplifies the vast differences in fixed and fluid people's tastes in style and form as much as their preferences about content.

The shows that lean Republican are much different from the Democratic shows. Republicans like reality shows such as *Duck Dynasty*, *Shark Tank*, *The Amazing Race*, *Survivor*, and *The Bachelor* more than Democrats do. Little wonder that Republicans' presidential candidate in 2016 was Donald Trump, the star of *The Apprentice*. Though there are exceptions, Republican-skewing shows feature "regular folks," whether it's the *Duck Dynasty* clan or ordinary-seeming fictional characters like the one Tim Allen plays in *Last Man Standing*. In reality shows, competition is at center stage, with clear winners and losers. In *Survivor*, for instance, the competition determines who will be voted off the island. In *The Bachelor*, it decides who will get the rose each week. In *Shark Tank*, the goal is to gain the financial backing of Mark Cuban or the other sharks. Clear-cut winners and losers and stock characters seem to appeal to Republicans more than Democrats.

Not surprisingly, then, microtargeting data also suggests that Republicans are more apt to watch sports than Democrats are. All the most popular sports on television, such as college football, the PGA golf tour, NASCAR, the Olympic Games, and the NFL, include audiences that tilt Republican. Among the few sports that Democrats seem to prefer, the NBA stands out, while Democrats are also more likely than Republicans to watch niche sports such as tennis, soccer, and extreme sports.

One consequence of the worldview divide is, as one commentator put it, the "politicization of everything." Amazingly, that now includes the National Football League, by far the most popular sports league in the

Donald Trump in April 2007, on the set of The Apprentice, *episodes of which often culminated in him telling contestants, "You're fired!" That uncompromising style appealed to fixed people's preferences for order and certainty when Trump ran for president in 2016.*
Mathew Imaging / FilmMagic

United States. Pro football has dominated television ratings, sports talk radio, and the sports internet for years. But in 2016, former San Francisco 49ers quarterback Colin Kaepernick began kneeling during the national anthem to protest police killings of unarmed black men. Kaepernick's protest soon became — pardon the phrase — a political football. A year later, with Kaepernick out of the league but other players taking up his mantle, President Trump excoriated players for disrespecting the American flag and called for them to be fired.

Quite predictably, the public split sharply along racial and political lines on the protests. Overall, 25 percent of Americans told Gallup in 2017 that they would boycott NFL games over the protests. Among Trump supporters, fully half said they would. Meanwhile, 97 percent of African Americans said Trump was wrong to criticize the players, while only half of whites did. Nearly nine in ten Democrats condemned Trump. Less than a quarter of Republicans did. For their part, the Redds don't watch football with the same relish anymore. They're sick and tired of the fact that *everything* is a political issue now and don't believe the anthem, in particular, should be one.

They're also not able to unwind in front of the TV for late-night comedy the way their parents did back when Johnny Carson ruled the airwaves. Jay Leno was fine, but David Letterman began showing his liberal colors long before his retirement, often disrespecting Donald Trump and other Republicans. His replacement, Colbert, is completely unwatchable, because of his steady drumbeat of smarty-pants criticism of anyone he disagrees with. Jimmy Kimmel used to be funny in their view, but his new vituperatively anti-Trump shtick is as bad as what Alec Baldwin and Kate McKinnon offer up on *Saturday Night Live*.

By contrast, in this dark and dismal time, the Bleus can't wait until ten thirty on Saturday evenings or really any evening, when they can get their fix of anti-Trump content. After watching *SNL*'s wicked jabs at Trump and his administration, they look forward to posting clips of it on Facebook the next morning. Of course, Seth Meyers, Trevor Noah, Samantha Bee, and John Oliver all provide them with great material, too.

● ● ●

If the Redds and the Bleus eschew books and TV, and instead listen to music to relax, they might gravitate toward some of the same artists—but any common ground is still likely to be limited. Musical tastes, like preferences about so much else, reflect fundamental differences between the parties, and once again worldview politics is the likely culprit.

A 2014 Facebook analysis of users revealed that partisan music differences are legion. Facebook identified users who had expressed a preference (via "likes") for both candidates running for office and popular musicians and their fan bases. Those who liked the pages of Democratic candidates had markedly different musical tastes from those who liked the pages of Republican candidates. Some of the differences can be explained by race and region. African American musicians, such as Michael Jackson, Mary J. Blige, Alicia Keys, and Beyoncé, are favorites of Democrats but not Republicans. The fans of noted Jamaican pacifist stoner Bob Marley lean particularly strongly to the left. But Democrats are attracted to more than just performers of color. Acts as diverse as Lady Gaga, Adele, Pink Floyd, and the Beatles are also especially popular in more-liberal precincts.

Country music dominates the acts favored by Republicans. New country, old country, all country—from Miranda Lambert and Lady Antebellum to Tim McGraw and Blake Shelton. From Jason Aldean and Kenny Chesney to Carrie Underwood, Brad Paisley, and Toby Keith. Old-time country legend George Strait is particularly popular among Republicans (and particularly unpopular among Democrats).

Although Republican-leaning artists are more country than Democratic-leaning artists are urban, Republicans do like a couple of rock acts. One is the southern rock group Lynyrd Skynyrd. Another is noted gun rights activist and Trump supporter Ted Nugent, the Motor City Madman. Recall that Nugent, in 2017, was part of an infamous picture taken in Donald Trump's Oval Office with Sarah Palin and fellow Michigander Kid Rock.

As interesting as the Facebook study is, its findings are likely self-evident to even the most casual observer of politics and culture. For instance, anyone tuning in to the two parties' national conventions in 2016 would have been hard-pressed to miss the differences between their soundtracks. The Republicans struggled to get musicians to play at their convention. G. E. Smith, the former front man for the *Saturday Night Live* band, ended up providing the entertainment and gave the crowd in Cleveland a never-ending stream of classic rock fare, with a few country songs mixed in. For fans of Paul Rogers, whether it was in his Free or Bad Company incarnation, the RNC did not disappoint. "My Sharona" by the Knack, "You Shook Me All Night Long" by AC/DC, and "Stay with Me" by the Faces (curiously, all odes to one-night stands) blared through the arena.

These songs and the others played at the convention were odd choices for the party of social conservatism, as liberal bloggers reminded their readers incessantly. Our best explanation for the dissonance is that conservatives' enjoyment of these songs is more a function of how the music sounds than the songs' lyrics. Indeed, no one on the convention floor seemed to bat an eye when Mike Pence took the stage to the Rolling Stones' "You Can't Always Get What You Want." Reportedly, it was not a shot at Pence, who was not Donald Trump's first choice for VP. Trump just likes the song.

The 2016 Democratic National Convention was much different. The organizers didn't rely on a cover band; actual recording artists showed up and played. They included big stars, such as Beyoncé, Lenny Kravitz, the Black Eyed Peas, and Katy Perry. Disproportionately populated by African Americans and featuring songs like "I Kissed a Girl" and "Ur So Gay" by Perry, the musical lineup was tailor-made to appeal to liberals' cultural tastes. Interestingly, too, while the Obamas and Clintons favored walk-up music from the 1970s, more than a few of the songs performed at the Democratic convention were penned in the twenty-first century, whereas contemporary music was all but absent at the Republican convention.

To give us a clearer sense of the differences in musical tastes between people on either side of the political spectrum, our April 2017 survey asked respondents about their favorite musical genre. The results are consistent with the worldview divide. The fluid reported that they love rap and hip-hop, along with a remarkable range of other favorites that include both widely popular genres (such as pop, rock, and classic rock) and a lot of niche interests. For example, a smattering of people identified world music, Korean pop, and electronic dance music, all of which have their roots outside the United States, as their favorites.

By contrast, not a single respondent at the fixed end of the world-view distribution identified either rap or hip-hop as his or her favorite, to say nothing of K-pop or EDM. Instead, the fixed especially love country, oldies, and old country. Country music turned out to be a very polarizing genre. A significant number of the fluid said that they like all music *except* country.

The fixed and fluid reported liking classic rock in about equal numbers. While our 2017 survey did not include questions about which types of classic rock people like, the aforementioned Facebook study did find a few classic rock bands that Republicans and Democrats were equally likely to be fans of. They included Bon Jovi, Aerosmith, Journey, AC/DC, and Metallica. We suspect that, if asked to clarify, the fluids likely would have identified boutique subgenres of classic rock, as opposed to usual guitar-riff fare. In contrast, it is hard to imagine a lot of people with fixed worldviews listening to psychedelic music from the 1960s, or gender-bending glam rock and atonal, melody-free '70s prog rock.

When James Redd and his fixed-worldview friends head out to a geezer rock show in Nashville, it is for the three-headed monster of Def Leppard, Styx, and Kansas, playing before a nearly sold-out audience at the eighteen-thousand-seat Bridgestone Arena. All were big sellers in their day, and even decades later they can still deliver their hits like pros — a win-win proposition, for someone who likes the tried-and-true and isn't looking for novelty or surprise when it comes to entertainment.

Finn and Phoebe and their crew of fluids, on the other hand, snag tickets to Steely Dan with special guest Yes at the intimate Ryman Auditorium. The Dan and Yes were critical darlings in the 1970s, but never attracted the same-size audience that the bands comprising the three-headed monster did. When Yes went more commercial in the 1980s, even their own fans decried them as sellouts.

After the shows end, both sets of concertgoers go home happy, although the fixed group is a little more content. The bands they saw trotted out their best-known material, and Leppard really nailed it on "Rock of Ages." While the Bleus and their friends in the fluid group enjoyed Steely Dan's performance, more than one of them were disappointed that the band didn't play a few of their more obscure numbers, such as "Time out of Mind," a criminally underappreciated song on side two of *Gaucho*.

In so many realms, it seems, there are stark differences between Democrats and Republicans, conservatives and liberals, the fixed and the fluid. What they like to eat, what shows they want to watch, where they choose to live—all of these preferences derive from their fundamentally different ways of seeing, sensing, and experiencing the world around them.

To be sure, different demographic groups have always gravitated toward different entertainment choices. Not many young people, after all, play shuffleboard and watch *Matlock*. More women than men make *Grey's Anatomy* appointment-watching television.

But the reason these red and blue choices matter is that they provide partisans with cues throughout their everyday lives—cues that people on the opposite side of the political divide are different.

For such a connection to occur, a few things have to happen. Most consequentially, Americans have to link specific personal tastes with specific political parties. If a Democrat hears someone likes *Duck Dynasty*, they'll likely start forming negative judgments about that person even before they've had a political conversation, because they know that is a show Republicans like. If a Republican partisan sees someone walking down the street carrying a yoga mat, she or he is very likely to categorize that person as a Democrat. The associations will be close to automatic— yoga mat equals contemptible liberal.

Emerging research demonstrates that Americans actually have a very easy time making such connections between cultural markers and political parties. In fact, responses to the study that tested the relationship between nonpolitical cues and partisanship showed that the connections people draw between *Duck Dynasty* and the Republican Party, and yoga and the Democratic Party, are at least as strong if not actually stronger than the connections people make between the political parties and their respective positions on abortion, which is a pretty high-profile partisan issue, to say the least.

People are able to make these connections so easily because the social groups Americans identify with the two parties are so clear—urban versus rural, white versus multiracial, southern versus coastal, young versus old, evangelical versus irreligious, hipster versus redneck. All these specific social markers have become affixed to the parties' identities because of the emergence of the fixed/fluid divide.

Take *Duck Dynasty*, for example. The show chronicles duck hunters from rural Louisiana. For an hour each week, they sing the praises of guns, rural life, and the South. All three of these groups (gun owners, rural dwellers, and southerners) found their way to the Republican Party because of positions the party took on worldview-tinged issues, which helps explain why the show is so disproportionately popular among fixed, Republican viewers.

On the other hand, the cultural taste that people most connect to in the Democratic Party is hip-hop music. The social groups associated with hip-hop are urban, young, and nonwhite—all social groups whose members have been pulled toward the Democratic Party because of its positions on issues connected to the fixed/fluid divide.

Everywhere you look these days, you see constellations of connections such as these. People effortlessly associate foreign films, yoga, veganism, atheism, rock climbing, Subarus, and farmers markets with Democrats. Similarly, the association between Republicans and hunting, the South, country music, action movies, steakhouses, and SUVs is all but automatic. Americans don't really have to think at all to know that someone is either with them or against them, when it comes to politics, even without any overtly political information.

Americans' ability to categorize cultural markers by party appears to have important implications. As we'll show next, partisans have been developing more strongly negative feelings about the other political party over the course of the twenty-first century than at any time back to the dawn of political surveys and probably further. The increased intensity of negative feelings Americans feel toward the other party coincides with the rise of the fixed/fluid party divide, which has been building for many years, but which became neatly sorted in the past two decades.

The result is a new form of prejudice taking hold in the United States: partyism. Partisans today are likely to express bias against people who identify with the other party even more than people of a racial or ethnic group do against people who identify with a different one. Many partisans no longer want their kids to marry someone from the other party. They are also more likely to withhold a scholarship from a qualified person from the other party than from a qualified person of another race. Considering the intensity of America's racial divisions, statements like these should give every reader pause.

Politics in the United States has often been ugly. Indeed, readers old enough to have lived through the 1960s can be forgiven for thinking that politics today is tame by comparison. Violence, assassinations, urban riots, antiwar protests, and general upheaval were the order of the day back then. Fear and loathing were facts of political life. But believe it or not, ordinary Americans, by and large, did not view other ordinary Americans who happened to belong to the other political party, even during that unsettling era, as threats to the nation's well-being. Conservative leaders have been castigating universities as hotbeds of radicalism and anti-Americanism for decades. But until a few years ago, a clear majority of Americans across the political spectrum believed those institutions played a positive role in American life. President Nixon made his hatred of the press abundantly clear. But in the 1960s and 1970s polls showed that media were among the most respected institutions in the United States. Republicans, even more than Democrats, admired their contribution to democracy.

Rancor in politics is nothing new. But leaving aside the always-theatrical nature of campaigns, the tendency of candidates to highlight the differences between themselves and their opponents and define themselves against troubling historical flashpoints has not traditionally provoked in ordinary Americans sustained, deep-seated fear of the opposition. The perfectly understandable, indeed inescapable, focus of news on political activists and politicians obscures the basic fact that most Americans don't spend a whole lot of time thinking about politics.

But now that worldview and political identity have become so intimately intertwined, the antipathy ordinary Americans feel toward their political opponents is greater than at any time in postwar history. The fixed and fluid, the anchors of the political divide, see the world in profoundly different ways. Those profound differences influence not only people's political preferences and choices; they have different preferences in myriad areas in life. As a result, the fixed and fluid do not live near each other, frequent the same restaurants, prefer the same music or television shows, or own the same types of pets. They drive different cars, watch different sports, and drink different beer. Because worldview animates both nonpolitical and political preferences, politics is no longer just about politics. It is about life.

In the chapters that follow, we will show some of the consequences that flow from a divide of this nature. One effect is that Americans have more reason, more motivation, to see the world the way they want to see the world rather than how it really is. Information isn't a tool for deeper and more dispassionate understanding. It's a weapon to be honed to defend one's side of the barricade. And when worldview politics dominates, even those with more-mixed worldviews and less passion for politics in general feel compelled to take sides. Normal human tendencies to "reason with bias" intensify greatly when worldview-based politics is ascendant.

A confluence of forces has transformed the media into the ultimate battleground for clashing worldviews—indeed, for wholly divergent views of reality. This conflict deepens the profound sense of bewilderment and alienation about their political opponents that Americans experience today. So does our worldview-centered party system, which is now arrayed in a way that increases the chances for challenges to seemingly bedrock and uncontroversial democratic principles. The current divide acts as a powerful gravitational device, pulling into its orbit even people whose worldviews are more mixed and who would otherwise feel less passionately about politics. Otherwise less engaged people not only feel like they have no choice but that they have to pick sides. They're also more likely to accept more extreme ideas simply because those are on offer, especially when the only alternative is to get in bed with forces even more dangerous and unpalatable.

Perhaps most troubling, these problems are not confined to the United States; the kind of worldview divide that has reshaped American politics has now appeared in Europe, with the same disturbing currents there that have come to characterize the United States.

5

Rattlers and Eagles

IF THE FIXED/FLUID DIVIDE only explained differing preferences for coffee, beer, cars, and the ideal neighborhood, it would be one thing. It takes all kinds, after all. But because the worldview divide has come to shape people's *political* choices along with these other, more personal preferences, it has increased the emotional intensity of politics to the point that rival partisans not only have difficulty comprehending each other—they actually *hate* each other.

Again, worldviews themselves do not ensure this kind of political polarization. They are not objects that people identify with—no one walks around saying he or she is fixed or fluid. For worldviews to be polarizing, they need to be connected to something that people do identify with— people *do* walk around saying they are Republicans or Democrats. Political parties themselves do not ensure polarization either—America has had them basically forever and the country hasn't always been polarized. For political parties to be polarizing, people need to feel that particular identity intensely.

The marriage between worldview and party creates polarization. Once the two have become one, people with worldviews fit into a well-established and long-standing social group—a political party—and this social identity breeds an "us versus them" mentality. Because the marriage is a passionate one, built on something as primal as a fixed or fluid worldview as opposed to something more anodyne like taxing and spending, the result is predictably intense and tumultuous. The consequences of these strongly negative feelings are legion. Many are deeply troubling.

Decades of research in social psychology reveal that group identities can matter profoundly to people. When they identify as members of groups and that identity becomes central to how they feel about themselves, they start to care—a lot—about even the most inconsequential matters. This is a product of our tendency to favor groups we belong to and denigrate those we do not: a central feature of human nature, and an outgrowth of fundamental survival strategies. It takes very little for humans to play the "us versus them" game, even when the categories of "us" and "them" are determined at random. When people are divided up into groups, things can get ugly fast.

This was made clear in one famous set of experiments from the 1950s, conceived and organized by the social psychologist Muzafer Sherif. Two dozen boys who did not know each other were recruited to a "summer camp" and placed at random into two groups. The researchers then took the boys to a state park in Oklahoma called Robbers Cave. Once there, they engaged in activities to create group cohesion. This was designed to encourage the boys to care about the group they were assigned to. By setting up tents, preparing meals, and engaging in other team-building projects together, they were creating a group identity.

Initially, the two groups camped at different sites and didn't really know about the other's existence. After a week, however, the self-described Rattlers and Eagles were pitted against one another in a series of competitions. The winning group and each member in it was awarded a trophy and prizes. The results of each day's competition were displayed for all to see. The competition and awards were designed to connect how the boys felt about themselves with the fortunes of the groups they belonged to. As a result, the boys' self-esteem was on the line when the groups competed.

The experiment showed how readily people can come to adopt group identities and how fiercely they can come to protect those identities.

Before long, the Rattlers versus Eagles competition turned ugly. They exchanged insults, referring to each other as "rotten pukes" and "dirty bastards." They vandalized each other's living quarters, and counselors had to break up their fights. The experimenters documented a rapidly escalating sense of mutual enmity among the boys and a growing desperation on both sides to win the contests. They quickly learned to "celebrate their victories and rationalize their defeats." Of course, some of this is what you would expect from any group of twelve-year-old boys in a camp setting. But the Robbers Cave experiment showed just how important people's group identities can become to members, leading to the demonization of those outside the group.

In the real world, people have multiple group identities. For example, the boys in the experiment could see themselves as Rattlers or as Oklahomans or just as boys, among other things. Depending on circumstances, one identity might come to matter to them more than the other alternatives, with important implications. Sherif's experiments made the boys' identities as Rattlers or Eagles most important, which made them aggressive toward their counterparts. Had the experiments encouraged them to think about themselves as Oklahomans—something all the boys had in common—no such aggression would have occurred. (Unless, perhaps, there were some Texans camping nearby.)

The consequences of group identities can run from mild to catastrophic. One example of a particularly devastating outgrowth of group identity is the Bosnian War, which lasted from 1992 to 1995. It resulted in over one hundred thousand dead out of a population of barely four million. And while the world came to understand that the war between Serbs, Croats, and Muslims resulted from "ancient" tribal conflicts, the reality was, if anything, more sobering. Before the war, the groups had lived among each other peacefully for generations. They even spoke the same language. When one of the authors was in Bosnia in 2004, as part of an election-monitoring team, he was astonished to learn that the local residents often couldn't say who was Serbian, Croat, or Muslim. They looked and sounded alike.

One reason these groups had lived peacefully next to each other for generations is because the leaders of the former Yugoslavia had incentives to submerge the country's ethnic differences to make governing a multiethnic state more manageable. During that period, people who lived in Bosnia could choose among a number of group identities — Yugoslav, Bosnian, or Serbian, in the case of those ethnic Serbs, to name just a few. Yugoslav leaders, of course, wanted those living in Bosnia, regardless of their ethnic identities, to identify as Yugoslavs.

After the disintegration of Yugoslavia, residents of Bosnia still had a range of group identities to choose among, although Yugoslav was no longer one of them. Slobodan Milošević, the leader of neighboring Serbia, who wanted to widen the boundaries of Serbia into Bosnia, had incentives to gin up animosities based on those ethnic differences to encourage ethnic Serbs in Bosnia to follow him, causing them to think of themselves primarily as Serbs, thus creating a new dominant group identity for them. In response to their group being under attack, Muslims and Croats stopped thinking of themselves as Bosnians and rather as enemies of the Serbs (as well as of each other). The results were catastrophic.

Ethnic identity in Bosnia plays the role that worldview plays in our story about the United States. It is always there, often lying dormant. When leaders connect those primal feelings to a cause, it magnifies the intensity of the resultant conflict. The result in Bosnia was civil war. In the United States, the result is partisanship that is completely out of control.

Americans also have a wide range of group identities to choose from. When it comes to politics, however, Americans are increasingly choosing only one — their party. Not all Democrats are fluid people and not all Republicans are fixed people. But in this environment, people feel forced to pick a team. Because of the marriage between worldview and party, partisans perceive the other party as a threat that needs to be stopped. Because today's political parties stand for issues and choices that people consider fundamental to their lives, and which tap into our deepest physiological and psychological impulses, the resulting group identity is more rabid, and those who identify strongly with their group regard their opponents with irrational fury.

As we've noted, politics in the United States has been ugly before, of course. But in previous eras of political conflict, like the 1960s, world-view-based issues, like race and war, divided the parties internally. Now they divide one party from the other. As a result, ordinary Americans feel sustained, deep-seated fear and loathing about their partisan opponents, with worldview and partisan identity intimately intertwined.

The antipathy ordinary Americans feel toward their political opponents is greater than at any time in postwar history, thanks to this marriage between politics and worldview. Because the bases of the respective parties differ in their fundamental outlooks on life and in personal preferences great and small, Republicans and Democrats look across the political divide and see people with whom they have precious little in common. These fundamental differences reinforce in Americans' minds the conviction that their political opponents aren't just sparring partners in a contest with a clear beginning and end. They're dangerous adversaries who threaten the nation's well-being. Thus, like a warring tribe, they must be beaten—whatever the cost.

And the costs, as we'll show, are astronomical. When roughly half of a democracy's electorate views the other half as mortal enemies, nobody wins. Quite the opposite, in fact: we are all sure to lose. Many Americans worry about the "partisan gridlock" that grips Washington right now. Congress can't agree on budgets, pass legislation, or fill administrative and judicial vacancies. Indeed, the last several Congresses have been the least productive since such records have been kept. That is regrettable, of course, but the consequences of worldview politics are much broader. The psychic animus partisans feel about their counterparts is so troubling because it draws on the kinds of tribal instincts on full display at Robbers Cave, motivating them to ignore, rationalize, and reinterpret political information in especially problematic ways.

One of the most immediate losses is already being felt: the sacrificing of truth and objectivity on the altar of partisanship. Partisan bias, and the rise of an entire media ecosystem to sustain it, have created some very pernicious trends, from the entrenchment of partisan divisions to the rise of fake news and antiscientific movements. All people have their biases, of course, but the degree of bias depends on the strength of their feelings. Stronger feelings motivate people to do the work necessary to see the world the way they want to see it, not how it really is. All of these developments are an outgrowth of the rise of worldview politics and the intense tribalism that it has created.

The skyrocketing intensity of negative feelings partisans express about the other party is surely one of the most consequential changes to have swept our political landscape since the 1990s, if not the 1960s.

The ANES has been asking people how they feel about different people and groups in society since the 1970s. Among the groups are the political parties. The questions use feeling thermometer scores, as described earlier.

The graph below tracks four average feeling thermometer scores about the Republican and Democratic parties from the Carter years through the Obama years. Solid lines represent partisans' feelings about their own party, and dashed lines represent partisans' feelings about the opposite party. Keep in mind that a score of 50 degrees is neutral.

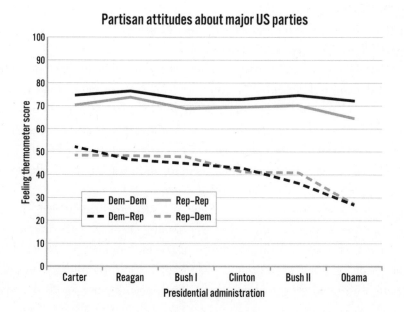

Partisans' feelings about the opposite party were pretty neutral from the Carter years through the George H. W. Bush years. During these three administrations, the average score Democrats and Republicans gave their opponents never dropped below 45 degrees.

Slowly, then more dramatically, however, things changed. The opposite-party averages dropped a bit, but only into the low 40s during the Clinton years. Then, during the George W. Bush years, Democrats' feelings about the Republican Party nose-dived into the 30s.

Feelings deteriorated even more dramatically during the Obama years, with both Republicans and Democrats rating the other party around 25 degrees. Feeling scores this low are what we'd qualify as political hatred, pure and simple. In 2016, during Obama's final year in office, the Democrats gave the Republican Party an average score of 25 degrees, and Republicans gave the Democratic Party a score of 27 degrees. To put that in some perspective, Republicans generally give "atheists" an average score a bit above 30, while white Democrats rate "Christian fundamentalists" with an equally cold score. (African American Democrats, who often belong to evangelical and fundamentalist denominations, score Christian fundamentalists much higher.) Republicans tend to score "illegal immigrants" at about 30 degrees, even with the word "illegal" in the label. The bottom two lines in the graph on page 127 are what gathering political hatred looks like in a public opinion survey.

Simply measuring partisans' average feelings about the opposing party doesn't tell researchers everything we need to know, however. It can't reveal whether there is just an increased *depth* of hatred among a relatively small group of true believers, or whether more and more people have come to share those negative feelings with the passage of time.

We can answer that question by looking at how many partisans, over the last several decades, have given a feeling thermometer score of 20 degrees or less to the other party. And the results are dismaying.

The percentage of partisans who really seem to hate the other party has skyrocketed since the turn of the millennium, as reflected in the graph on page 129. From 1980 through 2000, the number of partisans who rated their feelings about the opposing party as 20 degrees or less never exceeded twenty percentage points, and was usually much lower. After 2000, however, the percentage of partisans with hatred in their hearts rose with each election: from the 20s and 30s for Democrats and Republicans in 2008, to 48 and 50 percent, respectively, in 2016. Clearly, hating the opposite political party is no longer a fringe thing. The same can be said about hating the opposite party's standard-bearer—and even his wife. In a Pew Research Center survey taken in 2016, 59 percent of Republicans gave President Obama a score of zero, and even 40 percent gave First Lady Michelle Obama a goose egg.

This increase in negativity coincides with the alignment of Americans' worldviews and political identities. Recall that the fixed and fluid were pretty evenly split in their partisanship between Republicans and Democrats through the 2000 election. That changed in 2004 and deepened with nearly every subsequent election. Today, fixed voters are huddled in the Republican Party, while fluid voters are clustered in the Democratic Party.

Accompanying this political sorting by worldview is that people now harbor stronger negative feelings about the other party. Once worldview

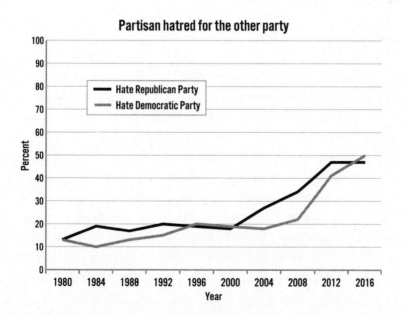

came to define the partisan divide, more and more partisans became heavily invested in their identity as partisans. America has, in effect, become a nation of Rattlers and Eagles.

Feeling thermometers also reveal something else of consequence about American politics that is deeply troubling—and also quite revealing about the way in which worldview politics has shaped Americans' attitudes toward partisans in the opposing tribe. It appears that partisans no longer distinguish between the Republican and Democratic *Parties* and the *people* who are Republicans and Democrats: multifaceted individuals who identify with one party or the other, but who are also moms and dads, students, employees, coaches, and sports fans, among myriad other nonpolitical identities.

Decades ago, people appreciated the distinction between partisans and parties. For instance, in 1980 the ANES asked half the people in their sample to evaluate "Republicans" and "Democrats" on the feeling thermometers and the other half to evaluate "the Republican Party" and "the Democratic Party." The average scores make clear that respondents distinguished between the people and the political institutions they supported: Democrats gave an average score of 51 degrees to the Republican Party, but a much higher average score of 61 degrees to Republicans in general. Republicans' feelings about the other side were similar.

Today, by contrast, partisans no longer seem to distinguish between people's political identities and the political parties they support. A 2017 survey that used the same approach as the 1980 ANES found that the average ratings that Democrats and Republicans gave the other party and the people who identify with the other party didn't differ at all.

This inability—or unwillingness—to differentiate partisans from their parties has given rise to a new form of prejudice in the United States, introduced in the last chapter as partyism. Americans harbor deep-seated, extremely negative biases about people in the opposing political camp—people with whom they disagree not only on politics, but also on the fundamentals of life. And while the country certainly has its fair share of prejudices, there is reason to think that the level of antipathy between members of different parties is coming close to outstripping any of the country's other biases, however deep-rooted they may be.

One quick and easy way that researchers have gauged Americans' relative levels of prejudice is to ask them about their children's potential marriage partners. This is because people are very good at hiding their prejudices, until the point where intermarriage is on the table. When, in 2010, researchers asked Americans whether they would be either "somewhat" or "very" concerned if their son or daughter married someone from the opposite party, fully one-third of Democrats said yes. Republicans expressed even more concern about the idea of their children marrying someone from the opposite party, with nearly half saying it would be a problem for them.

It didn't used to be that way. Back in 1960, not long after the dawn of survey research, Americans were asked whether they would find it discomfiting if one of their children married someone who belonged to the party opposite their own. Such concern was vanishingly rare. Only 4 percent of Democrats expressed unease about their child marrying a Republican, and 5 percent of Republicans expressed unease about their child marrying a Democrat. (Bear in mind that researchers can usually get about 10 percent of Americans to endorse even the most ridiculous ideas in a survey, whether it's that the remote Nevada military installation known as Area 51 holds captured aliens, that the Americans and Soviets fought a secret space war in the 1970s, or that Hillary Clinton is literally the spawn of Satan. The fact that only about 5 percent of partisans expressed concern about "interparty" marriage in 1960 suggests just how fringe a concern it was at the time.)

An experience with one of our friends suggests such blatant partyism exists in the real world and is not just something researchers conjure in academic experiments. A product of the Deep South, Dwight (not his real name) was born ten years before integration, and is a staunch conservative and deeply faithful Christian. Based on what we know about people who fit this description, we can assume that Dwight has a fixed worldview —with all of the preferences and biases that come with it, notably warier feelings when it comes to race. Yet he related to one of the authors that he found it much easier to have one of his daughters marry a politically conservative African American than to have another of his daughters marry a white liberal. This was true despite the fact that the white liberal in question here is a youth minister, which should have appealed to Dwight's religious sensibilities.

Like racial bias, partisan bias apparently occurs automatically, beyond the control of a person's conscious thoughts. That's not to say that people have no control over how they express these biases; for instance, Dwight didn't attempt to stop his daughter from marrying the white liberal minister. (At least, we don't think he did.) Rather, the point is simply that biases arise in our minds automatically, and uninvited. Researchers have demonstrated this again and again.

Social scientists test for the automaticity of biases by administering what they call an implicit-association test. In these tests, words with a positive connotation and words with a negative connotation pop up on a computer screen at random. The subjects taking the test are directed to associate the words with one group or another. Because the instructions tell the test taker to work as fast as possible, they cannot deliberate about their choices. Their responses are automatic, beyond their conscious control. To the extent that people who belong to a group associate the positive words with their group and the negative words with the other group more quickly than the reverse, these associations serve as evidence of implicit bias.

Research on race has shown for decades that implicit bias exists in most whites—but in applying the implicit-bias approach to the study of *partisan* bias, researchers have found that the automatic bias that partisans have against the other political party run even stronger than the automatic racial bias that whites possess about African Americans or African Americans possess about whites. In one notable study, people taking a survey were asked to decide between two (made-up) students competing to receive a college award. One résumé had a stereotypically African American name for the applicant, whereas the other had a stereotypically European American name. Half the résumés indicated that the applicant was president of the College Democrats at their school while the other half said the candidate was president of the College Republicans. This allowed researchers to compare whether the candidate's partisanship or race had a bigger impact on the subjects' decisions about awarding the scholarship.

The result: over 80 percent of partisans in the experiment chose for the scholarship the person who had headed the College Republicans or the College Democrats, whichever one matched their own party preference. This would not be much of a story if partisans only made this choice when the scholarship candidate of their party was the better qualified of the two candidates or even if the two were equally qualified. However, partisans chose the person of their party over 70 percent of the time when the applicant had a grade point average that was significantly lower than the candidate who had been the president of the other party's organization on campus.

Put bluntly, this study showed that partisans are willing to choose a demonstrably less qualified person to receive a scholarship, provided that person identifies with their party. And in making these decisions, partisans seem to care *much* more about political affiliation than race: while researchers found some racial bias reflected in the respondents' decisions, the amount was negligible compared with the partisan bias.

Consider that finding for a moment. Although people are aware of racial categories from near birth and come to understand party politics only much later in their lives, the political environment is such these days that Americans appear to have biases against the other party that are even stronger than the biases they have against those from other races —this, in spite of the fact that racial prejudice remains alive and well. All that is to suggest just how strong and potentially uncontrollable partisans' emotions have become in a worldview-divided party system.

If people make an effort, they can overcome their implicit biases. Just because they are biased before their conscious thought begins doesn't mean that they have to act on those biases, after all. To wit: almost all whites harbor some degree of automatic bias against African Americans, but a significant chunk of whites express positive feelings about African

Americans when they answer explicit survey questions. Although some may be hiding their true feelings, it is unlikely that anything close to all of them are lying. Rather, while their first instinct might be to discriminate, they have trained their conscious thoughts to overpower that first instinct.

Similarly, partisans could make a conscious effort to overcome their initial prejudices about people in the opposing party. Unfortunately, the evidence suggests that they don't. That may be because there are social costs associated with expressing prejudice against people who belong to different races, but there are no such costs associated with expressing prejudice against people who belong to different parties. People simply seem to have less motivation to do the hard work necessary to overcome their partisan biases than their racial biases.

Partisans' hatred of the opposing tribe has potentially devastating political implications. Such intense and widespread partisan enmity means more people than ever are highly motivated to process information about their own party and their opponents with bias—and more likely to discount information that threatens their perceptions of themselves, their tribes, and their rivals. Like the Rattlers and the Eagles in the Robbers Cave experiment, they "celebrate their victories and rationalize their defeats." Strong negative feelings increase the motivation people feel to do whatever is necessary to see the world the way they want to see it—to embrace facts that support their side and explain away those that don't.

The human desire to rationalize and reinterpret isn't new. As Anaïs Nin, or a Talmudic scholar, or any one of a number of writers over the past two hundred years who've been credited with the phrase once wrote, "We don't see things as they are; we see them as *we* are." People see things the way they want to see them, in other words. What *is* new is the increased incentive that an increasing percentage of partisans feel to rationalize and reinterpret when it comes to *politics*. Hate does that.

Strong partisan ties greatly amplify this human tendency to rationalize, to engage in what social scientists call "motivated reasoning." Humans are, in general, adept rationalizers—more like lawyers than scientists, as Jonathan Haidt puts it. Although people think they carefully weigh the pros and cons of different perspectives and reach reasoned conclusions based on the evidence, that's not the case. Instead, people start with certain beliefs, whether they are about their families, their friends, or their political tribes, and then interpret information in a way that comports with those beliefs. Of course, simply living life produces an avalanche of new information, some of which supports those beliefs and some of which challenges them. When it comes to new information that challenges their deeply held beliefs, however, people will do mental gymnastics to hold fast to these sacred truths. Failing to do so would cause them psychological pain.

But how much pain? If people care about something only a little, admitting their side is wrong will hurt only a little. They will therefore be only weakly motivated to reason with bias. When they care a lot, however, admitting their side is wrong will hurt a lot, which makes the motivation to rationalize and reinterpret much stronger. The complexity of the mental gymnastics people are willing to engage in is therefore a function of how much they care.

Because partisan feelings were not so strong a generation ago, fewer partisans cared enough to medal in Olympic-level rationalizations. With political identities entangled with their worldviews, however, today's partisans care a *lot* about their political identities—and thus are becoming as adept at these mental gymnastics as the Fierce Five were on the uneven bars at the 2012 London games. Even when it comes to objective matters like the state of the economy, partisans' assessments are so biased that it appears they must be living in different worlds. Despite experiencing the exact same conditions, one side is increasingly likely to say the economy is good while the other is increasingly likely to say it is bad. Differences in perceptions have always existed, but they appear to be two to three times larger than they were before worldview started to divide partisans.

Indeed, medal-worthy feats abound: for instance, right-leaning Americans have engaged in mental contortions of sufficient difficulty to believe that a certain president whose moral track record is spotty at best—who called African countries "shitholes," who apparently had multiple affairs, including with a porn star and with a *Playboy* model while his young (third) wife was home with their newborn son, and who, on average, has lied five times a day since assuming the office—is a good role model for children. Indeed, more than 70 percent of Republicans said as much in a 2018 poll.

According to the ANES survey, roughly 50 percent of Americans have an extremely dim view of their political opponents—and we can safely estimate that this same group will be willing to reason with *extreme* bias when it comes to politics. Even using a conservative metric of hatred— we used feeling thermometer scores of below 20 degrees for the other party when average Republican feelings about, say, atheists are above 30 degrees—it appears about half of each side, and probably more, will work as hard as they need to work to see the political world the way they want to see it rather than how it is.

This tendency toward hyperrationalization allows partisans on both sides to feel better about themselves and their political decisions. Unfortunately, it also undermines a central ideal of democratic citizenship, namely that citizens are capable of making rational calculations based on the world around them. With the rise of worldview politics, Americans seem more and more resistant to the information that they encounter, unless it confirms their preexisting ideas about how the world is organized, politically or otherwise.

The fact that so many Americans have such a strong motivation to reason with bias, even extreme bias, is not simply a historical anomaly. It has real and very serious implications for some of the weightiest issues in twenty-first-century politics. The Bush administration justified America's 2003 invasion of Iraq by pointing to evidence that Saddam Hussein's government was stockpiling weapons of mass destruction (WMD), but reality soon intervened. The United Nations weapons inspectors failed to find any such armaments before the US invasion, and American troops turned up nothing after their arrival in Iraq. But for a long time, Republican voters remained adamant: the weapons had been in Iraq at one point. Even after Bush's admission that no WMD had been located in Iraq, Republicans adopted a friendly *interpretation* for why none were found: the WMD had simply been moved from Iraq to Syria before American troops could find them. Such an interpretation, while possible, seems implausible.

Democrats' own view of the war changed fundamentally after Barack Obama became president. Suddenly, they had motivation to get behind a conflict they had previously viewed as an unmitigated disaster. When the Pew Research Center asked Americans in early 2008, months before Obama's election, whether the "US will succeed in achieving its goals in Iraq," only about 30 percent of Democrats said yes. When asked the same question in 2010, in the middle of Obama's first term, however, about 60 percent of Democrats said yes. Not surprisingly, Republicans' optimism about the war dropped by about fifteen points over the same period. Nothing about objective circumstances drove these changes in opinion. All that had changed was the tribe that controlled the White House.

Opinions about domestic surveillance follow a similar pattern. While there is no reason to think either set of American partisans should be especially enthusiastic about the idea of their government snooping on their phone calls, people with fixed worldviews tend to be more open to trade-offs that maximize safety — so it is reasonable to think Republicans would be more supportive of warrantless wiretapping and other forms of domestic surveillance. And indeed, that is how it was during the George W. Bush presidency, when revelations about surveillance programs first came to light. Over 80 percent of Republicans, according to a 2006 poll, supported the NSA "investigating people suspected of involvement with terrorism by secretly listening in on telephone calls and reading emails" without court approval. Democrats were much more reluctant, with only 32 percent supporting the program.

Once again, however, Democrats dramatically changed their tune during the Obama presidency. In the midst of Obama's second term, former National Security Agency contractor Edward Snowden leaked information showing the government was trying to identify terrorists by gathering mountains of data from telephone companies and websites without Americans' knowledge. In June 2013, soon after Snowden's revelations hit the news, the Pew Research Center asked a random sample of Americans whether it was acceptable that "the NSA has been get-

ting secret court orders to track calls of millions of Americans to investigate terrorism." Curiously, given Democrats' generally higher support
for maintaining civil liberties, they were significantly more supportive of
these intrusions than Republicans, by 64 percent to 52 percent. Democrats were nearly thirty percentage points more supportive of the Obama-
era program than the Bush-era one, and Republicans were more than
twenty points more supportive of the Bush-era program than the Obama-
era program. A more clear-cut example of motivated reasoning is hard to
imagine.

As with the war in Iraq and domestic surveillance, it is staggering how
much of a difference an election result can make when it comes to partisans' perceptions of economic conditions—something that, unlike these
other, subjective assessments, is actually measurable by hard, clear, and
widely accessible data. Gallup asked a sample of Americans whether the
economy was "getting better" or "getting worse" the week before the 2016
election and again the week after. In the preelection poll, only 16 percent of Republicans said it was getting better, whereas over 60 percent
of Democrats thought it was improving. In the postelection poll—administered only *days* later—48 percent of Republicans, triple the percentage before the election, suddenly thought the economy was getting better,
while the percentage of optimistic Democrats dropped by about fifteen
points. There were no new GDP numbers. The Labor Department hadn't
released a new jobs report. Inflation hadn't changed. All that was different was that Donald Trump had been elected president.

An *increase* in biased reasoning can be seen in the pattern of Americans' presidential approval ratings over time. The differences between
Republicans and Democrats in their approval of the president have never
been greater than they have been since the dawn of worldview politics.
George W. Bush's presidency marked the beginning of an era of dramatic increases in polarized approval ratings. An average of 84 percent
of Republicans approved of his performance in all the Gallup surveys
across his presidency, compared with only 23 percent of Democrats, producing a 61 percent spread. The difference was even larger for Barack
Obama. The average percentage of Democrats who approved of Obama

over his eight years in the White House was 83 percent, compared with 13 percent of Republicans—a seventy-point difference. At the time of this writing, Donald Trump seems poised to eclipse them both. His January 2018 numbers reveal better than 80 percent approval among Republicans, while only 5 percent of Democrats express approval. By contrast, from the 1950s through the 1970s, the average partisan spread in presidential job approval was only thirty-four points—about half that of the presidencies from George W. Bush to Donald Trump. In the past, Americans seemed to be relatively on the same page about the kind of job their president was doing; not so today.

It may be tempting to think that major differences of opinion such as these —especially about objective, measurable issues like the performance of the US economy—could be corrected with a healthy dose of accurate, impartial information. If people had the facts explained to them clearly and dispassionately, surely even ardent partisans would be forced to acknowledge the truth. Right?

As reasonable as that might sound, the evidence suggests otherwise. In fact, in this charged political environment, trying to present facts that challenge partisans' preconceived notions about a given issue probably won't make things better. It might even make them worse.

Partisans fail to acknowledge facts in the first place because they are protecting themselves from experiencing psychological pain—not necessarily because they haven't heard the facts. Acknowledging inconvenient truths also requires people to consider that they made a mistake —that semiautomatic weapons actually do kill young children in schools with great efficiency, for instance, or that their political commitments might be causing long-term harm to the planet. People are *really* resistant to facing up to facts this unpleasant. So not only will well-intentioned efforts to correct a person's misperceptions be unlikely to make much headway, such attempts might actually make him or her defensive about —and more resolute in—their mistaken beliefs.

Researchers have found evidence of this "backfire" effect in an experiment designed to measure the impact of scientific proof of climate change on people who are skeptical of climate change. Before providing the respondents with this scientific information, the researchers measured their subjects' capacity for mathematical reasoning. This step was important because, if people failed to update their opinions in response to scientific information, it might be that they simply didn't understand it—a possibility that researchers first had to rule out. Once they'd made sure that all the respondents could understand the information they were presenting, the researchers found that climate skeptics failed to become less skeptical after receiving the science on climate change. Not only that, but the ones with the highest capacity for scientific reasoning actually became *more* skeptical. It is likely that those with a high capacity for scientific thinking also have a high capacity to rationalize. Both take significant cognitive power.

More recent research suggests that partisans aren't generally as immune to facts as that. Indeed, in some recent experiments that use so-called corrective information, people often update their beliefs. This is the good news. The bad news is that even when people accept new facts as true, they don't necessarily change their behavior. For example, people who opposed vaccines because they thought they entailed serious health risks deemed them less dangerous after being presented with factual information about vaccine safety. Yet they remained unmoved about whether it was a good idea to give vaccines to their own kids; in fact, some members of the study groups became even less likely to say they would vaccinate. Similarly, during the 2016 campaign, Donald Trump repeatedly insisted crime rates were exploding across the nation when, in fact, they'd mostly been plummeting for decades. When researchers provided data about actual crime rates to Trump supporters, they adopted a more accurate view about crime rates in America. But it didn't change their opinions of Trump or their support for him. Instead, supporters minimized the significance of the new information.

In an ideal world, people would be less likely to support a politician who lied to them. But it seems that partisans' motivation to rationalize away information that threatens their political identities has simply become too high.

If new information corrects errors but does not lead people to change their behavior, one has to wonder whether people really *want* accurate information. What's clear is that people on one side of the aisle seem to want it more than people on the other. It's no coincidence that the preceding examples—misperceptions about climate change, crime rates, and the side effects of vaccinations—all find their staunchest defenders on the political right, rather than the left. Indeed, evidence is piling up that those on the political right seem to have a stronger tendency to take steps to buttress their worldview than those on the political left. This helps explain why right-wing media have always attracted much larger audiences than their left-wing counterparts, an issue we'll return to later in this chapter. (It also helps explain Republicans' especially resolute support for Donald J. Trump even when faced with what seem like Trump's obviously antidemocratic impulses, as we'll discuss in the next chapter.)

A good example of Democrats' and Republicans' respective relationships with new and uncomfortable information can be seen in the differing reactions that Republicans and Democrats had to the explosion of sexual-misconduct allegations beginning in 2016 and spilling into 2017. Some involved conservatives, such as Donald Trump; Bill O'Reilly, long Fox News's highest-rated host; and Roy Moore, the Republican Senate candidate from Alabama. Others involved liberal officeholders, such as Minnesota senator Al Franken and Michigan representative John Conyers. Of course, Bill Clinton's sexual misbehavior in the 1990s loomed over the entire discussion. According to a *Politico*/Morning Consult poll that asked a random sample of Americans about these figures and a range of media personnel brought down by allegations of sexual misconduct, Democrats were much less likely to be protective of those on their side than Republicans were. There was very little difference in how much Democrats and Republicans believed the charges against Bill Clinton and Al Franken —Democrats were four points and one point less likely, respectively, to believe them. By contrast, Republicans were twenty-six points less likely than Democrats to believe the charges leveled against Donald Trump, twenty-five points less likely to believe the charges against Roy Moore, and eighteen points less likely to believe the charges against Bill O'Reilly.

We see the same asymmetry when it comes to believing in political conspiracies and unsubstantiated rumors. The ANES asked a set of questions in 2012 about whether people believed a number of empirically false statements, but ones that had gotten some traction in the media. Specifically, they asked (1) whether President Obama was born in a country other than the United States, (2) whether Obamacare set up "death panels" to make end-of-life decisions, (3) whether people in the government knew about the 9/11 attacks before they happened but let them occur anyway, and (4) whether government directed flooding to impoverished parts of New Orleans during Hurricane Katrina. The first two are what might be considered conspiracies or rumors of the right, and the last two conspiracies or rumors of the left.

Predictably, the researchers found that Republicans were more persuaded by the rumors of the right than Democrats were, and Democrats were more persuaded by the rumors of the left than Republicans were. But the gaps between Republicans and Democrats on these matters suggest a marked asymmetry in this kind of thinking. Republicans were more than thirty points more likely than Democrats to believe the rumors of the right (44 percent to 10 percent on Obama's birthplace and 60 to 28 on death panels). Democrats, by contrast, were only an average of ten points more likely to believe rumors of the left than Republicans (41 percent to 33 percent on 9/11 and 23 to 11 on Katrina). Notably, Republicans with fixed worldviews were by far the most likely to embrace these rumors. On Obama's birthplace, 57 percent of the fixed believed it was probably not the United States, compared with 40 percent of less fixed Republicans. Similarly, 64 percent of fixed-worldview Republicans believed Obamacare included death panels, compared with 54 percent of less fixed Republicans.

It is possible that part of the reason Republicans were more likely to embrace the rumors on the right is that these rumors pertained to issues and events that were more recent than those that formed the basis of the rumors of the left. However, scholars asked two of these same questions four years later and the results suggest a different story. *Was Barack Obama born in the United States?* In 2016, 41 percent of Republicans still believed the rumor was probably true, statistically indistinguishable from the 44 percent who believed it in 2012. *Did government officials allow the 9/11 attacks to happen despite knowing of them in advance?* In 2016 the percentage of Republicans who believed that rumor actually topped the percentage of Democrats who believed it. While Democrats' belief in the 9/11 rumor actually dropped by eight percentage points between 2012 and 2016, Republicans' endorsement increased slightly.

Taken together, these results suggest that Americans on the political right may have a particularly strong propensity to reason with bias when confronted with information that challenges their preexisting beliefs. But the sad fact is that a good-sized chunk of Americans today encounter very little of this sort of information to begin with. In fact, they're much more likely to encounter information that confirms their beliefs—or that makes them more extreme, and they can pass it along, whether it is true or not, like a virus to others.

In May 2017 a former Fox News contributor, Tobin Smith, took to Medium .com to share a conversation he'd had with the late Roger Ailes. The former Nixon aide, political strategist, television producer, and founder of Fox News had passed away earlier that year, and Smith finally felt free to broadcast comments that Ailes had made to him in confidence about the Fox News network, its audience, and its goals.

According to Smith, Ailes envisioned Fox News as a network for people "55 to dead," viewers who "look like me . . . white guys in mostly Red State counties who sit on their couch with the remote in their hand all day and night." In Smith's retelling, Ailes said, "After the producers/host scares the shit out of them, I want to see YOU tear those smug condescending know-it-all East Coast liberals to pieces . . . limb by limb . . . until they jump up out of their LaZ boy [sic] and scream 'Way to go Toby . . . you KILLED that libtard!'"

Fox succeeded in everything Ailes envisioned, Smith observed. By marketing a powerful drug to a susceptible population (what Smith called "the most vulnerable and gullible senior Americans"), Fox gives those viewers "visceral gut feelings of outrage relieved by the most powerful emotions of all . . . the thrill of your tribe's victory over its enemy and the ultimate triumph of good over evil."

This tribal sense of enmity, which provides partisans with such strong motivation to see the world as they want to see it, has contributed to— and been exacerbated by—an efflorescence of partisan cable news channels and ideological internet news sites. The information these outlets provide confirms partisans' political beliefs and coheres with their worldviews. It also serves as ready-made ammunition for them to use against their political opponents.

For about two decades now, Americans have had access to one-sided partisan media options not available since the partisan press of the late nineteenth and early twentieth centuries. National political talk radio and television outlets such as the right-leaning Fox News and left-leaning MSNBC have enabled highly motivated denizens on each side of the worldview-politics divide to simply reject the basic facts that the other side views as given. These media bubbles have created a protective cocoon within which partisans with the desire to do so can avoid even talking about events or issues that make their team look bad, focusing instead on story lines that cast them in a positive light, or that denigrate the other side (or both).

It's not just the white, "55 to dead" crowd that falls into this trap. Because Americans' political identities and worldviews are now so closely intertwined, they are more susceptible than ever to the reassurance that partisan media provides, whether they receive doses of it directly or indirectly through their social networks. Outlets such as Fox News and MSNBC serve as elemental a need as there is: they tell stories, over and over again, that reinforce viewers' sense that their side is good and the other side is bad. In the process, this highly divisive media diet also reinforces fixed and fluid people's incompatible views of reality, and their sense that their political opponents are both aliens and enemies.

The media environment wasn't always like this. During the golden age of journalism in the 1960s and 1970s, when media were among the most respected institutions in the United States (in a 1972 poll, Walter

Cronkite, the CBS News anchor, was considered the single most trusted public figure in American life, with 72 percent of Americans expressing confidence in the legendary newscaster), the networks covered most of the same content, leading with the same story most nights. Today, on the other hand, partisan news channels and websites on the left and the right not only adopt different viewpoints, they often do not even cover the same events. Thus, the media tend to reinforce their audience's existing beliefs about the motives and character of the other side, while reaffirming the essential goodness of the home team.

Nothing close to all partisans consume cable news and ideological websites on the internet. But, among those who do, exposure to partisan media tends to harden viewers' extreme preferences about issues and to deepen their dislike of political opponents. Such forms of media also reinforce the worldview divide between Americans in other ways. Emotionally laden issues related to race and cultural change that are central to the current worldview divide are also economic opportunities for a profit-motivated industry like partisan news media, which have a strong incentive to focus on conflicts that draw in the largest number of viewers. If network executives are choosing between airing hearings about spending on highways and education, and shouting matches about gay rights and race, it's a pretty good bet they're going to pick the latter. And unlike mainstream news, which must maintain relative political neutrality, outlets like Fox News and MSNBC can give their viewers exactly what they want—a heaping helping of divisive issues served up in a fashion that caters to their audience's political and personal preferences—that is, their worldviews.

Media outlets serve up partisan content not only because it's in their economic interest to do so. A basic function of news organizations is to serve as a conduit for elite communication. As a matter of course, they record and broadcast what elected officials say. As elected officials in the two parties have become more polarized in recent decades, the messages that ordinary news consumers hear from them have become more clearly partisan in nature. Thus, even without highlighting conflict or engaging in sensationalized coverage that reduces complex debates to simple sound bites, media contribute to ordinary people's perceptions of the political world as a more starkly conflict-driven place.

The proliferation of cable television has also contributed to a hollowing out of America's political middle, and not just because it gave the country Fox News and MSNBC. Before cable, there were nearly no alternatives to watching the news; as Ted Koppel nostalgically noted, Americans everywhere used to "gather around the electronic hearth" every evening at 6:30 p.m. EST. In the 1970s, between twenty-seven million and twenty-nine million viewers nightly tuned in to watch "the most trusted man in America," Walter Cronkite, anchor the *CBS Evening News*. These were not all political junkies, not even close. But anyone watching television during that time frame simply had no choice but to get their daily dose of politics. News was all that was on.

Once cable, then the internet, entered people's homes, the number of viewing options skyrocketed. The average home had one television featuring five or six television channels in the 1970s; by 2016, the typical household had access to over two hundred channels, and everyone in the house could be using a different device either to get their news or, more commonly, watch something other than the news. Even accounting for the fact that the average household only watched about 10 percent of those channels in 2016, the menu of choices still increased fourfold over this time period. Whereas many occasionally interested and ideologically moderate voters in the 1970s tuned in to the evening news simply because nothing else was on, by the 1990s these same viewers had many other options to choose from.

This shift from a "low choice" to a "high choice" media environment is at least partly to blame for the growing polarization of the electorate. The occasional viewers who in the past were drawn to political news by sheer virtue of having nothing else to watch could drop out of politics altogether. The result has been a culling of political interest, leaving more ideologically intent voters to more greatly influence political conversations.

• • •

Partisan media don't just allow people to scratch an already-present partisan itch; they intensify that itch. Experimental research reveals that the current media landscape pushes people who are already extreme in their views to even more extreme positions: conservative individuals who watched an issue-based Fox News segment actually became more conservative on the issue after watching the segment, just as liberal viewers watching a liberal segment became more liberal. The backfire effect was at work in these studies, as well, with conservatives who watched MSNBC generally becoming more conservative. The same was true of liberals exposed to conservative media.

Partisan Americans' gravitation toward news outlets that match their worldview has only become more striking over time. In 2014, the Pew Research Center surveyed several thousand Americans for a series of studies of polarization in America. Summarizing their findings, Pew researchers wrote: "When it comes to getting news about politics and government, liberals and conservatives inhabit different worlds. There is little overlap in the news sources they turn to and trust." For example, Pew found that 47 percent of conservative respondents chose Fox News as their main news source. The next-most-relied-upon sources were local radio, with 11 percent; local television, with 5 percent; local newspaper, with 3 percent; and Google News, with 3 percent. In contrast, the most liberal respondents in the survey obtained information from multiple sources: 15 percent chose CNN as their main news source, 13 percent NPR, 12 percent MSNBC, 10 percent the *New York Times,* and 5 percent local television. Note that the only overlapping source was local television, and that accounted for only 5 percent of each group.

A relatively small percentage of Americans watch cable news, but its impact penetrates much more broadly and deeply into the American psyche. The best analogy might be that of a virus. Cable news infects the "carriers"—the 10 to15 percent of Americans who consume it—directly, and they in turn infect bystanders with the virus by talking to them about politics. While the politically uninterested moderate can always find a *Law and Order* episode or a particularly riveting installment of *Cake Boss* to watch, political junkies on the left and the right can flip to Fox News or MSNBC at any time of the day or night, receiving a dose of political vitriol that they later share with those otherwise less engaged *Cake Boss* viewers.

All that seems to be required for the virus to spread is that the newly infected people have the same basic political identity as the carrier. In one particularly fascinating study, two researchers recruited hundreds of subjects from the Philadelphia and Chicago metropolitan areas and asked them to watch twelve minutes of partisan media about the Keystone XL pipeline, a major project intended to bring crude oil from Canada to the United States, but with potentially adverse environmental consequences. After that, they created a number of discussion groups, some where everyone shared the same party identification, others with a mix of Democrats and Republicans, each including one of the people who had watched the partisan media and others who had not watched the clip. When a person watched a partisan news clip and then engaged in a discussion with a group of people who identified with the same party, the opinions of those who hadn't even watched the clip became more extreme.

Interestingly, when the discussion groups in this study included some people from the other party, the mix of Democrats and Republicans appeared to lessen the "secondhand" effect of partisan news. This suggests that contact between people from opposing sides of the world-view-political divide can stave off the worst effects of partisan media. Unfortunately, however, today this sort of contact is the exception rather than the norm.

These findings suggest yet another negative consequence of Republicans and Democrats being less likely to live near each other, to work with each other, and to share similar recreational interests because of the worldview divide. Increasingly, groups that talk about politics will be politically homogeneous. That means that the partisan news media contagion can spread like wildfire, passed along by political junkies who watch it all the time to like-minded neighbors, colleagues, and friends who don't watch it at all. In a bygone era, when neighborhoods and workplaces were more mixed by party, the fire would be more contained.

Social media have dramatically accelerated the spread of this partisan news "virus." Indeed, platforms such as Facebook and Twitter have altered the way Americans receive political information perhaps even more fundamentally than did the rise of cable television. The reach of social media is incredibly broad: nearly 90 percent of Americans are now online, and fully 80 percent use Facebook. More than three-quarters of users report logging in to social media daily. When they do, they leave themselves open to infection by partisan political news as well as by their friends in their social media networks.

Regardless of whether the people who consume this partisan news are highly politically active or vote only once every four years, the content takes a toll. When the fixed and fluid retreat to their media silos, they are exposed to a constant and damning stream of attacks directed at their opponents. These attacks activate their distinct worldview identities and generate an "us versus them" mentality, increasing people's dislike and distrust of the opposing side. Indeed, those self-identified liberals who watched an MSNBC clip in the lab exhibited less trust of and more antipathy toward the other side than those liberals who did not watch such a clip. Likewise, self-identified conservatives who watched Fox News clips had a greater dislike for and distrust of liberals. Both sides exposed to partisan media clips expressed much less interest in compromise.

Significantly, it appears that fluid, liberal people may be inoculated against this partisan news virus to some degree — at least, compared to fixed, conservative people. The reason has to do with the range of news media that each group consumes. A diverse diet of news media appears to boost the immune system of the people who ingest it, allowing them to better distinguish partisan news from objective news. On the other hand, a news media diet that is more limited, and that contains more partisan content, is likely to leave its consumers more susceptible to infection. And when it comes to media diets, fluid people's diet appears to be a whole lot more diverse than that of fixed people.

Just as fixed people gravitate toward tried-and-true choices when it comes to beer or coffee, they also seem to have a relatively limited and consistent intake of news sources. In 2017 the *Columbia Journalism*

Review (*CJR*) analyzed 1.25 million online stories that appeared between April 1, 2015, and Election Day 2016. The researchers found that a distinct right-wing information ecosystem developed around the hub of Breitbart News, an outlet founded by the conservative commentator Andrew Breitbart, which, under the leadership of media mogul (and onetime Trump presidential adviser) Steve Bannon, explicitly catered to hard-right nationalist and emergent alt-right viewpoints. *CJR* found that Breitbart anchored a successful effort by right-wing media to push a "hyper-partisan perspective" and, perhaps more importantly, "strongly influenced the broader media agenda, in particular coverage of Hillary Clinton."

One especially significant finding of the *CJR* study was that there was an asymmetric cast to the partisan media landscape. Whereas liberal audiences paid plenty of attention to explicitly partisan sites like Daily Kos, Huffington Post (where Breitbart worked before he formed his own site), and MSNBC, the information that formed the basis of their analysis and framed their discussions came from traditional media, including the network's nightly news broadcasts, which still try to maintain a degree of neutrality in their coverage and avoid more emotion-laden language in presenting it. By contrast, the right-anchored media existed almost wholly apart from traditional media, in a largely sui generis information environment. One consequence is that conservative news media consumers are less likely to encounter news narratives that are widely shared by those who are not part of their political tribe. At the same time, when they do, those narratives may well seem that much more alien and unbelievable to them.

This clustering of Republicans around a small number of highly partisan news outlets, and the grazing of Democrats on a wider, more varied media diet, reflects and reinforces the different levels of trust in specific media outlets expressed by liberals and conservatives. In 2014 the Pew Research Center asked respondents to rate how much they trusted three dozen news organizations, ranging from Breitbart to NPR. Respondents classified as "consistent liberals" trusted twenty-eight of the thirty-six sources, including the *Wall Street Journal,* which has a conservative editorial stance alongside a highly respected news-gathering operation.

"Consistent conservatives," by contrast, distrusted two-thirds of the news outlets, including CNN, all the major networks, *USA Today,* and the BBC. Consistent conservatives were as mistrustful of ABC's nightly news, an arguably very bland, down-the-middle newscast, as consistent liberals were of Sean Hannity, a highly partisan firebrand who leans heavily on outrage language to get his point across. Indeed, in the Trump era, Hannity has become the president's most stalwart high-profile media ally. One result is that conservatives' more limited exposure to at least somewhat varied information is likely to exacerbate their existing tendency toward mistrustfulness, which, in turn, is likely to reinforce both in them and their opponents the animus each side feels for the other.

This asymmetry in the way that people on the left and right consume news may, in turn, be related to instinctive differences in what kinds of news the fixed and fluid seek out. Numerous studies have shown that people who are more fixed in their worldview, and who thus have a greater need for cognitive closure, are also more likely to seek out information sources that reinforce their existing beliefs. One study asked people whether they wanted to read material about the death penalty that supported their existing view, opposed it, or presented a "balanced view." Before they received one of the articles about the death penalty, the study's subjects were exposed to ideas and images that raised questions about their own mortality. (Psychologists have long observed that "mortality salience," whereby individuals are prompted to think about their deaths, affects how much people then become rigid in their thinking and anxious about uncertainty.) All humans are inclined to retreat to certainty when confronted with their own mortality, but after contemplating their own deaths in this study, respondents on the right proved much more interested in reading material consistent with their own beliefs than did those on the left. This tracks with larger tendencies evident among the fixed and fluid: fixed people want to stick with what they know, while fluid people tend to be more adventurous, and more open to novel experiences and ideas.

Right-wing partisan media are also disproportionately powerful in shaping opinion. One study of more than thirty news purveyors—including the *New York Times,* the *Washington Post, USA Today, 60 Minutes,* Fox News, CNN, MSNBC, Rush Limbaugh, Bill O'Reilly, and Glenn Beck—found that conservative media, especially, influenced viewers' beliefs. For example, controlling for a range of demographic variables and political attitudes, researchers found that people who regularly watched Fox News were more likely to believe that President Obama was a Muslim or that the Affordable Care Act, aka Obamacare, included "death panels"—two widely discredited claims that nevertheless found traction with right-leaning viewers.

Fox's unique pull extends to shaping electoral outcomes. Between 1996 and 2000, Fox News spread to 20 percent of towns across America. Using this natural rollout, economists were able to estimate the effect of Fox News on election outcomes by comparing votes in towns without Fox in 1996 to votes in those same towns with Fox in 2000. They identified an increase in support for conservative positions in these towns as well as a 0.4 to 0.7 percentage-point increase in Republican vote share. This effect has only grown over time as Fox has further penetrated the cable market and solidified its fiery brand.

Another ominous trend is dovetailing with the asymmetric rise of partisan news media: an increasingly muddied distinction between mainstream news organizations that rely on an intensive editorial and fact-checking process, and information platforms that don't. The result is a blurring of the lines between fact and fiction, as stories more easily pass from one realm to the other.

A 2018 Rand study underscored this shift in the American information environment by placing it in a historical context. Earlier eras of contentious politics, including the Gilded Age (1890s), the 1920s and 1930s, and the 1960s, featured elements of what the authors describe as "truth decay": a pervasive blurring of the lines between facts and opinions in news outlets and increasing mistrust of formerly respected sources of factual information. But never before, the study's authors argue, have so many elements of truth decay been seen at once. Most notable and novel among these elements is something the study's authors describe as "increasing disagreement about facts and analytical interpretations of those facts." Unlike in previous eras, they observe, Americans seem less and less capable of agreeing on what is true and what is not.

There would not be the same appetite for the often untrue fare that "news-ish" platforms serve up if people's feelings about their opponents weren't so strongly negative. But the tribalism that has taken hold since the rise of worldview politics has intensified partisans' desire to seek out any information, true or not, that reinforces their existing beliefs. People who don't like immigrants, for example, are only too happy to consume and pass along dubious "facts" about beneficiaries of the Deferred Action for Childhood Arrivals (DACA) program. People who distrust organized religion, meanwhile, are excited to share stories about what *really* goes on at evangelical churches on Wednesday nights.

An asymmetry between the right and left also reveals itself when it comes to consuming "fake news"—and dismissing *real* news that leaders deride as fake. One study tracked traffic on fake news websites in October and November 2016, as the campaign reached its crescendo. The researchers estimated that over sixty-five million people consumed articles from these sites—but crucially, the pattern of consumption differed on the left and on the right. About 40 percent of Trump supporters consumed at least one story from a pro-Trump fake news site, while only about 10 percent of Clinton voters consumed news from a pro-Clinton fake news site. In fact, among Trump supporters, 6 percent of their total news diet appeared to come from fake news websites, specifically, compared with less than 1 percent among Clinton supporters.

Part of the difference observed in this study surely comes down to the relative supply of fake news for consumers on the left as opposed to consumers on the right; there were simply far more pro-Trump fake news sites than pro-Clinton ones. Part of it, however, can be attributed to differences in motivation. Conspiracy theories paint a world in broad black-and-white strokes. They identify clear villains and forces whose diabolical schemes and evil motives require no complex discernment. Such stories, while perhaps complex in their details, are simple and straightforward in their conclusions about right and wrong. These would appear to be more appealing to people for whom cognitive closure is more of a psychological necessity. One can, of course, find narratives on all sides that reduce reality to such simple themes. And sometimes, needless to say, people in power are up to no good and dishonest about their true motives. But there are clear differences in the tendency of the fixed and fluid to latch on to the kinds of far-fetched conspiracies that drive fake news. And particularly importantly, Republican officeholders have been much more likely to endorse and stoke those ideas than have prominent Democrats, President Trump being only the most obvious and high-profile example.

More recently, of course, the polarized political environment has given rise to the use of the phrase "fake news" as an epithet — one often hurled at news stories portraying oneself or one's tribe in an unfavorable light. Even if there is solid, accurate reporting behind such stories, calling them "fake" has proven to be an effective way of ensuring that one's supporters discount them — in effect, by giving them a leg up on their predisposed tendency toward motivated reasoning.

President Trump mainstreamed this usage of the term by labeling virtually every report unfavorable to him as "fake news." His tactic has now spread widely through American society, deepening the suspicion and mistrust that so pervades the nation's politics. According to a Gallup/Knight Foundation poll taken in early 2018, about 40 percent of Republicans believe that even *accurate* criticism of a political leader amounts to fake news. Only about 15 percent of Democrats agreed.

This finding is a perfect reflection of the worldview divide, and makes sense within that context. In a world rent by partisan news, it's not such a big step to argue that any negative information about a favored politician is only an effort to disparage and discredit that individual, and for necessarily nefarious reasons. The story itself might not be "fake" in the ordinary understanding of the word. But as far as partisans are concerned, the goal of the news is not to inform, but instead to attack and undermine their tribe. The contrast between real news and fake news is, for these people, a distinction without a difference.

• • •

The story we've told so far is admittedly discouraging. American politics is more polarized today than it has been in a hundred years, probably more, because Democrats and Republicans are now split not just by politics but also by worldview—by their natural human responses to the world, reactions that are more instinctive than rational. Not only do Americans' worldviews affect their political beliefs; they also affect their nonpolitical preferences, segregating fellow citizens by place and taste, and thereby deepening the divide.

In a perfect world, partisans would try to understand why their opponents believe what they do, and would explore places where they might find common ground. Unfortunately, most people are motivated to continue believing what they believe, not to reconcile their built-in preferences and prejudices with those of other people who don't think the way they do. This tendency toward motivated reasoning is especially strong today because partisans' negative feelings about the other party are so deep and pervasive. Our outlooks have drifted so far apart as to make it seem like we barely have any common ground left.

To make matters worse, mass media and social media now make it possible for Americans to live in partisan echo chambers that reinforce their preexisting beliefs while exacerbating their hatred of the opposing party and the people who support it. It's not simply that Americans listen to different music and watch different TV shows. They are also getting their information from completely different sources—from news media outlets that, in many cases, seem more interested in stoking their viewers' partisan animosity than in reporting news in the objective, balanced manner that is critical to the functioning of a liberal democracy. Even those who don't use these sources directly can be exposed to them through their like-minded friends.

This is not the only, or even the greatest, threat that worldview politics poses to American democracy, however. As we will show in the next chapter, the country's worldview-centered party system is now arrayed in a way that increases the chances for challenges to seemingly bedrock and uncontroversial democratic principles. Brazen appeals to xenophobia and fear are further undermining any sense of commonality the

American people might feel. That is opening the door wider for world-
view-motivated partisanship to enable a temperamentally authoritarian
president to undermine the pillars of US democracy, including the country's free press, judiciary, and institutions meant to check unchallenged
authority.

6

"You're Not Going to Be Scared Anymore"

UNTIL RELATIVELY RECENTLY, whatever else they thought, most Americans took for granted the basic stability of liberal democracy itself. The merger of Americans' worldviews and political identities, however, has a unique ability to open the door to leaders who challenge democratic norms and practices, and who therefore pose a unique threat to the country's most hallowed political principles.

Most Americans are proud of their democratic system, warts and all. Among the key pillars of that system is the Constitution, with its robust protections of individual rights, enshrined in the Bill of Rights; a free press tasked with holding those in power accountable to the public they are meant to serve; and broader limits on the power of those in authority provided for in the Madisonian system of checks and balances, in which the ambition of one branch of government is offset by the ambition of another.

There are countless caveats critics can offer about the viability of those pillars, how they don't, in practice, protect all Americans equally and how they've shifted and swayed over the course of America's history. But especially since World War II, most Americans have perceived the constraints on officeholders as foundational to our democratic system. Many Americans also take great pride and comfort in the long, if complicated, tradition of tolerance in the United States, and the advantages of maintaining moral authority in foreign affairs, especially insofar as they perceive the United States' system as an inspiration to those fighting for their own rights around the world.

Those pillars of democracy might be points of pride in the abstract. But for most, they are just that—abstractions. Where the rubber hits the road in people's day-to-day lives, abstractions matter less than their basic sense of safety and security. This is where worldview politics becomes so important. For those with more-fixed worldviews, especially, threats to safety and security are omnipresent. If certain aspects of the Bill of Rights—such as related Fourth and Fifth Amendment protections against unwarranted search and seizure and in favor of due process—are just tools for terrorists to hide behind, then those who invoke them aren't just naive. They're acting in bad faith in order to hurt America. And if a leader emerges who assures you that you don't have to be afraid anymore, then his or her word might mean far more than some lawyer's misguided beliefs about what the Constitution does and doesn't say.

We have already revealed that Donald Trump secured the Republican nomination with disproportionate help from those with fixed worldviews, a group central to the party's twenty-first-century base. By 2016 the vast majority of those with fixed worldviews had become Republicans, and they loved Trump's John Wayne, take-no-prisoners approach to the world. Yet fixed-worldview people are nothing close to a majority of Americans, or even a majority of Republican identifiers. Plenty of others had to vote for Trump to make him president. As we explained in the previous chapter, because worldview politics generates so much enmity toward the other party, partisans are all too willing to go along with things their side's candidates say and do even if they might sound excessive.

The story doesn't end there. People in the middle of the worldview spectrum—a group we call mixed—have their own distinctive outlook, not equal to the fluid or to the fixed. Although they might prefer a candidate who reflects their distinctive perspective, that's not what was available in 2016. Trump embodied the fixed worldview and Hillary Clinton the fluid one. So, while Democrats reacted with shock and horror at the thought that anyone could find it within themselves to pull the lever for

Donald Trump, it wasn't just fixed Americans who made that choice, and it might not have been particularly hard for the mixed given some of their preferences.

When it comes to issues such as race, immigration, and attitudes toward Muslims, the mixed are more like the fixed than the fluid. Put another way, while many may not have relished Trump's attacks on some of those groups, neither were they completely turned off by his comments. Indeed, they probably found them more palatable than the tendency of liberals to bend over backwards seemingly at every turn to defend groups of people who aren't exactly angels in the eyes of many Americans.

The truth is that, for better or worse, there's nothing wrong with Trump's followers—"wrong," at least, in the sense of "abnormal." Quite the opposite: the members of Trump's base, it turns out, are much more like the average American than are his staunchest opponents. A *lot* of Americans are susceptible to the kinds of rhetoric that won Trump the presidency, especially his appeals to people's innate xenophobia and fears of threats both internal and external. The liberals, people of color, and traditional conservatives who are outraged by Trump's comportment and who have vowed to oppose his every move—*these* are the real outliers.

As painful as it might be for fluid people to acknowledge, this yawning gap between the country's fluid citizens and the rest of its population is very real, and it has put the country in a serious predicament. Trump's seemingly antidemocratic propensities have already led to attacks on cornerstones of American democracy, including the free press, the judiciary, and other political institutions. These propensities were obvious when he was a candidate for president, and they have only become more so since his election. Although the Madisonian institutional structure has been robust so far in thwarting these attacks, they show no sign of relenting. Arguably, they have laid the kindling for an even greater conflagration.

Given what we know about partisans in this worldview-divided era, we can't count on them to behave soberly. Instead, partisans are especially motivated to rationalize and justify the behavior of those they support, no matter how extreme the conduct of those leaders may be. They are further egged on by partisan media outlets, which have declared total war on the president's enemies.

In this era of intense worldview conflict, in short, America has become a fertile market for the brand of politics that Donald Trump is selling. And there is a real risk that other enterprising demagogues, seeing his success, will try to build on it in the future.

Political psychologists typically use the term "authoritarian" to label those we call fixed in their worldview, believing such a worldview to be dangerous. This work argues that the fixed's preference for hierarchy, desire for order, and deference to authority makes them susceptible to an authoritarian leader, who vilifies "outsiders," criticizes the softness of past leaders, and promises a return to a simpler time by imposing a strong, uncompromising hand.

This harsh label — "authoritarian" — may seem out of place in today's debates about domestic politics. When it was first widely used, in studies of political psychology in the late 1940s and early 1950s, scholars were trying to explain why ordinary people would follow a leader like Adolf Hitler, who was determined to bring all of German society to heel as he carried out his genocidal vision and, in the process, brought total war to much of the planet.

Although it seems a stretch to argue that the United States is on the cusp of such rule today, the term "authoritarian" became part of the popular vernacular in 2016, as Donald Trump first emerged as a serious contender and front-runner for the Republican nomination. In a remarkable long-form piece titled "The Rise of American Authoritarianism," Amanda Taub highlighted a number of attributes in Donald Trump that many people — including many leading Republicans — saw as troubling. She pointed out that there was a segment of the population that would be especially attracted to a leader who promised to impose order using uncompromising force, to beat back the menace of unsettling change and uncertainty. Taken together, she argued, these attributes qualified Trump as an authoritarian leader.

Although Trump's time on the national stage has normalized his rhetoric, it was and is far outside the normal boundaries of American political discourse. For example, during the campaign, he promised not only to reduce immigration but to create deportation squads to expel the more than ten million people living in the United States without documentation. Not only would he beef up border security, he promised to build a giant wall on the southern border. His deportation squads conjured an image of a totalitarian-style secret police force. The extensive border wall he envisioned was at odds with the cherished notion of America as a melting pot of immigrants. Not only did he think the government should keep a closer eye on Muslims, he promised to ban them from entering the country altogether. He didn't just think the United States needed to take the fight harder to the soldiers of ISIS. He promised he'd "take out their families," using bullets dipped in pig's blood to send the strongest-possible message. And not only would he be tough on those captured and suspected of being in league with terrorists, he would bring back waterboarding and other forms of torture because "we have to beat the savages." As Trump made these promises, he made it clear that he, and he alone, had what it took to make America great again and keep us safe.

As president, at rallies for supporters, he continued to engage in demagoguery to whip his backers into a frenzy against his enemies; he continued to call for Hillary Clinton to be investigated and locked up; he derided as "so-called" judges who ruled against his proposed policies, and threatened to fire those in his administration who refused to do his bidding; he brazenly attempted to interfere in investigations into his campaign's alleged collusion with the Russian government, including by repeatedly demanding loyalty from officials bound to uphold the law.

To many who cherish the pillars of American democracy, his words and deeds conjured images of a strongman leader, not an American president. The question for these concerned observers, then, became: How could this have happened? What explains the wide support for Donald Trump in the 2016 presidential election and his enduring, if weakened, support as president? What explains the rise of a leader who seems so antithetical to cherished American norms and ideals?

Anyone trying to figure out how Trump ended up in the White House —and many experts have tried—would be mistaken to focus only on a relatively thin sliver of Americans. Trump's rise cannot be blamed solely on the "deplorables," whom Hillary Clinton memorably castigated in one September 2016 speech, or the approximately 20 percent of Americans who hold fixed worldviews. Trump won 46 percent of the popular vote, after all. It was not a small band of antidemocratic dead-enders alone who put him in the Oval Office. People with fixed worldviews may have started the Trump Train on its journey, but 90 percent of Republicans in the general election pulled it into the station.

Several clues point toward a more complex and complete explanation for Trump's rise to power. For starters, recall that all partisans in this age of worldview politics, not just the fixed or fluid, find themselves pulled to one side of the divide or the other. When people's political outlooks and their outlooks on life are intertwined, the choice of which side to align with is usually pretty clear. Partisans' inclination to reason with extreme bias—an inclination that is exacerbated by partisan news sources—also helps to explain why so many people supported Trump despite his often outlandish, offensive behavior; they were willing to do the hard work to rationalize it away. In a different, less polarized era, fewer would have done that work.

But there's something else to the story of Trump's surprise win in 2016: the outlooks of people with fixed worldviews (the purported authoritarians) actually aren't *that* extreme when compared with those of other Americans. In fact, people with mixed worldviews—that swath of Americans who are neither at the extreme fluid nor the extreme fixed end of the worldview spectrum—maintain attitudes on key issues that are more like those of the fixed than the fluid. While their worldviews might be halfway between the fixed and fluid, their policy preferences are not. Especially important, those attitudes that are closer to the fixed than the fluid are on issues, including race and immigration, that have centrally shaped the worldview divide. Although it might have *seemed* to fluid-worldview

Democrats that Trump's supercharged rhetoric—his claims about giant walls, bullets dipped in pig's blood, and, later, shithole African countries —would turn off all but a small basket of deplorables, the evidence suggests otherwise.

In addition, the fear felt by many Americans today helps to explain why people voted for Trump despite, or perhaps because of, his extreme positions on so many issues. Fear is the friend of a figure who flouts democratic norms, like Trump. His projection of strength is especially appealing to fixed voters, who find it attractive because of their baseline level of wariness. But in truth, when people *across* the worldview spectrum are afraid, they become more attracted to blunt projections of strength, one of Trump's calling cards. In particular, they become more supportive of blunt-force policies and the leaders who promote them—even if these policies challenge or undermine ideals that, in the abstract, many Americans would defend.

Indeed, if scholars of the 1950s could reconsider, with the sort of clarity that only the passage of time allows, their theories about what types of people followed Hitler, they might note that almost all Germans— not just the "authoritarians"—ultimately did fall in line with the Nazi regime. The deep social unrest and economic crisis during the Weimar years, combined with the rise of the Nazi Party's repressive state apparatus and, later, the horrors of World War II itself, all created intense fear and uncertainty among the German people. The resultant, crushing stress caused nearly everyone to submit to the authority of the Nazi state. In short, Germans didn't all fall into lockstep behind Nazism because they wanted to, so much as because they felt that they had no other choice.

It was context that conditioned Germans' responses to the Nazis. The mix of circumstances and psychology, not psychology alone, explains the opinions and behaviors of ordinary people in all kinds of situations. This is a lesson that Americans would do well to remember today, since circumstances and psychology are both crucial for explaining why Trump reached the heights that he did, and why his actions are as threatening as they are. Because of the aligning of worldview and politics, the especially intense partisanship that has resulted, and many Americans' wariness of the very diverse society in which we live, a leader like Trump was able to exploit an opening many could not even see until Trump had passed through it. Consequently, our democracy is not quite as secure as Americans would like to believe.

As we've noted, scholars of political psychology have typically argued that the fixed are the societal outliers, enough so to earn a label like "authoritarian." Having failed to adapt to the values of modern society, including respect for difference and acceptance of changing norms, they find themselves out of step, unable to face the cosmopolitan, multicultural reality of the modern world.

But what if that implicit assumption is wrong? What if it's fluid people whose worldviews are out of step with the attitudes of the average American, not people whose worldviews are fixed—or, more disconcertingly, "authoritarian"?

To assess whether the fixed's or the fluid's views more closely resemble those of the average American, we need to revisit some of the data presented earlier, comparing the fixed and fluid to people with a "mixed" worldview. These people, as the label would suggest, provide a mix of fixed and fluid answers to the questions about choosing desirable qualities in children. These mixed types make up a bit above two-thirds of the middle of the US electorate, and thus are a good representation of the average American voter. If the fluid are more like mixed Americans than the fixed are, the difference in beliefs between the mixed and the fluid will be smaller than the difference between the mixed and the fixed. If the fixed are more like the average American, the reverse will be true.

And indeed, the mixed mind-set is closer to the fixed than the fluid when it comes to a wide range of worldview-informed issues. To illustrate, consider one of the questions analyzed in chapter 2. It asked Americans whether they were bothered when they came into contact with immigrants who spoke little or no English. Among the fixed, 69 percent said it bothered them, while among the fluid only 26 percent said it did. The same data reveal that 53 percent of the mixed said that they were bothered when they encountered immigrants who spoke little or no English. The fixed, then, were sixteen points (69 minus 53) different from the mixed, while the fluid were twenty-seven points different (53 minus 26). The mixed's opinions were much closer to the fixed's opinions than to the fluid's. Other immigration questions, as well as questions about race and gender, yield similar results.

In nearly every area that we explored in chapter 2, the fixed are at least a little more like the mixed than the fluid are. For gender attitudes, the differences are small. On race and immigration, however, the differences are substantial. The fluid are nearly nine points further from the mixed than the fixed are on immigration issues. On racial attitudes, the difference is ten points. The fixed's attitudes about people who are racially and culturally different are not as far from the mainstream as Democrats would like to think. Rather, the fluid's are further from the mainstream. Indeed, the opinions of the fluid are more like those with mixed worldviews in exactly zero areas when it comes to race, immigration, and gender attitudes.

The relative similarity of the fixed and the mixed on racial issues should discomfit any fluid readers. More sobering still is the trend in Americans' racial attitudes over time. The graph on page 166 illustrates the average answers to the racial-attitudes questions in every ANES study between 2000 and 2016, broken down by worldview. Higher scores mean people harbor more resentment toward African Americans—that is, they agree that blacks only need to work harder to be as well-off as whites and disagree that generations of slavery and discrimination have anything to do with unequal outcomes between the races today. Lower scores reflect the opposite. The three lines on the chart track the average scores of whites with fixed, mixed, and fluid worldviews. The line for the mixed tracks the overall average for white Americans almost perfectly.

The fluid might expect that Americans—perhaps too slowly, but nevertheless surely—are all adopting more egalitarian attitudes about race. The numbers say otherwise. Only the fluid's attitudes are becoming more egalitarian, which is moving them further and further away from the rest of the public. Back in 2000, the fluid were about ten points more liberal than the mixed, while the fixed were about the same amount more con-

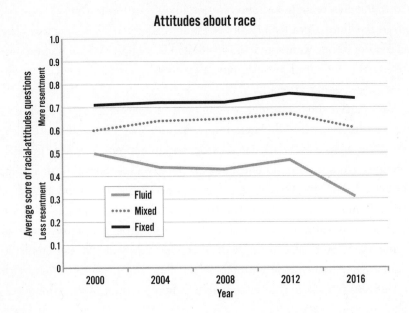

Attitudes about race

servative than the mixed. Since then, increasingly pro-black racial attitudes among the fluid have created a chasm between them and the mixed. Between 2012 and 2016 those with a fluid mind-set moved a staggering sixteen percentage points in a pro–African American direction, an absolutely remarkable shift in such a short time. Whereas the fluid were twenty points more liberal than they were in 2000, neither the fixed nor the mixed had changed in a statistical sense.

People with fluid worldviews are now in a completely different world when it comes to racial attitudes. They're the outliers. When Donald Trump opined that black youth lack spirit, or that their neighborhoods were besieged by "carnage," that smacked of old-fashioned racism to the fluid. They were outraged. Surely, they thought, Trump would pay a steep price for saying it. It would appear, however, that those with more-mixed worldviews are probably somewhat more apt to hear Trump's statement as hard truth telling (an interpretation consistent with the fixed's views on race) than as racism (an interpretation consistent with the fluid's views on race).

In fact, it is striking how resistant to change racial attitudes have been. Scholars first asked these questions tapping racial resentment back in 1986, barely twenty years after the Civil Rights Act of 1964 and the Voting Rights Act of 1965 became law. It seemed inevitable that more egalitarian racial attitudes would emerge as older voters passed from the scene. Yet the average amount of racial resentment whites expressed between 1986 and 2016 has remained pretty much the same. Imagine that: When the ANES started asking these questions, a high percentage of whites who had been active participants in segregation were still alive. By 2016, most of them were dead. Regardless, racial resentment has persisted at high levels, except among the fluid.

Maybe it shouldn't be that surprising. Americans romanticize the amount of support black civil rights enjoyed during the heyday of the civil rights movement. While it would be nice to believe most whites favored change, while only an intense minority of dead-enders blocked the popular will, the truth is that most Americans at the time were unenthusiastic about the idea of fully extending civil rights to African Americans. A May 1961 poll asked people whether they approved of the Freedom Riders' efforts. Only 22 percent did. The same poll asked whether sit-ins and other demonstrations would help or hurt blacks' chances of integration. Twice as many said these efforts would hurt: 57 percent, compared to 28 percent who said they would help.

Similarly, in 1966 a Harris poll asked whether Martin Luther King, specifically, was "helping or hurting the Negro cause of civil rights." Only 36 percent said helping while 50 percent said hurting. It wasn't just King. It was the whole movement. On the eve of the passage of the Voting Rights Act in the summer of 1965, a Harris survey asked whether demonstrations by African Americans had helped or hurt the group's cause. Given that the Civil Rights Act of 1964 had passed the year before and voting rights were on the cusp of passage, it is hard to imagine how a person could say the demonstrations had hurt. But that is what a plurality (45 percent) of Americans said, with only 36 percent saying they had helped.

Looking back over half a century, it's almost inconceivable to imagine that right-thinking people could have failed to support things like fair housing standards, interracial marriage, and desegregated schools. But most Americans initially resisted them, and they didn't much like the movement that forced them to think about these contentious matters either. Public opinion eventually came around, but most of this change occurred *after* officeholders enacted measures to ensure African American civil rights.

That is not to say the grassroots work done by the civil rights movement wasn't important. It was critical to raising awareness and shaping the political agenda. It also changed the opinions of some white Americans. But the rights and protections secured by these laws only became popular with the public much later. In fact, civil rights, specifically, is the issue area where (liberal) congressional action departed from public opinion by the largest amount over the past sixty years.

The fluid's racial attitudes suggest that, when they assess the causes of persistent racial inequality, they usually put the blame on the legacy of slavery and Jim Crow, as well as ongoing prejudice. Other whites diagnose the situation differently, placing more emphasis on the shortcomings of African Americans. Terms like "white privilege" and "institutional racism" resonate with the fluid, less so with the rest of the country. The fluid would like to believe that, if only the scourge of such prejudices were removed, their vision of a racially just and equal society could become a reality, and that just a small basket of deplorables stands in the way. But that view is not accurate. The mixed—those in the middle of the worldview spectrum—are ambivalent, at best, about that vision. And the differences between the fluid and the mixed are widening, not shrinking, with time.

What all of this means is that a presidential hopeful who talks about race like Donald Trump did during the campaign is likely to mortally offend a minority of American voters, while eliciting, at worst, shrugs from the rest. Just think about his inflammatory claims: Major urban centers are disaster areas. Crime rates are skyrocketing. President Obama might be from Kenya. Black youth lack spirit. All these statements seem racist—and hence disqualifying—to the fluid, but people on the rest of the worldview spectrum don't see it that way.

Immigration is another issue on which the fluid and the fixed/mixed are drifting further apart. As out-of-bounds as Trump's constant pillorying of immigrants, especially the way in which he demonized "Mexicans" to create an image of immigrants more generally as dangerous, might have seemed to the fluid, it didn't turn out to be disqualifying. The graph below reveals why.

The ANES has posed a question in every presidential election year since 2000 that asks Americans whether they think "the number of immigrants from foreign countries who are permitted to come to the United States to live" should be increased, decreased, or kept about the same. The trend over time is broken down by the three worldview categories.

It turns out that increasing immigration is incredibly unpopular. Only among Americans with the most fluid worldviews do a significant percentage support increased immigration to the United States. Support among the mixed has held constant over time at around 10 percent, while support of such increases among the fixed has never reached double digits. As with race, the mixed have been much more like the fixed than they

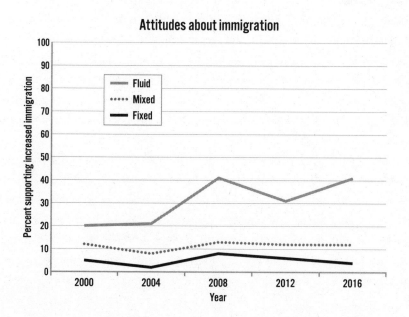

Attitudes about immigration

have the fluid over time. Indeed, over the sixteen-year period in question, mixed and fixed opinions have never been more than eight points apart.

As with their racial attitudes, the fluid's opinions on immigration are increasingly different from everyone else's. In 2004 the difference between the mixed and fluid was only 13 points. By 2016, 41 percent of the fluid wanted to see increased immigration while only 12 percent of the mixed did, placing mixed and fluid a whopping twenty-nine points apart. With 4 percent of the fixed supporting increased immigration, the mixed's opinions were a mere eight points from the fixed. It seems clear that immigration is not going to be a campaign issue that advantages the political left except insofar as it solidifies support with its Latino/a and Asian American base.

So when Donald Trump spoke in the harshest terms about immigrants, he probably was risking less than most people realized at the time. The fixed especially liked his stance, but many of the mixed probably weren't too troubled by it, either. Indeed that should have been obvious to any-one who was paying attention during the nomination season. Although Republican rivals criticized Trump's approach after he kicked off his campaign by calling those coming into the country from Mexico "rap-ists," it wasn't long before they followed Trump's lead to the far right on immigration. Marco Rubio went so far as to disavow the work he had done to chart a path to citizenship for the millions in the country illegally. In fact, he said during the primary process that he would no longer support the bill he himself had *sponsored* in the Senate. Among major immigra-tion issues, only DACA attracts widespread support across the political spectrum. That's probably why Trump felt he needed to at least pay lip service to "protecting those kids."

The same picture emerges when it comes to Muslims. Prospective leaders can readily whip up support by vilifying them, although the pat-tern is a little different in this case. The ANES has asked people to rate Muslims on a feeling thermometer since 2004. Back then, the fluid and mixed gave about the same rating, 58 degrees for the fluid and 54 degrees for the mixed. The outliers were the fixed, with an average score of 42 degrees. In 2016 the story was different. The mixed and fixed held pretty steady in their evaluations of Muslims, at 52 and 41 degrees, respectively. The fluid, however, grew warmer toward the group by 10 degrees. As such, the mixed went from being much closer to the fluid than the fixed in 2004, to being much closer to the fixed than the fluid in 2016.

On race and immigration, the fixed and mixed have much more in common than the mixed and fluid do. That suggests that while, in the minds of fluid people, Trump's language about these issues disqualified him from being president, few others felt the same way.

The only issue for which this pattern is different is gay rights. Three of our surveys between 2006 and 2016 asked people about same-sex marriage; the results reveal a dramatic increase in support for this issue over time. The results appear in the graph below.

The fluid have always been wildly supportive of same-sex marriage. When first asked about it in 2006, more than 80 percent expressed support, placing them in another world from the mixed and fixed. Not only were the fluid nearly sixty percentage points more supportive of same-sex marriage than the fixed in 2006, they were more than forty points more supportive than the mixed as well. If any group's position on gay marriage could have been described as "fringe" at that point, it was the fluid's. Lit-

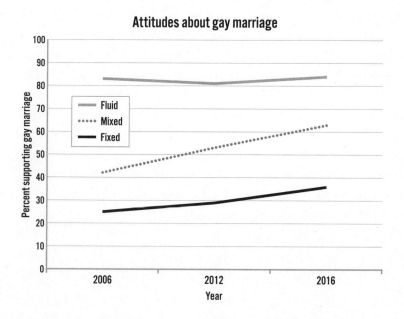

tle wonder Republicans hung the issue around the necks of Democrats like an albatross at that time.

Since then, fluid support for gay marriage has remained around 80 percent, but mixed worldview support has rocketed above 60 percent. Even fixed support ticked above 30 percent by 2016.

Trump made no effort to exploit Americans' differences on the issue of same-sex marriage. Of course, it is true that he expressed support for gay rights in the past, but he expressed support for abortion rights and a range of other things in the past that he has since repudiated. Perhaps he didn't pander to his base on gay marriage because the fluid, for the first time, had opinions more like the mixed than the fixed did.

In this sense, however, fluid people's more mainstream views on same-sex marriage are the exception rather than the rule. People with mixed worldviews have opinions that are consistently much more like those of the fixed than the fluid when it comes to race and immigration. In fact, the fluid's attitudes are growing further and further away from those of the rest of the electorate.

The persistence of negative attitudes toward historically marginalized groups is significant, because in a complex, diverse modern society, social tensions never go away entirely, even if they're often submerged. Opportunistic leaders can cause those attitudes to surface, by aggravating and playing upon those tensions to win support from people who feel most negatively about these "others." And then, when negative sentiment is widespread, such leaders will pay little price for scapegoating a minority group or removing safeguards that might protect it.

That's one reason a leader like Trump, despite the ways in which his rhetoric is so ugly and offensive to so many, could gain traction. Politicians have often found electoral success by demonizing certain groups. Donald Kinder has referred to the "electoral temptation of race" to describe how often candidates for office have found traction by implicitly or explicitly attacking African Americans—very tempting for politicians who want to play the "us versus them" game.

• • •

A second reason that a candidate like Donald Trump succeeded and, in turn, why key norms and institutions of American democracy are not as secure as citizens might believe is that people are more likely to adopt antidemocratic preferences when they feel enough stress. When humans are consumed by fear, their survival instincts come to the fore. Under those circumstances, high-minded principles and abstract ideals are unlikely to flourish.

The period right after the 9/11 terrorist attacks offered proof of how flexible Americans' staunch democratic ideals really are. Recall how afraid Americans were, especially the ones living in major population centers that might be a target for a future attack. This included many fluid people, since the same fears gripped most Americans. But public opinion surveys from that period bear out how willing these people, and the American populace as a whole, were to give up their principles for the promise of increased physical security. For example, five years after the 9/11 attacks, more than half of Americans said they approved of "President Bush authoriz[ing] government wiretaps on some phone calls in the US without getting court warrants." Similarly, although torture is inarguably anathema to what many Americans view as bedrock ideals, a majority of Americans supported its use to secure information from suspected terrorists during Bush's second term in office.

The anthrax scare that followed on the heels of 9/11 also had Americans on edge. An unknown assailant sent the poison through the US Postal Service, killing five people — several of whom were not even targets of the anthrax-laced letters. The reaction of our fluid-worldview friend Joseph was common. At the time, he lived in Princeton, New Jersey, not far from where the anthrax letters were postmarked, with his wife and infant son. He was terrified that trace bits of the poison might end up in his mail and harm his family. The probability was low, but Joseph's concern wasn't completely unfounded. A Connecticut woman died that November after contracting inhalation anthrax despite not being directly targeted. Her mail just happened to go through the same processing center that one of the anthrax-laced letters did.

Joseph told us he would have been fine with the government going through all his mail and gladly given up any privacy right to ensure the safety of his young family. His reaction is pretty typical. The desire to stay alive is primal. All types of people who had watched the collapse of the World Trade Center with their own eyes a few months or more before found themselves open to extreme measures to help secure their safety.

Stress and threat imperil liberal democratic ideals. Indeed the term "ideals" connotes an aspirational goal. They are principles people try to live up to. When people believe their well-being is under threat, they lapse into survival mode. Anyone who has ever been in a dangerous situation, such as getting lost on an unfamiliar hike as darkness is falling or hearing gunshots ring out close by, knows that higher-level thinking goes out the window. At best, people take protective action. At worst, they panic.

In politically stressful times, high-minded ideals fight a losing battle against the timeless instinct for self-preservation. No one is immune. The "lizard brain"—the amygdala, in particular—starts to run the show during times of stress and fear. The parts of the brain that govern higher-order reasoning become less involved. That is because aspirational ideals do the body little good if the body is no longer alive.

This understanding of the human condition suggests that times of national stress will cause the fluid (and the mixed) to be more like the fixed. In other words, the usually gaping differences in preferences between the fixed and fluid will narrow. The fixed won't change their beliefs much. The possibility that a catastrophic event could happen at any time is built into the fixed worldview and hence their political preferences. But fear spurs the fluid and mixed to adopt more restrictive and aggressive views.

To take an example outside the realm of politics, consider again that the fixed are much more likely to drive large SUVs and pickup trucks than people on other parts of the worldview spectrum. Part of that derives from the more rural places where fixed people tend to live, but safety is also a significant consideration. A big vehicle is a hedge against danger. Even the most careful drivers have to share the road with unsafe ones. Some could be drunk; they could be inexperienced; they could be texting. One way to deal with all the uncertainty is to drive a hulking mass of steel like a GMC Yukon XL, a Hummer H3, or a Ford F-150. If just about anything short of an eighteen-wheeler hits it, the other driver will be worse off than you.

During normal times, when the fluid buy cars, they have different things on their minds. An important criterion might be fuel economy. Because the fluid aren't as wary as the fixed, they are freer to pursue aspirational goals like saving the planet with their choice of transportation. Heavier vehicles require more power than light ones, so fuel-efficient vehicles tend to be small. Based on data from the US Department of Energy, the class leaders in fuel economy are all either tiny (two Smart car models), hybrids (two versions of the Toyota Prius), or both (the Hyundai Ioniq Blue and the Kia Niro FE). All get at least a combined thirty-five miles to the gallon and several get much more. Compare that with the most fuel-efficient versions of the Ford F-150, the GMC Yukon, and the Hummer H3. Their fuel efficiency is twenty-one, nineteen, and sixteen miles to the gallon, respectively.

But preferences can change in the face of a crisis. In chapter 4, we noted that the fixed and fluid were likely to make different choices about what kind of car to buy because they experience different levels of wariness and, therefore, apply different values when they make that purchase. But as we wrote in our 2009 book, in the moment before a collision, it would be difficult to deny that one would be better off in a Hummer than a Prius. That's because, under conditions of immediate threat, the preferences of the Hummer driver would remain the same, while the preferences of the Prius driver would likely undergo a sudden, dramatic change.

The same logic holds when it comes to politics. A crisis affects everyone's thinking, but some people's more than others. Just like the preference for safety of the fixed person driving the Hummer was already baked into her vehicle choice, her preference for safety is baked into her political views. As such, the fixed might tend to prefer high levels of defense spending or allowing government officials to wiretap without warrants no matter the circumstances. When it comes to keeping the country secure, it is always better to be safe than sorry.

Under duress, people's attitudes across the worldview spectrum will converge. Even those who don't have a fixed worldview are likely to adopt attitudes that look a lot like those of the fixed. Just as high-minded consumer principles about fuel economy are important to them until they are about to be trucked by a Hummer, high-minded political principles like due process for criminal defendants will go out the window when people fear their lives are threatened by terrorism. And if racial profiling is the price of safety, that might not seem like such a bad idea anymore.

An especially stark example of this phenomenon arose in 2003, when it came to light that American military and intelligence personnel were using the long-banned practice of waterboarding against terror suspects to get information about the al-Qaeda network and to head off future attacks. The Bush administration argued that using torture — or, to use its term, "enhanced interrogation techniques" — was justified to avoid a replay of 9/11 and many Americans agreed. In retrospect, it is something of a national embarrassment that public support was so high, far exceeding the percentage of "authoritarians" in the population. In fact, there was plenty of support for the use of torture across the entire worldview spectrum. Fear, that primal motivator, explains why torture became relatively acceptable even among Americans who tended to be less wary by nature.

Fear makes everyone more likely to support practices that, in the abstract, liberals especially would like to believe are outside the bounds of acceptable government conduct. This reality was confirmed by survey data collected in 2006 and 2008. These surveys included the four parenting questions and also asked whether people were afraid that they or a family member would be victims of a terrorist attack. Unsurprisingly, the fixed supported both torture and wiretapping without a warrant under any circumstances. Interestingly, however, among those who were mixed or fluid, fear of a terrorist attack also made them supportive of torture and warrantless wiretapping.

The results appear in the graph on page 177. When the fluid don't feel much threat from terrorism, they aren't big supporters of torture — about 20 percent approve. Among the fluid who express a lot of fear, however, the percentage supporting torture triples to nearly 70 percent. Similarly, the mixed who feel a substantial threat from terrorism are twenty-three points more supportive of torture than those who feel less of a threat from terrorism.

Based on questions asked in the 2006 CCES, a similar pattern holds when it comes to Americans' opinions about wiretapping without warrants. People with fluid worldviews who do not perceive much of a threat from terrorism are unlikely to support warrantless wiretapping — only 17 percent said yes. But, among fluids who are frightened, support jumps to 50 percent. Among the mixed, the jump is nearly as dramatic. When they feel little fear, 49 percent say they approve. Among the mixed who feel a lot of fear from terrorism, support increases nearly twenty points to 68 percent. In both cases, frightened fixed-worldview people are slightly more supportive than those who are less frightened, but, as expected, for them the increase in support is much smaller than for the mixed and the fluid. The fixed's general tendency to be wary is baked into their baseline preferences. In other words, under duress, attitudes converge — the mixed and the fluid start to think a lot more like the fixed.

Taken together, these results illustrate that all people, not just so-called authoritarians, are susceptible to antidemocratic thinking when

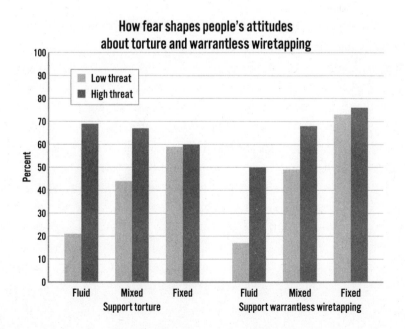

How fear shapes people's attitudes about torture and warrantless wiretapping

put under enough stress. Political conditions that are objectively frightening, or a political leader who can make people feel scared, will push
people's policy preferences in a fixed direction. If a political leader can
convince people that he can make them safe from the dangers around
them, it will bolster his candidacy. That is the story of Donald Trump.

Trump, as we have explained, was the choice of fixed-worldview
Republican primary election voters, with 50 percent expressing support
for him compared with 38 percent of those with less-fixed worldviews.
Given Trump's always aggressive and sometimes nativist campaign rhetoric, the fact that he was able to gain the support of fully 38 percent of the
less fixed requires additional attention. Although the mixed are not as far
from the fixed as they are from the fluid, it is still the case that they had
a lot of Republican alternatives available to them who were not quite so
"out there" as Trump. Yet high-quality candidates like Jeb Bush, Scott
Walker, and John Kasich failed to get any traction among less-fixed voters
despite Trump's liabilities.

Fear was a key reason that Americans—especially those with fixed
and mixed worldviews—flocked to Trump. Molly Ball summed up 2016's
political landscape well when she wrote, "Fear is in the air, and fear is
surging. Americans are more afraid today than they have been in a long
time: Polls show majorities of Americans worried about being victims of
terrorism and crime, numbers that have surged over the past year to highs
not seen for more than a decade." For example, a 2016 CNN/ORC poll
found that over 70 percent of Americans thought it likely or somewhat
likely that there would be "further terrorist attacks in the United States,"
the highest such figure since shortly after the US invasion of Iraq in 2003.
Trump took full advantage, selling himself as the antidote to the mayhem.
Republicans all across the worldview spectrum were buying.

Ball reported that "frightened people come to Trump for reassurance
[on the campaign trail], and he promises to make them feel safe. 'I'm
scared,' a 12 year old girl told the candidate . . . 'What are you going to do
to protect this country?' 'You know what, darling?' Trump replied. 'You're
not going to be scared anymore. They're going to be scared.'" Anyone
who has ever been afraid of a schoolyard bully knows how satisfying that

promise sounds. Not only do the targets of bullying want the fear to stop, the targets want the bully to feel that same palpable dread they have been feeling.

Nearly three-quarters of Republican primary voters reported feeling that terrorist groups posed a high risk to them, with 43 percent choosing the category expressing maximum fear. That fear benefited Trump among the less fixed. The graph below illustrates the pattern. Only 29 percent of Republican primary voters with less-fixed worldviews who reported feeling lower levels of fear about terrorism supported Trump. But among those less-fixed voters who felt the highest risk from terrorism, support for Trump jumped thirteen points (to 42 percent). As such, the differences in the voting preferences between the less fixed and the fixed who were not particularly frightened about terrorism was huge; the fixed were twenty-seven points more supportive of Trump than the less fixed. But the difference between the preferences of the fixed and less fixed shrank to only ten points among those voters who expressed extreme fear. In other words, fear made the fixed and less fixed more similar in their voting behavior.

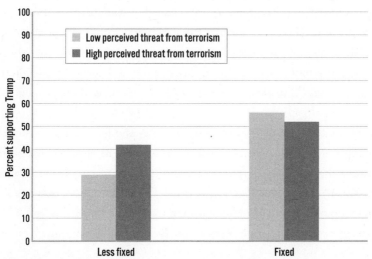

How fear of terrorism boosted 2016 primary support for Trump

Trump, of course, went on to win the nomination and later the general election. The latter was a cinch in a relative sense. The broad and deep hatred partisans feel for the other party these days makes it nearly impossible for many of them to defect to the opposing party. Add to this disincentive the fact that Hillary Clinton is, in the minds of many Republicans, as near to the spawn of Satan as any Democrat has ever been, and the motivation for GOP voters to find some way to look past Trump's liabilities was incredibly strong. When partisans believe the other side is a danger to the country's future, they can't vote for it. Partisans will vote for their party's standard-bearer almost no matter what, regardless of whether they said they'd "never vote for Donald Trump" only a few months before.

This is unchartered territory in America, at least since the late 1800s. Throughout much of the twentieth century, when the parties were not so polarized and worldview wasn't at the center of polarization, partisans regularly abandoned their standard-bearer if he didn't measure up. Roosevelt, Eisenhower, Johnson, Nixon, and Reagan all won landslides because partisans crossed over in droves to vote for them. If a party nominated a Goldwater or a McGovern or a Mondale, they paid a steep price. That is no longer true. Worldview-based polarization almost guarantees that a presidential candidate starts off with a high floor of support. It also ensures that he or she will be forgiven for what, in other circumstances, would be considered egregious or even otherwise "disqualifying" missteps. Trump's ability to survive his many self-inflicted wounds during the 2016 campaign brought that point home. And once elected, he was able, at a minimum, to tread water, even as his bull-in-a-china-shop rhetoric and approach to governing continued to offend and alarm so many.

After rising to power on a wave of xenophobia and fear, Donald Trump has attacked some of the most cherished institutions in our political system, including the judiciary, a free press, and the rule of law. To be sure, it is impossible to know how much of a threat Trump ultimately poses to these democratic institutions. But he has often lived up to his critics' worst fears. This may explain why Bob Woodward, the journalist who uncovered the

Watergate scandal in the 1970s, gave such a dire warning in November 2017: "Trump may be the final exam for the strength of our democracy."

Following Trump's inauguration, his administration imposed his promised ban on travel from several primarily Muslim countries. Although the ban was struck down in federal district court, Trump's response didn't comfort anyone who was concerned about the fact that he didn't acknowledge constitutional limits to his power. In a tweet after the negative ruling, Trump referred to the district court judge, James Robart, as "this so-called judge," and opined that his decision "essentially takes law enforcement away from our country" and would lead to "death and destruction."

This lack of respect for the independence of the judiciary—one of the core tenets of American democracy identified earlier—was a deviation from the norms of presidential conduct that shocked many observers. Beyond judges, moreover, Trump regularly ridiculed federal law enforcement. He derided the Justice Department as a "joke" and a "laughingstock" for resisting his wishes to investigate and prosecute political opponents. In particular, he repeatedly suggested that the department should prosecute Hillary Clinton and other Democrats for various misdeeds. The resistance he received from career prosecutors in the government seemed to drive him up a wall. As he said to Larry O'Connor in an interview in late 2017:

> The saddest thing is that because I'm the President of the United States I'm not supposed to be involved with the Justice Department, I'm not supposed to be involved with the FBI, I'm not supposed to be doing the kinds of things I would love to be doing and I'm very frustrated by it. I look at what's happening with the Justice Department, why aren't they going after Hillary Clinton with her emails and with the dossier and the kind of money . . . ?

These comments are reminiscent of Trump's unwillingness to discourage supporters at his raucous campaign rallies from chanting "Lock her up!" in reference to his Democratic opponent. It is not atypical for leaders of authoritarian regimes to jail their opponents after defeating them. Norms do not exist to prevent it. Such calls have no precedent in the United States — no major party candidate in modern times has threatened the arrest of a political opponent.

Trump has also tested other of the myriad boundaries that exist between the Department of Justice and the presidency. Feeling the stress of the FBI's probe into his campaign's potential collusion with Russia, he fired the agency's director, James Comey, who was leading the investigation. In the months that followed, Trump worked to force others in and around the FBI from their jobs as well, succeeding in firing former deputy director Andrew McCabe and making efforts to oust Attorney General Jeff Sessions and Sessions's deputy, Rod Rosenstein, not to mention the special counsel investing the charges after Comey's sacking, Robert Mueller.

Donald Trump campaigning in Iowa in January 2016. At rallies, Trump's supporters often chanted "Lock her up!" in reference to Hillary Clinton. Before Trump, no major American presidential candidate ever called for the jailing of a political opponent. AP Photo / Jae C. Hong

The impact of these dramatic actions on American public opinion was predictable, but still stunning. The amount of confidence that Republicans expressed in the FBI plummeted during Trump's first year in office. Because the Republican Party has traditionally been the party of law and order, party stalwarts' pre-Trump opinions of the bureau were very favorable. No longer. In a January 2018 survey, only 38 percent of Republicans expressed confidence in the agency compared with 64 percent of Democrats. Similar surveys taken around the same time a year earlier show that GOP support for the FBI dropped by over twenty points in just one year. This is Motivated Reasoning 101: Republicans who elected Trump president are motivated to believe just about anything, up to and including conspiracies about the FBI, to protect themselves psychologically after having pulled the lever for Trump in 2016.

Trump's attack on an independent free press has been withering as well. No politician likes to be criticized, and part of the press's job is naturally adversarial. Hence the relationship between the press and political leaders has always been a fraught one. But Trump's broadsides have been more extreme than any we are aware of. During his first six weeks on the job, for example, he twice referred to the news media as "the enemy of the American people." Retiring Republican senator Jeff Flake of Arizona took to the Senate floor to liken that language to that used by autocrats like Joseph Stalin to silence dissent. Although Flake's charge might have been a bit extreme, the last American president to target the press like that was, in fact, Richard Nixon during Watergate.

Again, the public response to Trump's criticism is predictable. A late-2017 survey of media attitudes found that, among Americans who said they approved of Trump's job performance, over 60 percent also said they believed the media are "the enemy of the American people." Among people who disapproved of Trump, only about 10 percent agreed. Similarly, among Trump supporters, over 40 percent thought the government should "be able to stop a news media outlet from publishing a story that government officials say is biased or inaccurate." So much for an independent press.

Indeed, Republicans' confidence in the news media has collapsed. Certainly, before Trump took office, GOP faith in the media already low. Only around 30 percent of Republicans expressed as much as a fair amount of confidence in the media. By late 2017, however, that paltry figure had dropped much further, into the low teens. More worrying still, Republicans with the most political knowledge were the ones who expressed the least confidence in the news media. That means precious few Republicans will be inclined to believe stories that are critical of the president even if they are demonstrably true, because people rarely believe sources they don't trust. These are all signs of a disturbing collapse in trust among Republicans of core American political institutions.

The United States is not safe from the dark pull of a leader with antidemocratic impulses. In fact, the American public is probably the least likely player in the nation's political process to put the brakes on such a leader. Motivated reasoning by his partisans will tend to keep close to half the public on Trump's side, no matter the facts. They can tune in to partisan cable news for whatever rationalizations and reinterpretations are necessary to maintain their current beliefs.

Runaway partisanship, fear, and xenophobia have propelled into power a man who is arguably America's most dangerous president ever. Exploiting racial and cultural tensions—the stock-in-trade of strongman leaders the world over—is always a shortcut to power for any politician, because unsympathetic views of those who are different are pretty common in the electorate. That means a would-be leader who vilifies minorities to drum up votes will repel far fewer people than one might hope. In addition, during times of crisis, almost everyone is prone to accepting limits on personal freedoms and other antidemocratic measures that they believe will ensure their safety. These factors explain how a norm-busting candidate like Donald Trump attracted broad-enough support to be elected. It happened once, and worldview-fueled polarization makes it more likely that it could happen again.

The erosion and collapse of democratic institutions is a more subtle process than we might think. This is in accordance with history. In a 2017 essay, Jessica Shattuck provided a real-life account. Shattuck's grand-mother was a young German who voted for Hitler. She never expressed anti-Semitic beliefs, at least not to her granddaughter. Instead, Shat-tuck said, her grandmother "joined the Nazis as an 'idealist' drawn to the vision of rebuilding Germany, returning to a simpler time and, perversely, promoting equality . . . She liked the idea of returning to 'traditional' Ger-man life, away from the confusing push and pull of a global economy."

Under especially stressful circumstances, people's capacities for rationalization and reinterpretation can become a bulwark of support for what they themselves might otherwise deem extreme and unacceptable actions. Sure, it might be wrong or unfair, in the abstract, to target cer-tain groups for harsh treatment or quarantine. But if those groups really threaten the well-being of the many, sometimes leaders have to make hard choices. Suspending certain freedoms or targeting some minor-ity group may not be ideal. But it could well be necessary. One doesn't have to be filled with instinctive hatred for certain groups to countenance harsh measures against them. All that is necessary is that people react fearfully to uncertain circumstances, at which point their very human instincts take over.

The conclusion to Shattuck's essay is chilling. "My grandmother heard what she wanted from a leader who promised simple answers to complicated questions. She chose not to hear and see the monstrous sum those answers added up to."

Fortunately, in the United States, at least, a leader with antidemo-cratic impulses has the constitutional framework of checks and balances to contain him. The most extreme elements of Trump's campaign agenda actually have not, so far, fared well since he became president. Federal courts have struck down numerous versions of his travel bans targeting Muslims. Similarly, Republican majorities in both houses of Congress refused to provide the Republican president with funding for anything like a deportation force to round up undocumented workers and eject them from the country. In addition, they gave no serious consideration to budgeting significant money to build a hard border wall between the United States and Mexico until it became linked to protecting DACA recipients from deportation. Moreover, the wall under consideration is taking shape more as a technological barrier than something like the Great Wall of China, which is at least symbolically less damaging to America's image as a melting pot, and contrary to Trump's repeatedly expressed wishes.

Likewise, when Trump pushed for prosecutions of his political enemies, the Justice Department resisted for the most part, regardless of how much he complained. Although Trump fired FBI director Comey, Republicans in the White House and in Congress dissuaded him from firing Robert Mueller, the special counsel investigating collusion between the Trump campaign and Russia. Even if we stipulate that Donald Trump actually does have antidemocratic impulses, then it appears that the political system has the capacity to contain them.

Of course, we may be overestimating the robustness of American institutions. One particular concern is how strongly Republican members of Congress will be willing to defend American institutions if confronting Trump increases the chances they might go down to defeat in a primary, where Trump's army of fixed-worldview voters have an especially strong influence. At the time of this writing, Special Counsel Robert Mueller's investigation into possible collusion between the Trump campaign and Russia is ongoing. What happens if Mueller's findings turn out to be damning, the president dismisses them as fake news, and the lion's share of his Republican followers in the electorate believe him? What will Republicans in Congress do? This is the stuff that constitutional crises are made of.

It is also possible that the system only *appears* to have performed so well because Trump has not been a particularly effective president. Even with a humming economy and a record stock market during his first year in office, he "achieved" the lowest approval rating of any new president in the seventy-year history of public opinion polling. His administration is widely reported to be divided and inept. Trump himself received low marks for his competence even from fellow Republicans in Washington. His lack of familiarity with basic policy issues and his often intemperate and ill-considered Twitter rants undermined congressional leaders' faith in him. From Roosevelt to Reagan, a president's political personal skill —his power to persuade—has always been central to his success. When fellow politicians perceive that the president lacks that ability, they provide him little help.

A more skillful president trading on antidemocratic ideas might have more success than Trump, particularly when advantaged by majorities in both houses of Congress. This possibility is especially troubling—and especially real—because the fact that the opinion climate for a leader who bucks democratic norms is more favorable than Americans would hope remains a critical feature of American politics. Fixed-worldview people are, not surprisingly, the least enthusiastic about small-d democratic principles, but their preferences are not especially fringe either. As evidence, we asked Americans in our 2017 survey a range of questions about whether certain seemingly bedrock characteristics of American democracy were, in fact, "very important" to ordinary Americans. When asked whether protecting the rights of people with unpopular views was an important characteristic of democracy, 70 percent of the fluid said it was "very important," but only a third of the fixed identified it as such. When asked whether it was an important characteristic of democracy that news organizations be allowed to criticize political leaders, three-quarters of the fluid said "very," while only a quarter of the fixed did. And, when asked the degree to which it was important for people to have a right to nonviolent protest, 78 percent of the fluid said it was "very" important, while barely half of the fixed did. On these three questions, the number of mixed who said "very important" was 42, 45, and 57 percent, respectively. On all three questions, then, the preferences of the mixed were *much* closer to the fixed than the fluid. The Framers who penned the First Amendment would surely be discomfited by these results.

The survey also included a couple of questions about whether certain characteristics were good or bad ones for a political system governing the

United States. Consistent with expectations, the fixed and fluid differed in the desirability of having "a strong leader who does not have to bother with Congress and elections." About 70 percent of the fluid labeled this as "very bad," while only 33 percent of the fixed did. Similarly, 80 percent of the fluid thought it would be "very bad" to have "military rule." Only 36 percent of the fixed were "very" averse to military rule. As with the questions about democratic principles, the mixed revealed preferences far closer to those of the fixed than the fluid. Only 45 percent of the mixed thought a strong leader who didn't have to worry about Congress and elections was "very bad," and only 48 percent of them saw military rule as "very bad."

Fortunately, the context in which such a movement could attract enough popular support to win power and, in turn, wreak havoc has been rare in established democracies since World War II. That said, because of the alignment of the worldview divide with partisan politics, the *potential* of such threats is greater in the tumultuous early years of the new century than at any time since 1945.

Regardless of Trump's middling success in undermining checks on his power, other deeply troubling developments have become all too normal. Perhaps emboldened by his inflammatory rhetoric, an increasing number of Americans appear to have more license to articulate vicious racist, sexist, and anti-Semitic rhetoric in settings that would have been previously assumed to be off-limits. That hasn't just coarsened America's civic discourse. It has also created an atmosphere of fear and terror for many vulnerable groups in the United States. Tellingly, hate crimes against many of these same groups, including transgender people, have spiked since Trump's campaign first got serious traction in 2015. The political atmosphere, stoked by worldview politics and the openings it has created for opportunistic leaders, has unquestionably become uglier and more dangerous.

These are daunting problems that could end up defining our era and resetting the course of American history—and they are not confined to the United States. As we will show next, the kind of worldview divide that has reshaped American politics has now landed on Europe's shores. The result is growing acrimony about matters Europeans thought they'd settled long ago, introducing new passion, intensity, and some of the same disturbing currents into the European environment that have come to characterize the United States.

7

Our Common Fate

DONALD TRUMP'S STUNNING VICTORY in the US presidential election of 2016 wasn't the only shock to the global system that year. A few months earlier, Britons had gone to the polls to vote on an oddly conceived but historically consequential referendum on whether the United Kingdom should leave the European Union. By a narrow majority, Britain said yes.

With two of the globe's largest dominoes seemingly falling in the direction of nationalist right-wing populism, supporters of more open borders in general and European integration in particular held their collective breath. Would the rest of the Western world follow the lead of these two great, pacesetting powers?

Concerned observers didn't have to wait long to find out. In 2017 parties and candidates with messages similar to Trump's enjoyed unprecedented support at the polls in other major European democracies. The far-right National Front in France, for instance, was a front-runner in pre-election rankings and finished second in the first round of voting before being defeated by the liberal-centrist La République En Marche! in the final runoff contest for the presidency. Similar developments were afoot in the Netherlands and Austria. Even voters in Scandinavian countries seemed to express unease about the changing nature of their demographics, although it would be difficult for an outsider to notice what was in actuality a very subtle change in their new migrant populations. Although parties in Europe did not ultimately enjoy the success that Trump and Brexit did, their unprecedented showing in the polls was proof that politics in Europe was changing.

The reason for this change is ominous: European politics appear to be reorganizing around a worldview-based divide like the one that has fractured the political system in the United States. Like voters in the United States, Europeans didn't wake up one day and suddenly decide their worldviews were going to start determining their political choices. Rather, the context of their political choices changed in such a way as to make worldview more central.

Immigration and open borders were the central characters. In the 1990s the European Union set the process in motion by expanding its membership into eastern Europe and deepening integration between member states. The result was easier movement between more countries. Countries whose populations had for centuries been relatively homogeneous were becoming more heterogeneous. By the 2010s, debates about the very concept of "the people" began to take center stage.

As in the United States, but contrary to conventional wisdom, Europeans' attitudes about immigration specifically and difference more generally have not been moving in a more populist direction. In addition, although the global financial crisis created more economic unease for a time, citizens' evaluations of their nations' economies have long since recovered. Instead, the attitudes of ordinary Europeans, just like those of ordinary Americans, have never been positive about outsiders. As Larry Bartels puts it, and contrary to much commentary about the European right in recent years, populist leaders did not create a wave. Rather, they tapped into a reservoir of negative attitudes that already existed. This is much more concerning. No "natural" forces, like ebbing tides, can be counted on to diminish the negative sentiment. It can be kept alive as long as those invested in doing so are able to.

People are naturally wary of strangers, some more than others. And as has been made abundantly clear in this book, variation in this human tendency can be revealed by people's worldviews. In short, the increased political salience of basic questions like who belongs and who doesn't has connected the political choices of ordinary citizens to whether their worldviews are more fixed or more fluid.

Although the specifics of the political situations in the United States and Europe differ, the parallels that brought us to this place are still noteworthy. In Europe, as in America, bread-and-butter economic issues dominated postwar politics, and voters, for the most part, identified with parties that represented their class interests. In Europe, leaders also had incentives to suppress nationalist expressions in the wake of the devastation caused by the two world wars. The project of European integration, beginning with the intertwining of the steel and coal sectors of France and Germany in the 1950s, was intended to short-circuit the sorts of nationalist impulses that for so long had plagued the historical antagonists. In addition, Europe entered a period of broad-based economic expansion, producing a large and secure middle class.

This combination—unifying policies, and a rising economic tide lifting all of Europe's boats—transformed the region's politics. As two scholars of European integration observed, "when the political gorilla of nationalism" was sidelined after World War II, domestic politics in most European countries essentially became focused on how much government ought to do and how social safety nets should be funded. The resulting style of politics in Europe bore some resemblance to the politics of post–New Deal America, in which worldview was not a salient political dividing line.

Like the United States following the civil rights and women's liberation movements, Europe in the wake of increased European integration became fertile ground for a new type of politics. Opportunistic political figures responded to the perception of growing discord in society by promising to restore order and reassert a "traditional" social and cultural hierarchy. This started with a *herrenvolk* vision of the welfare state whereby the benefits of living in Europe would remain the exclusive preserve of native-born Europeans. It began to dredge from the depths previously latent anger toward immigrants; ethnic, racial, and religious minorities; and the elites who allowed them into their countries.

In the process, xenophobic, nationalist leaders in Europe broke decades-long norms in Europe against speaking in the most strongly negative terms about minorities. These norms existed because of the atrocities of World War II, especially but not limited to the eliminationist anti-Semitism that helped bring Hitler to power and enabled his subsequent effort to exterminate Europe's entire Jewish population, along with other vulnerable ethnic and social minorities. In racially and religiously homogeneous European countries in the early decades of the twentieth century, Jews in particular had borne the brunt of European xenophobia. The horrific legacy of World War II effectively made anti-Semitism off-limits for any right-wing demagogue seeking to garner political support by demonizing a racial or ethnic minority.

But European nationalists and their leaders have found a new pool of minorities to disparage, thanks in large part to mass migration to Europe from the Middle East and North Africa. The vulnerability of these minorities has allowed right-wing populist candidates such as Geert Wilders, the leader of the Netherlands' xenophobic Party for Freedom, to compare the Quran to *Mein Kampf* and to call for the closing of mosques. It has made it not just acceptable but also advantageous for the leader of the Netherlands' newest and even-farther-right party, Forum for Democracy, to warn that, in a few decades, Europe will not exist "as a predominantly white-skinned, Christian or post-Christian, Roman-law-based kind of society." Although this superheated rhetoric is not especially common in Europe, it is exactly the kind of us-versus-them language that can appeal to voters with fixed worldviews — people who are primed by a combination of nature and nurture to fear racial, ethnic, and religious difference.

Of course, it takes two to tango. Plenty of other Europeans, in particular younger ones, have an affinity for political movements and parties that envision a cosmopolitan Europe, anchored in values of open borders and nontraditional lifestyles. The populist rhetoric of right-wing politicians such as Wilders in the Netherlands rankles these fluid-worldview voters. Sensing their ire, European politicians on the left — like Democratic Party leaders in the United States — are embracing openness: of borders, of family structure, and of culture more broadly.

Unlike in the United States, minor parties have captured the imagi-
nation of the fixed and fluid alike. One effect is that while the traditional,
mainstream parties are losing support (though they typically remain the
largest parties), green parties and other far-left formations are coming to
play a more significant role in European politics, just as the parties led
by the likes of Wilders and France's National Front leader Marine Le
Pen have on the right. For instance, in the Dutch parliamentary elections
of 2017, Wilders's party did worse than expected, while the GreenLeft
Party tripled its vote share with its youthful leader, Jesse Klaver, touting
the party's "pro refugee" approach. (Yes, he actually said "pro refugee.")
This far-left brand of politics, we can assume—and, in this chapter, will
demonstrate—is highly attractive to people with fluid worldviews. That
has certainly been the case in the United States. And just as in the United
States, as European voters' worldviews have increasingly become a central part of their political identities, politics has become nastier and more
caustic.

Although there are many similarities between the United States and
Europe, there are also important differences. Many of the worldview-
tinged issues that have consumed American politics in recent decades
—including guns, gay rights, and climate change—evoke little to no
controversy in Europe. In this regard, the United States really is an outlier—the only country in the world in which there is an acrimonious partisan debate about whether anthropogenic climate change is occurring
and is a serious problem. Likewise, only in the United States is there
intense disagreement about the regulation of guns for personal use.

As such, the far-right parties in Europe have not concerned themselves with these sorts of issues. Indeed, in 2017, when France's Le Pen
was campaigning for president (she would ultimately win 34 percent of
the vote), she sometimes expressed support for moving toward a zero-car-
bon economy and encouraged growing more organic food.

Of course, reducing carbon emissions isn't what Le Pen is known for.
Xenophobia is. And that is true of other emergent parties across Europe,
from Britain and Germany to Austria, the Netherlands, Italy, Scandinavia,

and beyond. In all of these places, right-wing leaders emphasize issues that seem tailor-made for a fixed worldview, zeroing in on the heart of what makes the fixed, fixed: their wariness of outsiders and of the change and uncertainty they represent. As in the United States, these European leaders, by catering to the fears of voters with fixed worldviews, have scored surprising electoral victories. The question now is whether these politicians will ride their victories to national power as Trump did in America.

In this chapter, we'll consider case studies from four nations: Germany, Great Britain, France, and Denmark. The first three countries are America's most significant European allies and, therefore, of particular significance. Denmark, for its part, is interesting because it is widely perceived as a bastion of tolerance. That right-wing populism has gained such traction there is a striking reflection of some of the larger arguments we're making—that there don't need to be profound, objective social changes for xenophobic nationalism to gain a foothold.

As we'll show, the same worldview-political divide that has recently emerged in the United States also seems to be taking root in these countries. We can say this with a degree of certainty because new evidence from Europe suggests that the four questions about the qualities people value in children, which originated in the United States and which we have used to pinpoint Americans' worldviews, can be used to successfully identify the worldviews of people there, as well. A fledgling organization called the Dalia Group included the parenting questions in a survey of Europeans back in December 2016. Its survey also asked a number of questions that worldview ought to be related to, such as how people feel about European integration, diversity, and other issues.

The Dalia Group also asked Europeans a question much like the one presented in the introduction to this book: do you think the world is dangerous, or is it a big, beautiful place to revel in and explore? Among fluid respondents, two-thirds perceive a big, beautiful world while only one-third think it's a dangerous place. Among the fixed, the percentages are basically the reverse—38 percent think the world is safe to explore while 62 percent are wary of it. These findings mirror those we have seen in

America, and suggest that the questions about the qualities people value in children can be used to pinpoint the worldviews of people in Europe, as well.

There also seem to be strong correlations between Europeans' worldviews and their political beliefs, just as we've seen among Americans. For instance, worldview seems to divide Europeans' opinions about the benefits of diversity, as it does in the United States. Asked whether they think diversity is a net positive or negative, fixed-worldview European respondents were pretty skeptical. Less than a quarter believe diversity has a positive effect. Among those on the fluid side, however, about twice that percentage do. Similarly, when Europeans are asked about nationalism, the familiar fixed/fluid differences reveal themselves again. When asked whether "country comes first," a majority of the fixed agree, but a majority of the fluid disagree.

In sum, the survey data suggest that the argument about worldview politics we've developed in this book has considerable potential to help explain public opinion in Europe, just as it does in the United States. As issues that play to people's worldviews become more salient in European politics, fixed and fluid people there have become more and more divided, with ominous implications for their democracies. Thus, in the ascendance of Donald Trump to the presidency in America, we may be seeing a glimpse of Europe's future, as well.

In Germany, the legacy of World War II has largely hamstrung demagogues. For example, after the war the state imposed strict prohibitions on the display of swastikas and other symbols that targeted minorities. Such steps helped to push far-right parties to the fringes of national politics after 1945.

In recent years, however, worldview politics appears to have come to Germany. As in the United States, resourceful politicians have tapped into Germans' latent, negative attitudes about race and ethnicity in particular, sparking a new political conflict that hinges on what is, for this history-haunted country, an incredibly loaded question: who does and doesn't belong in Germany?

Beginning in the 1960s and 1970s, a large influx of Turkish guest workers transformed German society, making Germany one of Europe's more diverse countries. Waves of violence against the migrants occurred periodically, but over time Germans became relatively hospitable to immigrants. Whereas in 1984 nearly 80 percent of all Germans said the country had too many immigrants, by 2008 just over half held that opinion. Notably, this was during a period in which Germany was making it far easier for migrants to remain in the country long term. Although Germans' worries about immigration had dropped significantly, the issue remained of enough concern for ambitious right-wing politicians to be able to take advantage of it.

No far-right party in Germany attracted significant national support until 2013, with the formation of the Alternative for Germany. At first, the AfD adopted a tone on immigration more strident than the more mainstream German parties, but it remained careful not to breach the clear norms of Germany's postwar consensus, which marked as verboten incendiary speech directed against minority groups. Instead, the AfD's main focus in 2013 was the EU itself, an inviting target for movements that want to raise the specter of threat about faceless outside forces. Bureaucrats in Belgium, the EU's administrative center, served the purpose. Whereas in 2010, at the height of the Eurozone debt crisis, German chancellor Angela Merkel could still rally support by proclaiming that "the euro is our common fate, and Europe is our common future," within a few years such appeals to Germans' neighborly spirit were beginning to seem less politically viable.

The 2015 Syrian refugee crisis and the resulting decisions made by political leaders seemed to provide something of a tipping point in Germany. In the midst of one of the deadliest conflicts in recent times, millions of Syrians fled their native land. As of this writing, over six hundred thousand people fleeing the war-torn nation crossed the border into Jordan. Another three million or so fled to Turkey. And at least another million tried to make their way to Europe. In response, Merkel, leader of the right-of-center Christian Democratic Union, insisted that Germany, and Europe, embrace the refugees.

While a majority of Germans accepted the new arrivals, the issue intensified German political divisions. And the AfD took full advantage of the political opportunity, stoking fears of an inundation of foreigners who would overwhelm and eventually undermine German culture. Crucially, however, anti-immigration sentiment did not increase in response to Merkel's policies. What changed was the issue's salience. Before 2015, immigration was a secondary issue for most German voters, but beginning that year the influx of refugees and the rise of the AfD as a political force caused more Germans to regard it as important—and the AfD's fortunes began to improve dramatically.

As the AfD became more strident, its popularity crept up. In the 2017 parliamentary elections, the AfD won 13 percent of the vote and ninety-four seats in the Bundestag, making it the third-largest party in the country. The AfD did especially well in its home base of Saxony, in eastern Germany, where it pulled in nearly 30 percent of the vote. It also drew support disproportionately from men and less educated voters, a profile consistent with support for Donald Trump in the United States and, indeed, other right-wing populist parties across Europe.

As important as the rise of the AfD is, it is not the only evidence of an emerging worldview-based politics in Germany. Just as the AfD's political platform seems tailor-made for fixed-worldview voters, the left-wing Green Party appears to embody the fluid worldview. The party has long been among the most consistent supporters of LGBT rights, favors legalized marijuana, and is a stalwart pro-migrant force. While support for Germany's mainstream, left-of-center Social Democrats is ebbing—the party has half as many seats in the German Bundestag as it did in 1998 despite the body's increased size—the Green Party has cemented its place as a significant political force, with its numbers creeping up toward 10 percent of the seats in the Bundestag. What's more, in an echo of trends in the United States, the Greens are particularly popular in the German state of Baden-Württemberg, where they pulled nearly 30 percent of the vote in the 2017 elections. Baden-Württemberg is like the Northeast Corridor from Washington, DC, to Boston in the United States. It is among the wealthiest regions in all of Europe and is home to many of Germany's most historic and prestigious universities.

The profound differences in outlook between the insurgent AfD and the Greens are consistent with the worldview divide. And data bear that out. The 2017 election offered a unique opportunity to put the four questions on qualities people value in children (determining their worldviews as more fixed or more fluid) on a major academic survey outside the United States, specifically the German Election Study. The results show that, among the fixed, fully 28 percent cast their votes for the AfD, compared with only 2 percent support among the fluid. Green voting, as expected, was the reverse. Among the fluid, 25 percent voted Green, while only 2 percent of the fixed did. It is hard to imagine that there is a better explanation for these voting patterns than worldview.

Based on the nature of the AfD's message in particular, moreover, it is reasonable to believe that the key issue dividing the fixed and fluid in Germany is immigration. The German Election Study bears that out. It asked respondents to place themselves on a ten-point scale between two poles labeled "laws on immigration should be easier" and "laws on immigration should be more difficult." People could place themselves at any of ten places on or between the two poles of the scale. The thrust of the question is similar to the ones that have revealed massive differences between fixed and fluid Americans' attitudes about immigration and immigrants.

The pattern is the same in Germany as it is in the United States. Among fixed respondents, the average score on the scale was 6.9, which is solidly on the more restrictive side of the immigration spectrum. The fluid's average response was only 3.9, solidly on the open side of the immigration spectrum. It is also noteworthy that Germans with "mixed" worldviews, like mixed-worldview people in the United States, are more similar to fixed than fluid people in their preferences about immigration. The average response of the mixed was 5.9, one point from the fixed but twice that far from the fluid.

Politically, then, Germany today bears an unmistakable likeness to the United States in 2016 and the years leading up to it. It is true that the migration crisis of 2015 was a major news story. But increasing support for the AfD preceded the crisis, and did not result from major changes in attitudes about immigration or from significant changes in permanent immigration levels. Rather, the AfD succeeded in attracting people who previously might have voted for another party, but found in the AfD a political force that spoke directly to that which mattered most to them—their wariness of outsiders. In the United States, similarly, a high percentage of Americans wanted to build border fences and slow immigration long before Donald Trump came along. Despite the fact that the country's immigration levels were holding steady or even declining, Trump's unique political skill made the issue salient to Americans. His distinctive way of talking about it seemed to resonate more deeply than when others did, convincing many Americans that he would actually *do* something to address their fears and worries. But importantly, he didn't create the attitudes; he merely harvested them.

In much the same way, the emergence of the AfD increased the salience of immigration in German politics. Until 2013 Germans were less likely than other Europeans to say that immigration was one of the key problems facing their country. By railing against it with increasing intensity, the AfD encouraged previously indifferent Germans to care a lot about it—and allowed many other Germans who actually *do* possess negative attitudes about immigrants to voice and channel those previously unspeakable opinions.

If this were the only change that worldview politics was having on Germany, the country might have escaped the sort of partisanship that is racking the United States. It is important to keep in mind, however, that the immigration issue has two poles, not just the anti-immigrant one. The increase in issue salience appears to have caused the Green Party, in particular, to perceive advantages to embracing the cosmopolitan side of the issue. As a result, some Germans now respond *more* favorably to questions about whether immigration is good for Germany as well. Worldview is not one-sided. It creates a divide between two sides with profoundly different ways of thinking about who belongs.

To the northwest of Germany, Great Britain appears to have been affected by worldview politics as well. Here, as in Germany, diversity has become a flashpoint for a volatile form of nativist, far-right nationalism. But more than in Germany, Britons' resistance to immigration especially has contributed to a much larger and, thus far, more successful resistance movement: the fight against European integration, in particular, the European Union.

Across the continent, the European Union has opened a deep fault line in European politics. Right-wing populist parties have pilloried bureaucrats in Brussels, the administrative capital of the European Union, as being out of touch and having priorities contrary to their nations' interests. The Dalia Group survey results suggest that this kind of rhetoric probably appeals to the fixed. Only about one-quarter of the fixed expressed any enthusiasm about the EU, while nearly half of the fluid did.

Nowhere has this backlash against the EU been more successful than in Britain. To be sure, Britain had, before and since its entry into the Common Market in 1973, always been something of an ambivalent partner in the European project. In the 1980s Prime Minister Margaret Thatcher resisted inclusion in labor and social accords she deemed antithetical to her brand of conservatism. And Britain never joined the single currency that bound together most of the other EU nations. Yet in other respects, Britain participated in the union wholeheartedly. By the 2010s, some three million EU citizens from the continent had settled in Great Britain, and over a million Britons had moved to the continent. Despite its arm's-length approach to aspects of EU integration, then, the United Kingdom was a full and central member. And until 2016, its role as a fulcrum in European and global finance seemed to ensure that it would remain so.

But the backlash against the EU had gathered enough force in Britain that Conservative prime minister David Cameron struck a deal with EU-skeptical backbenchers, including the upstart UK Independence Party (UKIP) and its ethno-nationalist leader, Nigel Farage. He promised to allow Britons to vote on a referendum on Britain's future in the EU if they reelected him in 2015. Cameron won the election and, true to his word, called a referendum on the subject. Held in late June 2016, it read simply:

Should the United Kingdom remain a member of the European Union or leave the European Union?

In what would become an eerily familiar script to Americans months later, the pundit class and most political elites regarded it as a given that "Remain" would win a decisive victory. Mirroring the US presidential election, the polls themselves, especially as the referendum approached, showed a narrow gap, a race that either side could win. But because it seemed unimaginable to a certain segment of British society that the people would engage in what they saw as such an obviously self-defeating political act, that meant it couldn't actually happen.

Until it did.

In the aftermath of the stunning 52 to 48 percent victory for "Leave," pundits scrambled to explain who voted to opt out of the EU and why. As was true after Trump's victory in the US presidential election later that year, many argued that the economically downtrodden, whose material circumstances had worsened due to globalization, were the primary constituency in favor of "Brexit." But as the writer Ronald Brownstein observed, a deeper look at the outcome of the Brexit vote "pointed to a reshaped U.K. political order that revolves more around cultural affinities—particularly attitudes toward immigration and diversity—than economic class."

It has been said of the United States that Americans love their immigrant past but dislike their immigrant present and future. Similar attitudes seem to prevail in Great Britain. One study that examined the plight of working-class communities in the East London borough of Barking and Dagenham observed that this formerly "homogenous refuge" for "London's white working class" had been riven by social conflict in recent years. Interviews with dozens of residents found many to be especially dismayed by an influx of non-English-speaking migrants.

As the borough transformed, nonimmigrant Britons expressed particular concern about the newer arrivals. One resident, a fifty-nine-year-old woman who'd lived there her whole life, took it upon herself to write a long letter to then–prime minister Cameron which echoed many of the major themes discussed throughout this book. Earlier generations of immigrants worked hard, she said. They expected nothing handed to them, and tried to learn English. By contrast, the new immigrants, including the "Nigerians," are indifferent to community norms and disrespectful of elders. People are afraid to go out because the streets have become so unsafe. The "natives" are second-class citizens in their own communities. *Sixty-seven* languages are said to be spoken at the local elementary school. The new arrivals carry diseases with them and all need to be checked for infections. And so on. Such complaints, about violent, disease-ridden foreigners who are a threat to existing communities, are probably familiar to the American ear, particularly given looming fears among many white Americans that half the country will soon be nonwhite.

Like the United States, Great Britain has become increasingly nonwhite. In parts of Britain, that has stoked an increase in anti-immigrant politics, including in Barking and Dagenham. But in general, in the places in which the migrant population has been the largest, Britons themselves have been relatively supportive. Indeed, the regions of Britain that have witnessed an influx of migrants below the national average were twice as likely to vote for Brexit than those areas experiencing higher-than-average immigration.

A demographic picture of Leave's victory will ring familiar to any casual observer of America's worldview-divided politics. "Leave" won big outside of major cities, and it carried over three-fifths of those without four-year college degrees as well as a clear majority of seniors and whites. "Remain" drew the votes of over two-thirds of nonwhites, nearly three-fifths of college graduates, and solid majorities among younger and urban residents. In London itself, 60 percent voted to stay.

This pattern sounds almost precisely like the residential demographics of the fixed/fluid divide in the United States. The fixed, who perceive more danger in the world and hence prefer racial, ethnic, and cultural sameness, choose to live in less densely populated areas. The fluid, who perceive less danger and are thus more open to diverse cities with people who challenge existing norms, opt to live in more densely populated areas.

The demographics of Britain's "Leave" and "Remain" voters track to some degree the "somewheres" and "anywheres" that David Goodhart identifies in his book *The Road to Somewhere*. Goodhart argues that

about a quarter of the population are "anywheres"—highly educated and
mobile, and who tend to be university-educated and to live in Britain's
larger cities, most notably London. Because London is such a culturally
and economically dominant place, it "sucks in" an enormous proportion
of the professional class. The "anywheres" tend to value, in Goodhart's
words, "openness and autonomy and fluidity." They're comfortable with
social change and they're "less attached to place or to groups." Goodhart's "somewheres," in contrast, sound a lot like the fixed. They tend to
have less formal education and "to value familiarity and security." They
are less comfortable with change and diversity. That divide, as we suggested above, seems to have tracked very closely with recent British elections, including the 2016 Brexit vote.

Indeed, numerous analyses, including a postelection survey conducted by the veteran American pollster Stanley Greenberg, found that
"opposition to immigration" was the single best predictor of support for
Leave. Another poll of twelve thousand Britons found that 62 percent
of Leave voters said immigration was a "force for ill." And yet another
reported that 80 percent of Leave voters said the same about "multiculturalism."

The Dalia Group survey also asked a question about Brexit of its British respondents. The results reveal that worldview was strongly related to
voting on the referendum. Fully 60 percent of those on the fixed side of
the worldview spectrum supported Leave. Only half that percentage on
the fluid side of the worldview spectrum did. Once again, the four simple
questions asking people to choose between desirable qualities in children provided a remarkable window on political conflict.

It is unclear whether Brexit will drive a new fault line into British party politics. Much is working against it, particularly the traditionally class-based conflict that has defined British politics for ages.
That being said, the results of the 2017 parliamentary elections identified an element of worldview politics—place of residence—as critical
to voting behavior. Those living in small towns supported the Conservative Party by big margins, while city dwellers voted in larger numbers for Labour. As is true elsewhere, British cities are younger and

more racially diverse, and they have more college graduates. In outlying areas, the population tends to be older and have less formal education. These demographic and geographic factors are all consistent with
the fixed/fluid divide. This fault line was clear in the Brexit vote, and it
bears watching to see if it will come to influence British party politics
more generally in the years to come.

Ask anyone from France and he or she will tell you that the French are
different from the Germans and British. When it comes to politics, France
has a longer history with a popular right-wing political party, the National
Front. The recent implosion of the traditionally dominant parties in France
made it a particularly striking battleground for what looks an awful lot like
the worldview divide.

Unlike the AfD, the National Front (FN) in France did not come out of
nowhere in the 2010s. Jean-Marie Le Pen founded the FN in the 1970s.
In the 1980s he ran on an explicitly anti-Europe, anti-immigrant, and
anti-Semitic platform, including dabbling in Holocaust denial. In the
2002 presidential elections, Le Pen shocked the world by earning 17 percent of the vote in the first round, good enough to qualify for the second-
round runoff. He lost that election by over sixty points to Jacques Chirac
and support for the FN under his leadership declined significantly after
that.

His daughter, Marine Le Pen, became the leader of the FN in 2011.
She toned down some of the uglier aspects of her father's rhetoric and
sidled away from his anti-Semitism. Indeed, she expelled her own father
from the party in 2015 after he made yet another round of controversial
statements minimizing the Holocaust. The younger Le Pen focused like
a laser on France's growing immigrant population and its putative threat
to the French nation. This approach had much more potential to resonate
widely than the older Le Pen's approach. France's national ethos centers
on preserving its unique culture, which has set off major controversies in
the past, including a 2011 law to ban wearing the burka in public.

Le Pen argued that a rising tide of foreigners, many of whom are Muslims of North African descent, was changing France for the worse. Left

unchecked, these immigrants would undermine the French nation itself. When she first ran for party leader in 2011, Le Pen told a gathering of supporters that the desire of some Muslims to pray in public in the streets of Paris was akin to the Nazi occupation of France. This has led many to argue that the new, softer image of the FN is just that, an image, an attempt to put a "human face" on a far-right party.

A tragic bit of political context gave the FN a boost. In 2015 and 2016 France was victimized by a series of terrorist bombings and other attacks, carried out by Islamic extremists claiming allegiance to ISIS. One series of attacks, in November 2015, left over 130 people dead in Paris. Recall from chapter 6 that the fear and stress caused by terrorism is a boon to parties and candidates whose message caters to voters with fixed world-views. Not only does it attract the fixed; those with less fixed worldviews become more like the fixed in their preferences during those times of fear. As expected, the violence increased support for Le Pen as the 2017 presidential elections approached. With the dominant establishment parties of the center-left and center-right falling by the wayside, Le Pen emerged from the first round of the elections with the second-most votes.

The failure of the usual centrist alternatives also paved the way for a new cosmopolitan and multicultural party, led by a thirty-nine-year-old bureaucrat, Emmanuel Macron. He was the first-round winner and faced off against Le Pen in the runoff election between the top two vote getters. Pundits in the United States and Europe feared a replay of Brexit and Trump's victory. Of course, not everyone agreed that a Le Pen victory would be a bad thing. One of the engineers of Trump's campaign, Steve Bannon, viewed it as another step in the restoration of a Judeo-Christian Western civilization that he and other right-wing populists believed was under assault from the forces of multiculturalism. It is noteworthy that the Trump adviser most committed to this version of populism in the United States expressed such enthusiasm for Le Pen.

Proponents of European integration feared the worst. One observer noted that cosmopolitan centrist parties of the sort that Macron built were failing throughout Europe because they were losing their "old base by appearing to care only about free trade, technological progress, and limitless diversity." In other words, they appealed too much to those with fluid worldviews at the expense of support from those in the middle of the world-view spectrum.

In the runoff election in May 2017, Macron won a smashing victory, defeating Le Pen 66 percent to 34 percent. This was not a triumph for the ideas preferred by fluid people, however. In contrast to the United States after Trump won the Republican nomination, right-of-center parties and their leaders did not fall in behind Le Pen as Republicans did behind Trump. Indeed, all the mainstream candidates, including the conserva-tive François Fillon, who received the third-most votes in the first round, immediately called for all French to rally around Macron to defend the Republic. Signals like these made clear to their supporters that Macron was the superior alternative.

Although defeated soundly, Le Pen's showing in 2017 demonstrated that her views are far from fringe. Qualifying for the runoff and winning 34 percent of the vote in the second round does not suggest that only a small group of dead-enders back the FN. Instead, a sizable segment of French society finds a program that appeals to fixed-worldview people to be attractive. Had the French center-right alternatives not thrown their support behind Macron, things might have turned out better for Le Pen.

Fortunately, the fixed/fluid questions appeared on the French Elec-tion Study in 2017. And, again, the results demonstrate the clear impor-tance of worldview in shaping voting behavior. In the second-round contest in which Macron defeated Le Pen head-to-head, an astounding 91 percent of the fluid preferred Macron, with only 9 percent support-ing Le Pen. Those with fixed worldviews were much friendlier to Le Pen. Although she won only about a third of the vote overall, well over 40 percent of the fixed voted for her over Macron. Fixed/fluid differences shaped voting behavior in the first-round elections as well, particularly in explaining support for Le Pen. In fact, fixed-worldview voters were fully five times more likely than fluid-worldview voters to cast their ballots for the National Front leader in the first round.

In France as in Germany, it appears the central issue dividing the fixed and fluid is immigration. The French Election Study asked people whether they thought there were "too many immigrants" in France. Among the fluid, the most common answer was to disagree—44 percent either said they "totally disagreed" or "rather disagreed." In contrast, these categories were the least common choices among the fixed, with only 8 percent of them falling into either of the disagree categories. Instead, 72 percent of those with fixed worldviews agreed that there were too many immigrants. Importantly, there is one more notable parallel between the German and French survey results. The mixed's preferences on immigration were closer to the fixed's than they were to the fluid's. Only 19 percent of the mixed disagreed with the notion that France had too many immigrants, eleven points more than the fixed but fully twenty-five points less than the fluid.

The FN's recent rise did not follow a large influx of immigrants and French attitudes about immigrants and immigration have not changed dramatically over the last couple of decades, which has to come as a surprise to readers given the breathless reporting about growing anti-immigrant sentiment in Europe. Instead, what changed was that an entrepreneurial leader, Le Pen, combined with the terrorist attacks in 2015 and 2016 to *activate* attitudes about immigration. As a result, the country became more sharply divided over the issue, as the two most significant political forces in the country took opposite positions.

A rising wave of anti-immigrant sentiment might in itself be troubling, at least to those on the fluid side of the worldview divide. But the analogy of a wave suggests an eventual cresting and breaking, leaving in its wake a more "normal" level that is more welcoming of those who are different. But attitudes about immigration have not changed appreciably in Europe. There is no wave. That might sound comforting to the ear, but it is not. When parties like the AfD and FN are marginal political players, it might seem like anti-immigrant sentiment doesn't really exist. But recent developments suggest that this sort of xenophobia does exist even if it is dormant at times, awaiting a skillful leader and the right set of circumstances to bring it to life. To return to Bartels's metaphor, it is like a reservoir that nationalists and xenophobes can always tap into. Those attitudes are always available for harvesting by power-hungry elites. That means the threat posed by parties like the AfD and FN is not going away any time soon.

The story from Germany, Britain, and France—the biggest countries in Europe—is sobering. But so, too, is the situation in smaller nations across Europe. Few countries in the region, it seems, are immune from the appeal of leaders who prey on voters' fears of the cultural change, physical threats, and pure *otherness* of immigrants. And perhaps no country demonstrates this susceptibility better than the small Scandinavian nation of Denmark.

In a (very) informal survey following Trump's victory in 2016, we asked many of our fluid friends whether they had thought about leaving the United States for a foreign country—and if so which country they wanted to flee to. By a wide margin, their first choice was Canada. But Denmark—a small, wealthy country with a seemingly congenial political climate for people who value openness—was second.

Its liberal credentials seem rock solid. Denmark is a bastion of progressive policies, with arguably the most highly developed and thoroughgoing "cradle to grave" welfare state of any country in the world. It established universal health care for all citizens in 1973. It has robust paid family-leave policies for mothers and fathers. The most popular mode of transportation in Copenhagen, Denmark's cosmopolitan capital, is the bicycle. Not only that, Denmark was the first country in the world to legalize same-sex unions. It did so in 1989, more than twenty years before the United States.

A recent survey reported that Denmark was the happiest country on earth. But some observers are starting to see dark clouds encroaching on this sunny picture. Denmark is facing some of the same challenges that much of continental Europe is, most notably a growing population of migrants and refugees seeking asylum. And those challenges appear to be prompting the beginning of a process of political sorting based on worldview differences. At the heart of it appear to be divergent orientations with respect to strangers.

Denmark sits between the two European countries that attract the most refugees, Germany and Sweden, and its leaders and citizens worry that a surge of new arrivals would drain its generous welfare benefits. As a result, Danes are taking steps to erect barriers. For example, the Danish parliament passed a law in 2016 that requires the government to seize any assets over the equivalent in Danish kroner of $1,450 from asylum seekers, the stated purpose of which is to defray the costs of their resettlement. Danish officials have also considered plans to move new immigrants from urban apartments to camps outside cities, the better to convey the government's intention that asylum seekers would only be granted temporary respite before being repatriated. In an especially striking move, one Danish city council passed a law requiring that pork be placed on menus of municipally run eateries, including in schools and day care centers. While this was probably a nice sop to the Danish pork industry, its primary purpose seems to be to unfurl a very clear unwelcome banner for the growing Muslim population in the country.

Europe's multiparty systems make it easier for parties to occupy distinctive niches, including smaller parties that would appeal most directly to a fixed-worldview constituency. In Denmark, the Danish People's Party (DPP) appears to be the fixed-worldview option. Its founder, Pia Kjaersgaard, argued in the late 1990s that Denmark's embrace of "multiculturalism" would be a "national disaster" for the nation. In 2005 she said of Denmark's neighbor Sweden—which has long had the most generous immigration laws in Europe (though a backlash is brewing against immigration policies there, as well)—"If they want to turn Stockholm, Gothenburg or Malmo into a Scandinavian Beirut, with clan wars, honour killings and gang rapes, let them do it. We can always put a barrier on the Oresund Bridge" (the bridge connecting Sweden and Denmark).

The party proudly touts its "anti-Muslim" bona fides and says its priority is to maintain Danish culture against the influx of non-Christian foreigners. One party leader has called for Muslim asylum seekers to be barred from Europe altogether, because Europe needs "a respite after recent terrorist attacks" and derides as "naive" those who believe that Islam is a "religion of peace." The DPP supports the continuation of a strong welfare state, but insists that it be maintained for the benefit of Danes only.

Ideas such as these used to occupy the political fringe in Denmark. When it first started running candidates for Denmark's parliament in 1998, the Danish People's Party garnered only 7 percent of the vote. But it received triple that percentage in 2015, making it second-largest in parliament. And its influence, on issues like immigration, exceeds its numbers, as mainstream parties have been nervous about being outflanked as hard-liners on immigration. The aforementioned law to seize migrants' assets passed parliament by an overwhelming margin.

This is a bit of a puzzle. Unlike Germany, Britain, and France, Denmark has experienced no recent mass-casualty terrorist attacks. What's more, the last outburst of violence in Denmark that could be construed as such was a brief rampage in 2015 by a Danish man of Palestinian descent, including a shooting outside a synagogue that left a Jewish security guard dead. Investigators quickly discovered that the shooter, who was killed by police, was a disaffected young man with a history of violence but little in the way of ideological motivation. While tragic, this attack bears little resemblance to the large-scale, coordinated assaults by hardened jihadists in Germany, the United Kingdom, and France. Yet despite the fact that Denmark has been almost entirely spared from this type of violence, anti-Muslim sentiment runs high in the country.

One close friend of ours, a non-Danish European who has lived in Copenhagen for two decades and raised kids there, says that, while Muslims comprise about 5 percent of Denmark's population, from reading local newspaper coverage you might think it was 85 percent. This anecdote might help to explain why a poll in 2016 found that fully one-third of Danes agreed with the statement that Denmark is "at war with Islam."

As in Germany, Britain, and France, Denmark has experienced an increase in foreign-born residents since the turn of the new century, but not an especially dramatic one. According to OECD data, about 6 percent of Danish residents in 2000 were foreign-born. In 2013 about 8.5 percent were. That's an increase of a little over 100,000 people in a country whose population is 5.5 million. But, as we have seen elsewhere, even small demographic changes — or maybe just the perception of such changes — can be exploited by right-leaning politicians and sympathetic media outlets. In Denmark, of all places, wary native-born people, believing that a multicultural tide is rushing toward them, are seeking safety and comfort in the arms of leaders who promise that they don't need to be afraid anymore. And whereas other European countries that have experienced this shift have seen a spike in support for left-wing parties to balance the growth of the far right, in Denmark there is little evidence of a similar counterbalancing taking place.

These developments in Europe have been discomfiting to many political observers. It is jarring and, for many people, frightening to hear demagogues spouting xenophobic rhetoric. It is even more disturbing to observe voters responding favorably to it. Given Europe's long history of wars and other forms of conflict, it is similarly troubling to see efforts to undo the project of European integration, which has appeared to lessen old nationalist instincts.

Yet scholars of right-wing populism in Europe do not agree about whether parties like the UKIP in Britain, the AfD in Germany, the FN in France, and the DPP in Denmark pose a serious threat to democracy itself. Cas Mudde, among the most prominent of them, argues that western Europe's populist right-wing parties are likely to be much more successful in tapping latent prejudice to foment anger at outsiders than they are in undermining democratic institutions themselves. Mudde observes that these parties have especially targeted the courts and the media, but that their main successes have been more rhetorical than institutional. That being said, their demagogic appeals and reckless and relentless assault on "counterbalancing institutions," including the aforementioned courts and media, are dangerous and unnerving, threatening to undermine social cohesion and to make it harder and harder for leaders to find common ground to address critical issues.

Similarly, though social safety nets have frayed to varying degrees in much of Europe in recent decades, they remain robust, virtually everywhere, by American standards. And though inequality has increased substantially in some countries, like Britain, it has scarcely changed at all in others, like Denmark. And in no case does inequality approach the extraordinary levels the United States has witnessed over the past thirty years. What has changed in Europe is the emergence of significant new fault lines in response to either the perception or actuality of significant social and demographic change. And that new divide should be familiar by now—between those who find the world a dangerous place and those who think it is safe to explore. In much of Europe, opportunistic politicians have jumped on the emotional power of social and demographic change to create powerful new parties and reorient the political map in ways that look a lot like the worldview divide in the United States.

Catastrophic terrorist attacks make people more willing to fall in line behind leaders promising to deal ruthlessly with danger and insecurity. But national tragedies aren't necessary for such political reorientations to occur. Populist right and xenophobic parties have seen their fortunes surge in much of western Europe, both in places where attacks have happened and in places where they haven't. And in eastern Europe, in Poland, Hungary, and elsewhere, they've managed to come to power, not just increase their vote shares and parliamentary representation.

Right-wing populist successes have spanned a range of circumstances. They've succeeded even in the absence of terrorism; they've fared well where there's been relatively little increase in immigration; they've scored impressive victories in countries in which there has been little change in the economic fortunes of ordinary citizens. And these parties have accomplished all of this despite the fact that Europeans' attitudes toward immigration have not gotten more negative in recent years.

The common thread in the rise of anti-immigrant, populist parties has been leaders and parties committed to emphasizing those issues in circumstances where there's been just enough change to make their warnings about decline and dissolution plausible. Enough people maintain anti-immigrant, anti-Muslim beliefs that, even if they don't normally express them in the stark form of the AfD or ultranationalists like Geert Wilders, their beliefs align well enough with those of their leaders.

Other parties have also been increasingly committed to promoting a pro-cosmopolitan vision for their societies, highlighting the stark worldview differences this book has emphasized. Unlike the United States,

where the two major parties reflect almost all of the country's major political conflicts, in Europe, minor parties have represented most clearly the
poles of the worldview divide, while mainstream parties sometimes have
and sometimes haven't reoriented themselves to the new fault lines. But
the power of those issues—their visceral appeal—is such that it's impossible to escape completely their siren song.

In sum, a variety of circumstances, in some cases not even objectively all that dramatic, have proved to be fertile ground for the appeals
of right-wing populism to attract those with a fixed worldview and those
who, though they might be of a more mixed disposition, share enough of
the former orientation to support parties carrying the torch of the fixed
worldview. And that same dynamic has created space for more left-wing
parties like the Greens, intent on appealing to a fluid worldview. As is
true in the United States, only time will tell whether these liberal, fluid
parties will ultimately be able to challenge fixed opinion successfully.

CONCLUSION

PRIOR TO THE 2016 ELECTION, many liberal, fluid people in the United States had cause for optimism. In style and temperament, Barack Obama embodied many of the attributes that these Americans prize most: a sense of nuance, a measured appreciation of the complexities of the world, a fundamental tolerance for difference, and a willingness to embrace social and cultural change. And the fact that this first-ever African American president won resounding victories in the 2008 and 2012 presidential elections was a sign to many fluid people the world over that America was changing.

The country, it seemed clear, was becoming less white and more liberal when it came to many cultural issues. Younger Americans demonstrated increasing tolerance for diversity. Most of them seemed to think it laughable that issues like gay marriage were even issues at all. They related to the young, hip Obama. The Republican Party, by contrast, was the party of older white men, retrograde in its views and increasingly out of touch with where America was heading. Anybody with a passing acquaintance with pop culture knew this much to be true.

After Obama won reelection in 2012, the Republican Party itself seemed to recognize the demographic problem it faced. In a 2013 report, commonly referred to as the "autopsy," Republicans acknowledged that they needed to expand beyond their white base if they were to be competitive in presidential elections in the future. The fast-growing population of Latinos had swung Democratic in recent elections and had already helped turn California into a single-party state. Other states, like Nevada, Colorado, and New Mexico were moving in that direction. Large and growing Latino populations in Texas, Arizona, and even Georgia and North Carolina would spell long-term disaster for the party, unless the GOP could rebrand itself as hospitable to them.

This was a frightening prospect for Republicans and a comforting story for liberals—not only because of the hard numbers that seemed to lay behind it, but also because it tickled the fancy of fluid-minded folks everywhere. The reason Democrats would ultimately and decisively triumph over Republicans was because of women, people of color, and the LGBT community. For fluid people, this sort of diverse coalition was as good as it got.

But that rosy picture obscured a different political reality. Since 2010, Democrats were getting shellacked in elections at all levels of government. By 2014, Republicans had retaken control of both houses of Congress and occupied more governorships and controlled more state legislatures than they had since the 1920s. Outside of metropolitan areas, they were the dominant party almost everywhere.

When Donald Trump emerged as the Republican nominee, many fluid observers assumed that his boorish behavior would derail his surreal candidacy. He said things that many Americans knew were simply "disqualifying." But a significant portion of Americans—the members of the nation's electorate with a more-fixed worldview, and the people who lived disproportionately outside the country's metropolitan areas—saw it differently.

Trump may have breached some long-cherished norms of our democracy, but doing so did not disqualify him electorally. The same is true of xenophobic and nativist parties in Europe. There, as in the United States, attitudes about race and immigrants are not changing. Anti-other attitudes have always been widespread, even if they have been voiced more rarely in recent decades than in the more-distant past. What's more, they are ripe for manipulation by political elites who are willing to exploit voters' biases to gain power. Trump was the first of these success stories, if you can call it that. It's unlikely that he will be the last.

Political elites don't need to capitalize on voters' biases by being as nakedly racist as Donald Trump; as Lee Atwater memorably observed, dog whistles have often sufficed to get leaders elected. But if the 2016 US presidential election taught the Western world anything, it is that dog-whistle politics is an anachronism. "Bull-horn politics" is now the name of the game.

Trump typically did not try to conceal his contempt for outgroups, beginning with his campaign kickoff event, when he described many Mexicans coming across the border as rapists and drug dealers. A typical Trump rally began by reading the names of people killed by illegal immigrants, as if those crimes were qualitatively different from any of the other ten thousand murders that take place in the United States every year. Trump often contradicts himself on policy matters—there seems little there in the way of a governing philosophy—but he has been consistent in his desire to signal whose lives he believes matter most. When neo-Nazi protesters marched through Charlottesville in 2017 and one of them killed a counterprotester, Trump took days to issue a proper condemnation. Before he did, he insisted that there were good people on "both" sides, the neo-Nazis very much included. When it emerged that one of his aides was a serial abuser of women, including his two ex-wives, Trump, in his first remarks, defended the man and said that many men were being accused unfairly. At every turn, he has stoked racial, ethnic, and gender-based grievances and, when called on it, is as likely as not to double down. And while the president remains unpopular by historic standards, he shows no sign of changing his ways. Why would he, when his base seems to welcome his approach, and when it clearly hasn't stopped people beyond his base from supporting him?

Ordinary people—you, us, anyone—can be manipulated to some degree. Just as advertising executives know how to persuade us to buy particular products by appealing to our emotions, political elites can win voters' support by tapping into their subconscious minds and their very physiologies.

This can produce intense, acrimonious partisan conflict, as Americans and Europeans have witnessed. For politicians, the benefits of such conflict are obvious: it means more votes, more donations, and more power. But the benefits for voters themselves are less clear.

When politicians leverage voters' worldviews for political gain, it is deeply polarizing and can be deleterious to democracy. In America, it has caused partisan hatred to grow for decades; in recent years it has exploded, allowing politicians to pursue dysfunctional strategies with little concern about losing their jobs in the next election. They can shut down the government or fail to compromise when it comes to needed legislation, and actually score points with their most loyal constituents. They are being rewarded for failure. It doesn't take a PhD in political science to know that nothing good can come of that.

Worldview politics helped bring Americans Donald Trump and an especially intense era of polarization. And polarization has created the kind of legislative gridlock that has made the US Congress dysfunctional. Still, it's worth recalling that bipartisanship can be overrated, at least for people who are seeking to level a playing field that has historically been tilted against them.

In a democracy like America's, political conflict can be a prerequisite for healthy change. Although it hasn't been an explicit part of our story in this book, the fact is that the civil rights and women's liberation movements were the earliest causes of the worldview rupture that began to divide Americans from each other in the 1960s. Both of these movements were hugely disrupting and, as a consequence, polarizing. Race, family structure, and culture emerged as key political battlegrounds, driving many Americans with fixed worldviews into the hands of the Republican Party, while white Americans with fluid worldviews, as well as minority groups, fled the growing hostility they perceived from Republicans, and wound up in the Democratic camp.

As unmanageable as political conflict has become, it would be impossible to argue that African Americans and women would have been better off if not for the polarization caused by these disruptions. In more recent years, the LGBT movement has had success effecting social change, too.

As with civil rights and women's rights, the fight for LGBT rights also required political disruption and polarization.

In short, although it is easy to forget, polarization historically has helped certain groups of people a great deal. Indeed, we would argue, it has made America a better, more just place — in some respects, at least.

Although it is not possible to draw a direct causal link, it appears that wealthy US economic interests also have been well served by polarization, at the expense of Americans who are less well-off. The focus on racial and cultural issues may have something to do with the steep rise in inequality since the 1970s. Republican business interests have signed off on this approach for decades. More recently, Democrats' growing reliance on Wall Street for financial support and well-off people with fluid worldviews for votes has made many more socially liberal elites comfortable with joining the ranks of the corporate titans.

So while political conflict has done a great deal of good, it also has engendered a new political divide that has effectively hobbled the US federal government; this dysfunction, in turn, has disproportionately hurt poorer Americans. The have-nots need government programs, whereas the haves generally do not. If health care reform had not been enacted, for example, the less well-off would have been the worse for it, not those at the top of the income ladder. The adverse consequences of Obamacare repeal, which President Trump and Republicans have pursued doggedly, will likewise fall on have-nots. The same is true of efforts to weaken regulation of the financial sector and consumer protections.

In general, it seems, worldview politics helps the rich and hurts the poor. It is noteworthy that the period characterized by the lowest levels of polarization in the twentieth century — the post–World War II years — produced the lowest levels of income and wealth inequality. Even though worldview politics is not centrally driven by concerns about redistribution, it appears to have deeply negative implications for those who would benefit from more of the latter. Indeed, in addition to the racial and ethnic hostility they face from much of the GOP, redistributive concerns help explain why African Americans and most Hispanics, in particular, are so favorably disposed toward Democrats, regardless of how fixed or fluid they are in worldview. Of course, non-college-educated whites have been adversely affected by the fraying social safety net as well. Especially alarming, the economists Anne Case and Angus Deaton have found that life expectancy is actually dropping among a substantial swath of non-college-educated white Americans, a consequence of their stagnating economic fortunes and an explosion in drug fatalities, including as a result of the raging opioid epidemic. Yet this group's response to the circumstances could not be more different from that of minorities.

The reason is racial politics, a key feature of worldview conflict. In *Strangers in Their Own Land*, Arlie Hochschild explains why economic suffering has pushed working-class whites toward Republicans. She uses the metaphor of cutting in line to characterize their experience. They believe they have worked hard their whole lives just to grab the smallest share of the American dream. While they've patiently waited in line, minorities have jumped the queue, snatching, unfairly, that which the aggrieved in this metaphor believe was rightly theirs. That sense of grievance is precisely what Trump promised to redress to, in the words of conservative *New York Times* columnist Ross Douthat, "protect a once-dominant majority, to restore its privileges and reverse its sense of cultural decline."

But while many low-income white voters saw salvation in Donald Trump's victory and the politics of grievance he championed, it is hard to imagine that the national Republican Party is the best vehicle to solve their economic problems. Indeed, its focus on cutting taxes for the rich at the expense of other programs will almost certainly hurt these same working-class whites who so eagerly cheered on Trump's often xenophobic message. Trump's victory may cause this group to *feel* like they, too, are winners, but it's unlikely his presidency will do much to make them tangibly better off economically. In this sense, at least, they are in the same boat as many of their compatriots — fixed and fluid alike.

Elites won't change their behavior to reduce polarization, even if doing so would be good for the country. They will need a different set of incentives. The Republicans came up with the southern strategy, for example, because they were consistent losers along the old battle lines of the New Deal and needed to redraw them. Today, they have no such incentive. The idea that they will need to stop race-baiting if they're to attract minority voters—a concept cherished among liberals—does not actually hold much water. Around the turn of the twenty-first century, left-leaning political analysts suggested that when the nonwhite segment of the electorate reached 25 percent, it would be all but impossible for Republicans to win anymore unless they changed their positions relating to race. Yet that number is nearing 30 percent now, and Republicans still managed to win in 2016. One reason is that as the proportion of nonwhites in the electorate has grown, nonfluid whites have increasingly thrown their support to the GOP. In 2000 Democrat Al Gore won 42 percent of the white vote. In 2016, however, Hillary Clinton got only 37 percent. Although whites may be a shrinking percentage of the population, their loyalty to the Democratic Party has not remained constant but rather continues to wither.

If Republicans were losing, they would change. But they are not, so they won't. The same basic calculus holds true for Democrats. As we've just made clear, many of their constituency groups have benefited from worldview politics. Moreover, even though Republicans had the upper hand in 2016, their margins are small, at least in Congress. And Donald Trump failed to win a plurality of votes even though he won in the electoral college. Despite their sense of doom about who is running the country, Democrats still have reason to be optimistic that time is on their side.

Some party leaders on both sides might be tempted to deemphasize the issues that have been most divisive. But that risks alienating more of their diehard supporters, the fixed and the fluid, than attract new voters.

Leaders outside the parties might have better luck. For example, many CEOs who normally support the GOP were especially turned off by Donald Trump, at least during the 2016 campaign. Whereas a third of Fortune 100 leaders had endorsed Mitt Romney by the third quarter of 2012, none had endorsed Trump at the same juncture four years later. Of course, many of these business leaders fell in line with Trump after his election. But the reasoning behind their hesitation is clear: while Republican candidates may be able to win elections with mostly white voters, businesses can't maximize profits with mostly white customers. The costs of being associated with a party whose message is widely viewed as intolerant when it comes to race, ethnicity, and sexual orientation are increasing. As Chick-fil-A, Target, Cracker Barrel, and other big companies have learned, being on the culturally conservative side of the divide is often not good for business. They want to sell their products to 100 percent of Americans, not 50 percent.

Generations ago, when the Democratic Party's main benefactor was organized labor and the Republican Party's was big business, a marriage between Democrats and business would have been unthinkable. Not anymore. As old-time labor Democrats will remind you, today's Democratic Party is not particularly hostile to big corporations. Indeed, many of these companies have their headquarters in big cities located in blue states and hence have been doing business with elected Democrats for decades. And their transnational interests and orientation make for an easier cultural fit with today's Democratic Party than with the GOP, especially in its Trumpian incarnation.

This creates an uneasy coalition of business interests, fluid white liberals who are more likely to benefit from those interests, and nonwhite Democrats, but it might nevertheless eventually prompt a reckoning for the GOP.

Changing elite behavior is one path. Another might be the role events play in reshaping politics in unanticipated ways. For example, if changes in the natural environment accelerate in the years ahead, it could direct conflict away from the worldview divide. Serious and prolonged drought, endemic water shortages in some areas, or flooding that makes other areas uninhabitable — natural disasters such as these could make unavoidable a reckoning with climate change. This could also reconfigure the political map. For example, areas hardest hit by the adverse effects of climate change would presumably demand federal action. Areas less affected would want the opposite. Hot, dry places might benefit from a redistribution of water. Cool, wet places would rather hang on to their water. The resulting conflicts between climate haves and have-nots could redefine political conflict and, in turn, submerge the worldview divide.

Of course, we're not rooting for an environmental cataclysm. The important point here is that new circumstances like the one we just sketched could change politicians' incentives in ways that reorient politics. In turn, such a reorientation could weaken the foundations of the worldview divide. A chunk of the fixed and a chunk of the fluid might end up on the same team as was the case during the New Deal party system.

Apart from transnationally oriented CEOs, and Mother Nature, what about ordinary people? What might they do?

Grassroots activists played a critical role in bringing into being and providing the electoral muscle behind both modern conservatism and contemporary liberalism. Activism sparks conversation, and elites often have to respond. With that in mind, new generations can create a distinctive style of politics. The people who came of age in the 1960s have disproportionately shaped the current divide. Similarly, younger generations now coming of age have the opportunity to reshape the political landscape around the issues they care most about.

New generations can decide to take on different causes. Or maybe they can find ways to take on the same issues in different ways. Either might serve to reorient political conflict. The key, however, is a group of people who decide that they're fed up with the status quo and have enough motivation to sustain political engagement and influence the political conversation. We've recently seen perhaps the first promising signs of something just like this. In early 2018 high school students took it upon themselves to do something different from what people have done before in response to a school shooting. After the horrific massacre at Marjory Stoneman Douglas High School in Parkland, Florida, where a previously expelled student murdered seventeen students and teachers, young people in Florida and around the country said, in effect, "We are going to use our voice to change the conversation on guns."

Of course, it is not a given that such a change will occur. But such initiative is one of the mechanisms by which Americans might begin to upend the worldview divide, and repair, at least partially, the country's fractured politics. And it's not just this country's future that hangs in the balance. When Abraham Lincoln warned in 1858 that "a house divided against itself cannot stand," he was referring to the United States, but his warning could equally apply to any nation. The worldview-political divide has given modern democracies around the world the opportunity to either test the truth of Lincoln's warning or echo his message of unification. The choice, ultimately, is up to us.

ACKNOWLEDGMENTS

In one way or another, we've been discussing these ideas for more than fifteen years. Hence it is impossible to recognize all the people who have provided us helpful conversation and thoughtful feedback along the way. Paul Sniderman's work motivated our inquiry from the beginning. Jim Stimson championed our ideas from that stage. And Larry Bartels questioned, doubted, encouraged, and mentored us through many years.

As for this project, however, a number of people require recognition. We thank Amanda Taub for bringing our scholarly work to the attention of a broader audience in early 2016. Ben Hyman, then an editor at Houghton Mifflin Harcourt, was one who noticed, and reached out to ask whether we'd consider revisiting our academic work on worldview. This book would not have existed without Ben's foresight and insight. We cannot say enough about Alex Littlefield, who took over as our editor when the writing began. Alex devoted superhuman time, energy, and intelligence to making this book as engaging and as rigorous as possible. Jill Grinberg, our wonderful agent, whose initial support, incisive mind, and dogged work ensured that we put together a worthwhile proposal. She has also provided wise and invaluable counsel throughout the writing process. Thanks also to her great team at Jill Grinberg Literary Management.

A number of remarkable graduate students at Vanderbilt University gave Herculean efforts on our behalf, none more than the dynamic duo of Drew Engelhardt and Michael Shepherd. Their dedication and attention to detail—not to mention their kindness and enthusiasm—were irreplaceable. Carrie Roush, Meri Long, and James Martherus also played key roles along the way. Two very talented undergraduate students, Zoe Gelman and Alexandra King, made important contributions as research assistants.

A number of professional colleagues offered critical feedback on all or part of the manuscript. And, more important, most on this list provided friendship as well. Thank you to Jon Hurwitz, Mike Nelson, Mark Peffley, Bruce Larson, Kathy Cramer, Wendy Rahn, Zeynep Somer-Topcu, Bob Luskin, Lisbet Hooghe, Efren Perez, Tom Mann, Aaron Martin, Jennifer Hochschild, Stanley Feldman, and Jamie Settle. The work we did with European data collections would not have been possible without the help of Scott Matthews, Rudiger Schmidt-Beck, Pavlos Vasilopoulos, and Martial Foucault. Finally, Suzanne Globetti listened, read, and improved our work more than even the most committed spouse could be expected to.

Others in Hetherington's network of friends—some more fluid and some more fixed—provided feedback on the manuscript and inspiration throughout. They include Carol Montano, Hagan Rose, Dewey Green, Brian Overton, and Fred Lamb. Ben Hetherington read several chapters and made a number of observations that are reflected in the book. Sammy Hetherington might not have been as interested in the book as Ben, but he contributed to it in his own unique ways.

Weiler wishes especially to acknowledge Anne Menkens and Lillian Menkens-Weiler, who have cheerfully listened to endless talk about "the book." Jesse Kalisher and Dustin Howes, two dear friends who passed away in 2017, were always supportive and encouraging about these ideas. And thanks go to Yonat Shimron, a loving partner with an eagle editorial eye.

As our dedication suggests, the imprint left by all four of our wonderful and loving parents shows up in everything we have ever done. The two of us come from very different worlds (one suburbs, one city), very different backgrounds (one Catholic, one Jewish), and have very different loyalties (one Red Sox, one Yankees). Our parents also brought us up in different ways (one more fixed, one more fluid). Yet the two of us find ourselves with more in common than not, which gives us some hope about the future, if people from different backgrounds talk to each other.

NOTES

Introduction

PAGE

x   *"My parents chose John Wayne": All the President's Men Revisited,* directed by
Peter Schnall, Discovery Channel, aired April 21, 2013, available at YouTube,
https://www.youtube.com/watch?v=Xo7KWzOgnf8. We realize, of course, that Jane
Fonda did not arrive on the political scene until after 1968, but, in the interview,
Scarborough connected her trip to Hanoi to the events of 1968.

xii   *Nearly 80 percent of:* Douglas Rivers, "What the Hell Happened? The Perils of
Polling in the 2016 US Elections" (presentation, Harvard University, Cambridge,
MA, April 24, 2017).

xiv   *But the Scarboroughs:* Joe Scarborough, Twitter, February 27, 2009, https://twitter
.com/JoeNBC/status/1260057924; Jeff Miller, "Recognizing the Life of George
Francis Scarborough," Congressional Record 157, no. 63 (2011), E840, https://www
.gpo.gov/fdsys/granule/CREC-2011-05-10/CREC-2011-05-10-pt1-PgE840/content
-detail.html.

xv   *Hence both sides:* To keep the coalition together, Democratic leaders had to avoid
talking about race. When they failed to, as Harry Truman did when he signed
Executive Order 9981, which integrated the armed forces in 1948, they ran the risk
of losing the South and, with it, its political dominance.

xvi   *Another result of the recent convergence:* Amnon Cavari and Guy Freedman, "From
Public to Publics: Variations in Issue Priorities of Americans" (prepared for presentation at the Annual Meeting of the Comparative Agendas Project, Edinburgh,
2017).

228

In a Pew Research Center poll: Pew Research Center, "Partisanship and Political Animosity in 2016," June 22, 2016, http://www.people-press.org/2016/06/22 /partisanship-and-political-animosity-in-2016/.

xx *They simply need to know:* James N. Druckman, Matthew S. Levendusky, and Audrey McLain, "No Need to Watch: How the Effects of Partisan Media Can Spread via Interpersonal Discussions," *American Journal of Political Science* 62, no. 1 (2018): 99–112; Jaime Settle, *Frenemies: How Social Media Polarizes America* (New York: Cambridge University Press, 2018).

1. Republicans Are from Mars, Democrats Are from Venus

2 *Most research on ordinary citizens:* David O. Sears and Christia Brown, "Childhood and Adult Political Development," in *The Oxford Handbook of Political Psychology,* ed. Leonie Huddy, David O Sears, and Jack S. Levy, 2nd ed. (New York: Oxford University Press, 2013), pp. 59–95.

Moral psychologist Jonathan Haidt: Jesse Graham et al., "Moral Foundations Theory: The Pragmatic Validity of Moral Pluralism," *Advances in Experimental Social Psychology* 47 (2013): 55–130.

3 *In fact, it is very common:* Christopher Ellis and James A. Stimson, *Ideology in America* (New York: Cambridge University Press, 2012).

4 *The most important of these differences:* Our thinking here borrows from the work of the psychologist John Jost. See especially John T. Jost et al., "Political Conservatism as Motivated Social Cognition," *Psychological Bulletin* 129 (2003): 339–75.

In their book Predisposed: John R. Hibbing, Kevin B. Smith, and John R. Alford, *Predisposed: Liberals, Conservatives, and the Biology of Political Differences* (New York: Routledge, 2013).

Given that the exercise: Ibid., p. 132.

5 *But the researchers also found:* Douglas R. Oxley et al., "Political Attitudes Vary with Physiological Traits," *Science* 321, no. 5896 (2008): 1667–70.

6 *It is plausible that humans:* Jonathan Haidt, *The Righteous Mind: Why Good People Are Divided by Politics and Religion* (New York: Vintage, 2013).

7 *In response to disgusting images:* Kevin Smith et al., "Disgust Sensitivity and Neurophysiology of Left-Right Political Orientations," *PLOS One* 6, no. 10: e25552, https://doi.org/10.1371/journal.pone.0025552.

These tendencies and reflexes: Olivia Goldhill, "The Shape of Your Brain Influences Your Political Opinions," Quartz, March 28, 2018, https://qz.com/1238929/your -political-views-are-influenced-by-the-size-of-your-brains-amygdala/. See also Kanai Ryota et al., "Political Orientations Are Correlated with Brain Structure in Young Adults," *Current Biology* 21, no. 8 (2011): 677–80.

These studies have their critics: David Sears levels what is probably the most critical treatment in David O. Sears, "College Sophomores in the Laboratory: Influences of a Narrow Data Base on Social Psychology's View of Human Nature," *Journal of Personality and Social Psychology* 51, no. 3 (1986): 515–30.

8 *For example, people who report:* Lene Aarøe, Mathias Osmundsen, and Michael Bang Petersen, "Distrust as a Disease Avoidance Strategy: Individual Differences in Disgust Sensitivity Regulate Generalized Social Trust," *Frontiers in Psychology* 7 (2016): 515–14.

People who report, for example, being particularly grossed out: Cindy D. Kam and Beth A. Estes, "Disgust Sensitivity and Public Demand for Protection," *Journal of Politics* 78, no. 2 (2016): 481–96.

10 *These two traits, openness and conscientiousness:* Alan S. Gerber et al., "Personality and Political Attitudes: Relationships Across Issue Domains and Political Contexts," *American Political Science Review* 104, no. 1 (2010): 111–33.

These people are, as a team of researchers has put it: Hibbing, Smith, and Alford, *Predisposed*, p. 104.

11 *As Jack Nicholson's Colonel Jessup:* Wikiquote, *A Few Good Men*, https://en .wikiquote.org/wiki/A_Few_Good_Men. Accessed February 5, 2018.

Describing one of her subjects, Janice: Arlie Russell Hochschild, *Strangers in Their Own Land: Anger and Mourning on the American Right* (New York: New Press, 2016), p. 166.

12 *One promotes homogeneity:* It is certainly true, however, that liberals' strong attachment to these values will create homogeneous groups of liberals, driving away those who don't agree.

13 *The four questions used:* Paul Sniderman actually used several of these items to great effect before Feldman did as part of his pathbreaking book with Thomas Piazza, *The Scar of Race* (Cambridge, MA: Harvard University Press, 1993). Feldman's work with the ANES created the four-item battery used here.

One area Feldman thought: This material is based on a personal interview with Professor Feldman, carried out on February 9, 2018.

16 *Thus, these people's political preferences:* George Lakoff, *Moral Politics*, 3rd ed. (Chicago: University of Chicago Press, 2016).

19 *For instance, the 2012 Cooperative Campaign Analysis Project:* This survey collected data from 44,998 United States citizens eighteen and older. Respondents were selected from YouGov's nonrandom online panel, with the final survey set to population benchmarks through a combination of matching and weighting. On the validity of using opt-in surveys, see Lynn Vavreck and Douglas Rivers, "The 2006 Cooperative Congressional Election Study," *Journal of Elections, Public Opinion & Parties* 18, no. 4 (2008): 355–66.

2. "A Hell of a Lot More Abstract"

22 *Even opposition to the Vietnam War:* Michael Dimock, "The Iraq-Vietnam Difference," Pew Research Center, May 15, 2002, http://www.pewresearch.org /2006/05/15/the-iraqvietnam-difference/.

But because of the centrality: Christopher H. Achen and Larry M. Bartels, *Democracy for Realists: Why Elections Do Not Produce Responsive Government* (Princeton, NJ: Princeton University Press, 2016).

23 *In survey after survey, US partisans:* See, for instance, Alan I. Abramowitz and
 Steven Webster, "The Rise of Negative Partisanship and the Nationalization of
 U.S. Elections in the 21st Century," *Electoral Studies* 41 (2016): 12–22.

24 *Nearly half of both Republicans and Democrats:* Pew Research Center,
 "Partisanship and Political Animosity in 2016."
 Partisans today demonstrate more prejudice: Shanto Iyengar and Sean J. Westwood,
 "Fear and Loathing Across Party Lines: New Evidence on Group Polarization,"
 American Journal of Political Science 59, no. 3 (2015): 690–707.
 Two-thirds of Americans: Michael X. Delli Carpini and Scott Keeter, *What
 Americans Know About Politics and Why It Matters* (New Haven, CT: Yale
 University Press, 1996).

25 *Since the late 1960s:* The term itself is Herbert McClosky's. The best-known treat-
 ments of Americans' lack of ideology from the era are Philip E. Converse, "The
 Nature of Belief Systems in Mass Publics," in *Ideology and Discontent*, ed. David
 Apter (New York: Free Press, 1964), pp. 206–61, and Lloyd A. Free and Hadley
 Cantril, *The Political Beliefs of Americans: A Study of Public Opinion* (New
 Brunswick, N.J.: Rutgers University Press, 1967).
 a term that two scholars: Donald Kinder and Nathan Kalmoe, "The Nature of
 Ideological Innocence in Mass Publics: Meaning and Measurement" (work-
 ing paper, 2013), https://nkalmoe.files.wordpress.com/2013/09/kinder-kalmoe-
 apsa2008.pdf.
 These "conflicted conservatives": Ellis and Stimson, *Ideology in America*.
 This suggests that the operational dimension: Larry M. Bartels, "Partisanship in the
 Trump Era" (working paper, Vanderbilt University, 2018).

26 *As a result, they needed to live under institutions:* Herbert McClosky, "Conservatism
 and Personality," *American Political Science Review* 52, no. 1 (1958): 27–45.

27 *William Jennings Bryan:* It is interesting to note how similar electoral college
 maps from the present day and the late 1800s look, just with the parties switched.
 William Jennings Bryan, the wild-eyed populist Democrat, won the states that
 Republicans tend to win these days. See Gary Miller and Norman Schofield,
 "Activists and Partisan Realignment in the United States," *American Political
 Science Review* 97, no. 2 (2003): 245–60.

28 *Over the last decade or so:* At our request, the CCAP began to include the four parenting items in 2008 to track its relationship to Americans' political behavior. After
 the publication of our first book in 2009, the CCES began to include the questions
 in its presidential election year surveys as well, allowing scholars to track the deepening and widening of the partisan-based worldview divide.
 People of a fixed: Our thinking here and throughout the book is heavily influenced
 by George Lakoff's work. See Lakoff, *Moral Politics: How Liberals and Conservatives
 Think*, 3rd ed. (Chicago: University of Chicago Press, 2016).

29 *Although it is difficult to find:* While we do not have 2012 data, Mitt Romney was a
 candidate in 2008 as well, and it seems unlikely that his appeal—that of a wealthy
 Mormon businessman—would have been any different with the fixed in 2008 than

it was in 2012. Because there are so few fluid Republicans, it is necessary to lump together those who provide either zero, one, or two fixed answers to the four parenting questions to provide a large-enough comparison group.

About 27 percent: The candidate who attracted a disproportionate share of the fixed vote in 2008 was former Arkansas governor Mike Huckabee. Among those with fixed worldviews, 21 percent of Republican primary voters cast their ballots for him. Only 13 percent of the less fixed did.

30 *Based on the primary voting results*: Some political scientists think worldview had a less important role in the 2016 primaries than we suggest. For example, in their March 2016 *Monkey Cage* blog post for the *Washington Post*, "Trump's Voters Aren't Authoritarians, New Research Says. So What Are They?" Eric Oliver and Wendy Rahn argue that "Trump voters are no more authoritarian than supporters of Ted Cruz or Marco Rubio." When we reanalyzed these data, we found Trump was clearly the choice among those with fixed worldviews. Among the fixed, 35 percent favored Trump, compared with 19 percent for Rubio and 13 percent for Cruz. The reason Rubio and Cruz supporters had, on average, high fixed worldview scores was because so few people with more fluid worldviews supported them. As we discuss in chapter 6, Trump attracted a relatively large chunk of less-fixed-worldview supporters, specifically those who also reported feeling very threatened by terrorism. We find the same pattern in the Democracy Fund's VOTER survey. Thanks to Eric and Wendy for generously sharing their data with us.

31 *Only he was necessary:* Yoni Applebaum, "'I Alone Can Fix It,'" *Atlantic*, July 21, 2016, https://www.theatlantic.com/politics/archive/2016/07/trump-rnc-speech -alone-fix-it/492557/.

32 *Among the latter group:* We covered some of this ground in our first book, *Authoritarianism and Polarization in American Politics* (Cambridge: Cambridge University Press, 2009).

While campaigning for the presidency: Jeffrey Goldberg, "Obama on Zionism and Hamas," *Atlantic*, May 12, 2008, https://www.theatlantic.com/international/archive /2008/05/obama-on-zionism-and-hamas/8318/.

Back in 2004, President George W. Bush: Richard Cohen, "Bush's War Against Nuance," *Washington Post*, February 17, 2004, https://www.washingtonpost.com /archive/opinions/2004/02/17/bushs-war-against-nuance/1f2af155-c701-47f9 -8dc0-84d270b4d1c5/?utm_term=.77729ad9878c.

Former Louisiana governor: Jonathan Chait, "Bobby Jindal: President Obama Caused Trump by Being Too Intellectual and Mature," *New York*, March 4, 2016, http://nymag.com/daily/intelligencer/2016/03/jindal-obama-caused-trump-by -being-too-mature.html.

33 *The response of one liberal:* Steve Benen, "Mitt Romney, Pandering Robot," *Washington Monthly*, March 22, 2011, https://washingtonmonthly.com/2011/03/22 /mitt-romney-pandering-robot/.

In the spring of 1974: David Skinner, "A Battle over Books," *Humanities* 31, no. 5

(2010), https://www.neh.gov/humanities/2010/septemberoctober/statement/battle
-over-books.

One activist, driving perhaps: This account is drawn from Rick Perlstein, *The Invisible Bridge: The Fall of Nixon and the Rise of Reagan* (New York: Simon & Schuster, 2015).

41 *That is not to say* everyone *is untrustworthy:* See Jeffry A. Simpson, "Psychological Foundations of Trust," *Current Directions in Psychological Science* 16, no. 5 (2007): 264–68.

Evolutionary psychologists believe: For example, see Michael L. Manapat, Martin A. Nowak, and David G. Rand, "Information, Irrationality, and the Evolution of Trust," *Journal of Economic Behavior and Organization* 90 (2013): S57–S75.

42 *To the fluid, the fixed:* Mario Procaccino, the working-class Democrat who ran against liberal Republican John Lindsay for mayor of New York City in 1969, accused Lindsay of being a "limousine liberal" for advocating fair housing policies that would never touch the kinds of neighborhoods Lindsay and his better-heeled supporters tended to live in.

43 *When people view themselves:* Naomi Ellemers, Russell Spears, and Bertjan Doosje, "Self and Social Identity," *Annual Review of Psychology* 53, no. 1 (2002): 161–86.

Steve Bannon: Alex Eisenstadt, "Bannon to Alabama, 'They Think You're a Pack of Morons,'" *Politico*, September 25, 2017, https://www.politico.com/story/2017/09/25/alabama-senate-bannon-strange-moore-243131.

44 *And only 16:* 2010 General Social Survey: 5 percent of whites said they'd not vote for a black presidential candidate; 2016 General Social Survey: 16 percent of whites oppose a close relative marrying a black person (down from 30 percent in 2006); 2017 Reuters/Ipsos: 5 percent of whites disagree that all races are equal, and 8 percent support white nationalism.

44 *The graph on page 45:* Only survey respondents who identify as white are included in the analysis for reasons that will become clear momentarily. It is not that the opinions of racial minorities do not matter; they matter profoundly. But the relationship between worldview and politics differs for whites and nonwhites.

47 *Similarly, our 2017 survey:* Martin Gilens, *Why Americans Hate Welfare: Race, Media, and the Politics of Antipoverty Policy* (Chicago: University of Chicago Press, 1999).

48 *Researchers typically measure:* Efrén O. Pérez, *Unspoken Politics: Implicit Attitudes and Political Thinking* (New York: Cambridge University Press, 2016).

50 *Although American Muslims:* Pew Research Center, "U.S. Muslims Concerned About Their Place in Society, but Continue to Believe in the American Dream," July 26, 2017, http://www.pewforum.org/2017/07/26/findings-from-pew-research-centers-2017-survey-of-us-muslims/.

51 *In fact, African Americans:* Hetherington and Weiler, *Authoritarianism and Polarization in American Politics.*

It is possible: See, for example, Efrén O. Pérez and Marc J. Hetherington,

"Authoritarianism in Black and White: Testing the Cross-Racial Validity of the Child Rearing Scale," *Political Analysis* 22, no. 3 (2014): 398–412.

Republicans have targeted: Donald R. Kinder and Lynn M. Sanders, *Divided by Color: Racial Politics and Democratic Ideals* (Chicago: University of Chicago Press, 1996); Tali Mendelberg, *The Race Card: Campaign Strategy, Implicit Messages, and the Norm of Equality* (Princeton, NJ: Princeton University Press, 2001).

Crime, urban unrest: Ian Haney López, *Dog Whistle Politics: How Coded Racial Appeals Have Reinvented Racism & Wrecked the Middle Class* (New York: Oxford University Press, 2014).

Given the way Republicans: Mark Peffley and Jon Hurwitz, *Justice in America: The Separate Realities of Blacks and Whites* (New York: Cambridge University Press, 2010).

52 *This turn among Republicans:* See, for instance, the argument in Shaun Bowler, Stephen P. Nicholson, and Gary M. Segura, "Earthquakes and Aftershocks: Race, Direct Democracy, and Partisan Change," *American Journal of Political Science* 50, no. 1 (2006): 146–59. The spread of anti-immigrant policies nationally can be seen as an outgrowth of this California-specific experience.

Increasingly representative of the party's views: Elspeth Reeve, "Steve King Wants to Protect the Border from Cantaloupe-Sized Calves," *Atlantic*, July 23, 2013, https://www.theatlantic.com/politics/archive/2013/07/steve-king-wants-protect -border-cantaloupe-sized-calves/312984/.

53 *Perhaps it ought not be:* Thierry Devos and Debbie S. Ma, "Is Kate Winslet More American Than Lucy Liu? The Impact of Construal Processes on the Implicit Ascription of a National Identity," *British Journal of Social Psychology* 47, no. 2 (2010): 191–215.

One striking experiment: Alexander Kuo, Neil Malhotra, and Cecilia Hyunjung Mo, "Social Exclusion and Political Identity: The Case of Asian American Partisanship," *Journal of Politics* 79, no. 1 (2017): 17–32.

54 *White eligible voters:* Jens Manuel Krogstad, "2016 Electorate Will Be the Most Diverse in U.S. History," Pew Research Center, February 3, 2016, http://www .pewresearch.org/fact-tank/2016/02/03/2016-electorate-will-be-the-most-diverse -in-u-s-history/.

56 *After Obama's endorsement:* Scott Clement and Sandhya Somashekhar, "After President Obama's Announcement, Opposition to Gay Marriage Hits Record Low," *Washington Post*, May 23, 2012, https://www.washingtonpost.com/politics /after-president-obamas-announcement-opposition-to-gay-marriage-hits-record -low/2012/05/22/gIQAlAYRjU_story.html?utm_term=.43c612009cfd.

57 *But a closer look:* Theda Skocpol and Vanessa Williamson, *The Tea Party and the Remaking of Republican Conservatism* (New York: Oxford University Press, 2012). *Fully 60 percent:* Marc J. Hetherington and Jonathan D. Weiler. "Authoritarianism and Polarization in American Politics, Still?," in *American Gridlock: The Sources, Character, and Impact of Political Polarization*, ed. James A. Thurber and Antoine Yoshinaka (New York: Cambridge University Press, 2015), 86–112.

Beginning with the war on poverty: Gilens, *Why Americans Hate Welfare.*
Fifteen years later: Michael Tesler, "The Spillover of Racialization into Health Care: How President Obama Polarized Public Opinion by Racial Attitudes and Race," *American Journal of Political Science* 56, no. 3 (2012): 690–704.

58 *By 1981:* Rick Perlstein, "Exclusive: Lee Atwater's Infamous 1981 Interview on the Southern Strategy," *Nation,* November 13, 2012.

3. Worlds Apart

63 *Rather, those with a fluid:* It is true that self-conscious consumer choices are increasingly and expressly political. Many liberals have boycotted Chick-fil-A in recent years because of the company's stated opposition to equal rights for gays and lesbians. Starbucks has been the target of conservative boycotts because of the perception that some of its holiday-season mugs and products represent a rejection of Christmas. Amazingly, the National Football League, perhaps America's most popular entertainment diversion, has become a focal point of growing partisan political tension, because of a series of protests during the national anthem, initially led by Colin Kaepernick and other black players objecting to police violence. In turn, President Trump has expressly called for the league to be shunned until the protesting players are disciplined or fired.

65 *Political consultant James Carville:* Carville made the comment in 1986, while working on a gubernatorial race. See Carrie Budoff Brown, "Extreme Makeover: Pennsylvania Edition," *Politico,* April 1, 2008, http://www.politico.com/news /stories/0408/9323.html.

66 *People who are fluid:* In an analysis of population density of the zip codes in which people live and their worldviews, we found a moderately strong correlation, suggesting the fixed prefer places with lower population density than the fluid do.
Arlie Hochschild observed: Hochschild, *Strangers in Their Own Land,* p. 19.
By an equally stark: Pew Research Center, "Political Polarization in the American Public," June 12, 2014, http://www.people-press.org/2014/06/12/political-polariza tion-in-the-american-public/.
Worldview, not politics: A similar dynamic can be seen in dating. Just as it shapes people's choices about where to live, the worldview divide also plays a clear role in guiding people's selection of romantic and life partners. Research suggests that people tend to date and marry those they agree with politically, despite the fact that politics is a low priority for most people. What brings these couples together is a shared worldview; the political connection, for most, is secondary. Just as few prospective home buyers would grill their real estate agents about where all the liberals live, few people think to put "seeking Democrat" or "seeking Republican" in their Match or Bumble profiles. People simply seem to prefer other people who match their sensibilities, just as they prefer residential areas.

67 *For most of the twentieth century:* Bill Bishop, *The Big Sort: Why the Clustering of Like-Minded America Is Tearing Us Apart* (Boston: Mariner Books, 2009).
In 1976: Ibid.

68 *Over the same period:* Emily Badger and Quoctrung Bui, "Why Republicans Don't Even Try to Win Cities Anymore," *New York Times,* November 3, 2016, https://www .nytimes.com/2016/11/03/upshot/why-republicans-dont-even-try-to-win-cities -anymore.html.

69 *It's this vision:* John B. Judis and Ruy Teixeira, *The Emerging Democratic Majority* (New York: Scribner, 2004).

    Each school district: Clare Malone, "One Pennsylvania County Sees the Future, and Not Everyone Likes It," FiveThirtyEight, October 17, 2016, https://fivethirtyeight .com/features/one-pennsylvania-county-sees-the-future-and-not-everyone-likes-it/.

    When the journalist: Joe Bageant, *Deer Hunting with Jesus: Dispatches from America's Class War* (New York: Broadway Books, 2008).

70 *When supervisors express:* Ibid.

    And people who have: Preelection polls in 2016 revealed that, among white voters, Trump led over Clinton by very wide margins among those who never moved from their hometowns. Conversely, Clinton attracted much more support than Trump from Americans who did leave home. And the farther they moved from their home-towns, the more supportive of Clinton these Americans were. Andrew McGill, "Many of Trump's Supporters Never Left Their Hometowns," *Atlantic,* October 6, 2016, https://www.theatlantic.com/politics/archive/2016/10/trump-supporters-hometowns/503033/.

71 *Such trips are time-intensive:* Daron R. Shaw and Scott Althaus, "Electoral College Strategies of American Presidential Campaigns from 1952 to 2016" (manuscript, University of Texas at Austin, February 2018).

    This was demonstrated: "Democratic vs. Republican Occupations," Verdant Labs, June 2, 2015, http://verdantlabs.com/blog/2015/06/02/politics-of-professions/. Accessed August 21, 2017.

72 *In 2016, Donald Trump:* Jon Huang et al., "Election 2016: Exit Polls," *New York Times,* November 8, 2016, https://www.nytimes.com/interactive/2016/11/08/us /politics/election-exit-polls.html.

    John Judis and Ruy Teixeira: Judis and Teixeira, *The Emerging Democratic Majority.*

73 *One such study:* Eitan D. Hersh and Matthew N. Goldenberg, "Democratic and Republican Physicians Provide Different Care on Politicized Health Issues," *Proceedings of the National Academy of Sciences* 113, no. 42 (2016): 11811–16.

75 *It probably helps:* Keith Laing, "Santorum Defends Calling Obama a 'Snob,'" *Ballot Box* (blog), The Hill, February 26, 2012, http://thehill.com/blogs/ballot-box/gop -presidential-primary/212593-santorum-defends-college-snob-remark.

76 *In July 2017:* Pew Research Center, "Sharp Partisan Divisions in Views of National Institutions," July 10, 2017, http://www.people-press.org/2017/07/10/sharp-partisan -divisions-in-views-of-national-institutions/.

    But perhaps the most: Hannah Fingerhut, "Republicans Skeptical of Colleges' Impact on U.S., but Most See Benefits for Workforce Preparation," Pew Research Center, July 20, 2017, http://www.pewresearch.org/fact-tank/2017/07/20

/republicans-skeptical-of-colleges-impact-on-u-s-but-most-see-benefits-for
-workforce-preparation/. Accessed August 21, 2017.

Nearly half of the Americans: Huang et al., "Election 2016."

78 *In 1963 conservative activist:* "William F. Buckley Jr. Harvard Faculty Quote,"
YouTube, https://www.youtube.com/watch?v=2nf_bu-kBr4.

The following year: Ronald Reagan, "Address on Behalf of Senator Barry Goldwater:
'A Time for Choosing,'" American Presidency Project, University of California at
Santa Barbara, http://www.presidency.ucsb.edu/ws/index.php?pid=76121.

Rick Santorum put it: Quoted in Neil Gross, "The Indoctrination Myth," *New York
Times,* March 4, 2012, http://www.nytimes.com/2012/03/04/opinion/sunday/college
-doesnt-make-you-liberal.html.

79 *Around the same time:* Geoffrey Layman, *The Great Divide: Religious and Cultural
Conflict in American Party Politics* (New York: Columbia University Press, 2001).

With Ronald Reagan promising: Ibid; Ryan L. Claassen, *Godless Democrats and
Pious Republicans? Party Activists, Party Capture, and the "God Gap"* (New York:
Cambridge University Press, 2015).

After all, evangelicals: Hetherington and Weiler, *Authoritarianism and Polarization
in American Politics.*

80 *Of all groups:* Ibid.

The result is that: Peter Beinart, "The Failure of the American Jewish Establishment," *New York Review of Books,* June 10, 2010, http://www.nybooks.com
/articles/2010/06/10/failure-american-jewish-establishment/.

Trump won by: Huang et al., "Election 2016."

The latter group: Ibid.

Other research has shown: Michael Barone, "The 49 Percent Nation," *National
Journal* 33, no. 23 (2001), available at http://www.uvm.edu/~dguber/POLS125
/articles/barone.htm.

82 *Asked about denomination:* Some might wonder about non-Christian religions.
These groups tend to be either overwhelmingly nonwhite (Muslims and Hindus) or
tiny in size (Jews). Hence they don't make much of a ripple in these analyses.

84 *Only with the forcible:* Howard Schuman et al., *Racial Attitudes in America: Trends
and Interpretations,* 2nd ed. (Cambridge, MA: Harvard University Press, 1997).

Contact is necessary: Gordon Willard Allport, *The Nature of Prejudice* (New York:
Perseus Books, 1979).

Scores of studies: Thomas F. Pettigrew and Linda R. Tropp, "A Meta-Analytic Test of
Intergroup Contact Theory," *Journal of Personality and Social Psychology* 90, no. 5
(2006): 751–83.

85 *Using door-to-door canvassing:* David Broockman and Joshua Kalla, "Durably
Reducing Transphobia: A Field Experiment on Door-to-Door Canvassing," *Science*
352, no. 6282 (2016): 220–24.

86 *A major turning point:* Jeremiah J. Garretson, "Exposure to the Lives of Lesbians
and Gays and the Origin of Young People's Greater Support for Gay Rights,"
International Journal of Public Opinion Research 27, no. 2 (2015): 277–88.

In his masterwork: Robert D. Putnam, *Bowling Alone: The Collapse and Revival of American Community* (New York: Simon & Schuster, 2001).

87 *More time spent:* Matthew S. Levendusky, James N. Druckman, and Audrey McLain, "How Group Discussions Create Strong Attitudes and Strong Partisans," *Research & Politics* 3, no. 2 (2016): 1–6.

4. A Day in the Life

93 *A recent estimate:* "The Political Fertility Gap," ABC News, August 23, 2006, http://abcnews.go.com/GMA/Politics/story?id=2344929&page=1.

94 *But the data show:* J. Eric Oliver, Thomas Wood, and Alexandra Bass, "Liberellas Versus Konservatives: Social Status, Ideology, and Birth Names in the United States," *Political Behavior* 38, no. 1 (2016): 55–81.

Its state-by-state map: Roberto A. Ferdman and Christopher Ingraham, "Where Cats Are More Popular Than Dogs in the U.S.—and All Over the World," *Washington Post*, July 28, 2014, https://www.washingtonpost.com/news/wonk/wp/2014/07/28/where-cats-are-more-popular-than-dogs-in-the-u-s-and-all-over-the-world/?utm_term=.70611a468164.

95 *Other studies:* Chris Wilson and Jonathan Haidt, "It's True: Liberals Like Cats More Than Conservatives Do," *Time*, February 18, 2014, http://time.com/8293/its-true-liberals-like-cats-more-than-conservatives-do/.

97 *Better still, they:* Kali Wilder, "The 2016 50 Best Companies for Diversity," *Black Enterprise*, November 9, 2016, http://www.blackenterprise.com/2016–50-best-companies-diversity/.

98 *This allowed YourMechanic:* Maddy Martin, "Politics and Personal Driving Preferences: Do Republicans and Democrats Drive Different Cars?," YourMechanic, February 12, 2016, https://www.yourmechanic.com/article/red-car-blue-car-do-political-views-predict-car-preferences.

99 *By driving one:* Dan Pera, "The Most Liberal Cars in America . . . and What We Need to Do About It," *I'm Right, Everyone Else Is Wrong* (blog), November 13, 2008, http://dantheman85x.blogspot.com/2008/11/most-liberal-cars-in-america-and-what.html.

In 2012: Amy Friedman, "Red and Blue Brands: How Democrats and Republicans Shop," *Time*, June 19, 2012, http://newsfeed.time.com/2012/06/19/red-and-blue-brands-how-democrats-and-republicans-shop/.

102 *A 2012 study:* Reid Wilson, "What Your Beer Says About Your Politics, in One Chart," *Washington Post*, January 8, 2014, https://www.washingtonpost.com/blogs/govbeat/wp/2014/01/08/what-your-beer-says-about-your-politics-in-one-chart/.

102 *Those on the political left:* Romana Khan, Kanishka Misra, and Vishal Singh, "Ideology and Brand Consumption," *Psychological Science* 24, no. 3 (2013): 326–33.

103 *An ingredient:* This is too good of a line to claim as our own. Our old friend Henry Laurence is the source.

There may be: Alan S. Gerber et al., "Personality and Political Attitudes: Relationships Across Issue Domains and Political Contexts," *American Political Science Review* 104, no. 1 (2010): 111–33.

104 *Some people have:* Hibbing, Smith, and Alford, *Predisposed.*

106 *In 2016,* Time: Chris Wilson, "Do You Eat Like a Republican or a Democrat?," *Time,* July 18, 2016, http://time.com/4400706/republican-democrat-foods/.

108 *Goodreads:* Patrick Brown, "You Are What You Read: Reading Habits of Voters," Goodreads, October 8, 2012, https://www.goodreads.com/blog/show/388-you-are -what-you-read-reading-habits-of-voters.

110 *TV shows like:* James Hibberd, "Republican vs. Democrat Survey: Who Watches the Best TV Shows?," *Entertainment Weekly,* December 6, 2011.

112 *"politicization of everything":* Tim Morris, "NFL, ESPN, Starbucks and the Politicization of Everything," *New Orleans Times-Picayune,* November 17, 2017, http://www.nola.com/opinions/index.ssf/2017/11/the_nfl_papa_johns_and_the _pol.html.

113 *Less than a quarter:* Jennifer Agiesta, "CNN Poll: Americans Split on Anthem Protests," CNN.com, September 30, 2017, https://www.cnn.com/2017/09/29 /politics/national-anthem-nfl-cnn-poll/index.html.

114 *A 2014 Facebook:* Winter Mason, "Politics and Culture on Facebook in the 2014 Midterm Elections," Facebook, October 27, 2014, https://www.facebook.com/notes /facebook-data-science/politics-and-culture-on-facebook-in-the-2014-midterm -elections/10152598396348859.

117 *Emerging research demonstrates:* Maggie Deichert, "The Content and Consequences of Partisan Cultural Stereotypes" (working paper, Vanderbilt University, February 2018).

118 *Similarly, the association:* Ibid.

119 *They are also more:* Iyengar and Westwood, "Fear and Loathing Across Party Lines."

5. Rattlers and Eagles

123 *This is a product of our tendency:* Donald R. Kinder and Cindy D. Kam, *Us Against Them: Ethnocentric Foundations of American Opinion* (Chicago: University of Chicago Press, 2010).

This was made clear: The succeeding treatment of the Robbers Cave experiment is paraphrased from ibid., pp. 4–5.

Two dozen boys: Muzafer Sherif et al., *Intergroup Conflict and Cooperation: The Robbers Cave Experiment* (1954/1961), Classics in the History of Psychology, http://psychclassics.yorku.ca/Sherif/. In narrating this story, we rely on Kinder and Kam's telling of it in *Us Against Them.*

126 *Indeed, the last several Congresses:* Marc J. Hetherington and Thomas Rudolph, *Why Washington Won't Work: Polarization, Political Trust, and the Governing Crisis* (Chicago: University of Chicago Press, 2015).

129 *In a Pew Research Center survey:* Pew Research Center, "Partisanship and Political Animosity in 2016.

130 *A 2017 survey:* The means were the following: Democrats rated the Republican
     Party at 27 degrees and Republicans at 25 degrees, which is not a statistically
     meaningful difference. Republicans rated the Democratic Party at 20 degrees and
     Democrats at 22 degrees — again, not a statistically meaningful difference.

131 *When, in 2010, researchers:* David A. Graham, "Really, Would You Let Your
     Daughter Marry a Democrat?," *Atlantic,* September 27, 2012, https://www.the
     atlantic.com/politics/archive/2012/09/really-would-you-let-your-daughter-marry
     -a-democrat/262959/.

132 *Research on race:* Iyengar and Westwood, "Fear and Loathing Across Party Lines."

133 *from near birth:* Lawrence A. Hirschfeld, *Race in the Making: Cognition, Culture,
     and the Child's Construction of Human Kinds* (Cambridge, MA: MIT Press, 1996).

134 *Rather, while their first instinct:* E. Ashby Plant and Patricia G. Devine, "Internal
     and External Motivation to Respond Without Prejudice," *Journal of Personality
     and Social Psychology* 75, no. 3 (1998): 811–32.
     As Anaïs Nin: Anaïs Nin uses this phrase in *The Seduction of the Minotaur* (1961),
     but credits the Talmud for the words. The reference probably comes from an
     English translation of the Talmudic tractate Berakhot (55b) by Rabbi Shemuel
     ben Nachmani. Similar statements have been made in an 1801 sermon by Sydney
     Smith, Henrik Sharling's *Nicolai's Marriage: A Picture of Danish Family Life*
     (1876), and many others. More information can be found at http://quoteinvestigator
     .com/2014/03/09/as-we-are/#note-8403–3.
     Humans are, in general, adept rationalizers: Haidt, *The Righteous Mind.*

135 *Instead, people start with certain beliefs:* Ziva Kunda, "The Case for Motivated
     Reasoning," *Psychological Bulletin* 108, no. 3 (1990): 480–98.
     Differences in perceptions have always existed: Hetherington and Rudolph, *Why
     Washington Won't Work.*

136 *five times a day:* Glenn Kessler and Meg Kelly, "President Trump Has Made More
     Than 2,000 False or Misleading Claims over 355 Days," *Washington Post,* January
     20, 2018.
     Indeed, more than 70 percent: 72 percent of Republicans reported believing that
     in January 2018 right after reports arose suggesting that Trump had paid porn star
     Stormy Daniels $130,000 to keep quiet about their affair.
     But for a long time: Brian J. Gaines et al., "Same Facts, Different Interpretations:
     Partisan Motivation and Opinion on Iraq," *Journal of Politics* 69, no. 4 (2007):
     957–74.

137 *All that had changed:* Pew Research Center, "A Decade Later, Iraq War Divides the
     Public," March 18, 2013, http://www.people-press.org/2013/03/18/a-decade-later
     -iraq-war-divides-the-public/.
     Over 80 percent of Republicans: "Post-ABC Poll: Privacy Rights and the War on
     Terrorism (March 5, 2006)," *Washington Post,* March 5, 2006, https://www
     .washingtonpost.com/page/2010-2019/WashingtonPost/2013/06/06/National
     -Politics/Polling/question_11096.xml?uuid=_QS_Cs64EeKFczuu6momRw.

138   *Curiously, given Democrats':* Pew Research Center, "Majority Views NSA Phone
      Tracking as Acceptable Anti-Terror Tactic," June 10, 2013, http://www.people
      -press.org/2013/06/10/majority-views-nsa-phone-tracking-as-acceptable-anti
      -terror-tactic/.
      All that was different: Justin McCarthy and Jeffrey M. Jones, "U.S. Economic
      Confidence Surges After Election," Gallup, November 15, 2016, http://news.gallup
      .com/poll/197474/economic-confidence-surges-election.aspx.
      An average of 84 percent: If one excludes the anomalously high approval ratings
      from Democrats in the months after September 11, 2001, the differences approach
      those of Obama.

139   *By contrast, from the:* Jeffrey M. Jones, "Obama Job Approval Ratings Most
      Politically Polarized by Far," Gallup, January 25, 2017, http://news.gallup.com
      /poll/203006/obama-job-approval-ratings-politically-polarized-far.aspx.
      Researchers have found evidence: Dan M. Kahan et al., "The Polarizing Impact
      of Science Literacy and Numeracy on Perceived Climate Change Risks," *Nature
      Climate Change* 2, no. 10 (2012): 732–35.

140   *Not only that:* In fact, numerous studies have shown that more educated conser-
      vatives are *more* likely to reject climate science than are less educated ones. One
      reason for this could be that the better educated pay more attention to news. And if
      the news sources they're paying more attention to include science-denying entities
      like Fox News, their cue-taking will filter the information about climate science in
      the ways we've described. It's also likely that better-educated people may simply be
      more adept rationalizers.
      More recent research: Brendan Nyhan and Jason Reifler, "When Corrections Fail:
      The Persistence of Political Misperceptions," *Political Behavior* 32, no. 2 (2010):
      303–30.
      For example, people: Brendan Nyhan and Jason Reifler, "Does Correcting Myths
      About the Flu Vaccine Work? An Experimental Evaluation of the Effects of
      Corrective Information," *Vaccine* 33, no 3 (2015): 459–64.
      When researchers provided data: Brendan Nyhan, "Fact-Checking Can Change
      Views? We Rate That as Mostly True," *New York Times,* November 5, 2016,
      https://www.nytimes.com/2016/11/06/upshot/fact-checking-can-change-views
      -we-rate-that-as-mostly-true.html?mcubz=3.

141   *It's no coincidence:* "Anti-vaxxing" ideas have been more commonly associated with
      the left, but polling shows that Trump voters were much more likely to be skeptical
      of vaccines than were Clinton voters.
      According to a Politico/*Morning Consult poll:* Steven Shepard, "Poll: Democrats
      More Likely to Believe Allegations of Sexual Misconduct," *Politico,* November 29,
      2017, https://www.politico.com/story/2017/11/29/sexual-misconduct-democrats
      -poll-267201.

142   *On Obama's birthplace:* There are so few fluid Republicans that we have to lump
      together those who provided 0, 1, or 2 fixed answers to create a large enough group
      for comparison.

143 *By marketing a powerful drug:* Tobin Smith, "FEAR & UNbalanced: Confessions of a 14-Year Fox News Hitman," Medium.com, May 26, 2017, https://medium.com/@tobinsmith_95851/how-roger-ailes-fox-news-scammed-americas-la-z-boy-cowboys-for-21-years-1996ee4a6b3e.

144 *During the golden age of objective journalism:* Jonathan Ladd, *Why Americans Hate the Media and How It Matters* (Princeton, NJ: Princeton University Press, 2011).

145 *Nothing close to all partisans:* Markus Prior, *Post-Broadcast Democracy: How Media Choice Increases Inequality in Political Involvement and Polarizes Elections* (New York: Cambridge University Press, 2007).

146 *The proliferation of cable:* Ibid.
   Before cable: Ted Koppel, "Olbermann, O'Reilly and the Death of Real News," *Washington Post,* November 12, 2010, http://www.washingtonpost.com/wp-dyn/content/article/2010/11/12/AR2010111202857.html.
   In the 1970s: By 2016, the three networks *combined* failed to best Cronkite's tally.
   Even accounting for: Ladd, *Why Americans Hate the Media.*
   The result has been: Prior, *Post-Broadcast Democracy.*

147 *The same was true:* Matthew Levendusky. *How Partisan Media Polarize America* (Chicago: University of Chicago Press, 2013).
   Note that the only: Amy Mitchell et al., "Political Polarization and Media Habits," Pew Research Center, October 21, 2014, http://www.journalism.org/2014/10/21/political-polarization-media-habits/.

148 *In one particularly fascinating study:* Druckman, Levendusky, and McLain, "No Need to Watch."

149 *The reach of social media:* Settle, *Frenemies.*
   Both sides exposed: Levendusky, *How Partisan Media Polarize America.*

150 *The researchers found:* A *New York Times* profile of Breitbart in 2017 noted a "strategic inversion of identity politics" in Breitbart's inflammatory and racially and culturally charged content. An article sounding alarm bells about black criminality was written by an African American writer. Anti-immigration content was sometimes penned by a Latino. And so on. Wil Hylton, "Down the Breitbart Hole," *New York Times,* August 16, 2017.

151 *more interested in reading material:* Howard Lavine, Milton Lodge, and Kate Freitas, "Threat, Authoritarianism, and Selective Exposure to Information," *Political Psychology* 26, no. 2 (2005): 219–44.
   One study of more than thirty news purveyors: Gary C. Jacobson, "Partisan Media and Electoral Polarization in 2012: Evidence from the American National Election Study," in *American Gridlock: The Sources, Character, and Impact of Political Polarization,* ed. James A. Thurber and Antoine Yoshinaka (New York: Cambridge University Press, 2015), 259–86.

152 *They identified:* Stefano Della Vigna and Ethan Kaplan, "The Fox News Effect," *Quarterly Journal of Economics* 122, no. 3 (2007): 1187–1234.

Most notable and novel: Jennifer Kavanagh and Michael D. Rich, *Truth Decay: An Initial Exploration of the Diminishing Role of Facts and Analysis in American Public Life* (Arlington, VA: Rand Corporation, 2018). The authors note that "when referring to increasing disagreement about facts, we mean increasing disagreement in areas where the existing data or analytical interpretations have not changed, or where they have been strengthened by new data and analysis."

153 *One study:* Andrew Guess, Brendan Nyhan, and Jason Reifler, "Selective Exposure to Misinformation: Evidence from the Consumption of Fake News During the 2016 U.S. Presidential Campaign" (manuscript, Dartmouth College, Hanover, NH, 2018), https://www.dartmouth.edu/~nyhan/fake-news-2016.pdf.
Part of the difference observed: Hunt Allcott and Matthew Gentzkow, "Social Media and Fake News in the 2016 Election," *Journal of Economic Perspectives* 31, no. 2 (2017): 211–36.

154 *According to a Gallup/Knight Foundation poll:* Knight Foundation, American Views: Trust, Media, and Democracy, January 15, 2018, https://knightfoundation .org/reports/american-views-trust-media-and-democracy.

6. "You're Not Going to Be Scared Anymore"

160 *When it was first:* Theodore Adorno et al., *The Authoritarian Personality* (New York: Harper & Brothers, 1950).
In a remarkable long form: Amanda Taub, "The Rise of American Authoritarianism," Vox, March 1, 2016, https://www.vox.com/2016/3/1/11127424/trump-authoritarian ism.

161 *And not only would he:* Jeremy Diamond, "Trump on Torture: 'We Have to Beat the Savages,'" CNN, March 6, 2016, http://www.cnn.com/2016/03/06/politics/donald -trump-torture/index.html.

163 *Indeed, if scholars of the 1950s:* Stanley Milgrim's famous experiments on confor- mity are something of an exception.

164 *These people, as the label would suggest:* Someone with a mixed worldview might have expressed a preference for, say, children who are independent (fluid) rather than respect their elders, obedient (fixed) rather than self-reliant, have good man- ners (fixed) rather than being curious, and are considerate (fluid) rather than well behaved.
If the fluid: To compare the fixed's or fluid's views with the mixed's views, we simply subtract the percentage of mixed-worldview people who believe something from the percentage of fluid who do or from the number of fixed who do.

165 *Other immigration questions:* Specifically, we followed the same process we described in the previous note but then averaged together the differences to each of the questions asked across four of the different issue domains examined in chapter 3.

166 *Between 2012 and 2016:* We leave to others the task of pinpointing the exact rea- son for such a dramatic change at that point in time, although a number of possible explanations do spring to mind. Most plausible to us is the violence perpetrated

against unarmed African American men by police and some private citizens during Barack Obama's second term in office. The killings that fostered the birth of the Black Lives Matter movement might have caused those already sympathetic to African Americans to become even more so. And after eight years of the Obama presidency, the persistence of such jarring and disturbing events might have reinforced those sympathies. In a similar vein, Donald Trump's attacks against African American culture in 2016 were more explicit than the usual Republican fare in presidential election campaigns. This, too, might have elicited a more pro–African American response than usual from those with fluid worldviews.

167 *Only 22 percent did:* Elahe Izadi, "Black Lives Matter and America's Long History of Resisting Civil Rights Protesters," *Washington Post,* April 19, 2016, https://www.washingtonpost.com/news/the-fix/wp/2016/04/19/black-lives-matters-and-americas-long-history-of-resisting-civil-rights-protesters/?utm_term=.73e47b33c9ea.

168 *In fact, civil rights:* Martin Gilens, *Affluence and Influence: Economic Inequality and Political Power in America* (Princeton, NJ: Princeton University Press, 2012).

172 *Donald Kinder:* Kinder and Sanders, *Divided by Color*, chap. 8.

173 *For example, five years:* "Poll Finds U.S. Split over Eavesdropping," CNN, January 11, 2006, http://www.cnn.com/2006/POLITICS/01/11/poll.wiretaps/.
Similarly, although torture: "Poll Results: Waterboarding Is Torture," CNN, November 6, 2007, http://www.cnn.com/2007/POLITICS/11/06/waterboard.poll/.

175 *That's because, under conditions of immediate threat:* Hetherington and Weiler, *Authoritarianism and Polarization in American Politics*, p. 114.

177 *In other words:* For a more detailed treatment of these issues, see Marc Hetherington and Elizabeth Suhay, "Authoritarianism, Threat, and Americans' Support for the War on Terror," *American Journal of Political Science* 55, no. 3 (2011): 546–60.

178 *Molly Ball summed up:* Molly Ball, "Donald Trump and the Politics of Fear," *Atlantic,* September 2, 2016, https://www.theatlantic.com/politics/archive/2016/09/donald-trump-and-the-politics-of-fear/498116/.
For example, a 2016 CNN/ORC poll: Jennifer Agiesta, "Poll: Concern About Terrorist Attack at Highest Level Since 2003," CNN.com, June 23, 2016, https://www.cnn.com/2016/06/23/politics/terror-attack-poll/index.html.
Ball reported: Ball, "Donald Trump and the Politics of Fear."

180 *This may explain why Bob Woodward:* Julia Fair, "Bob Woodward on Trump's Presidency: 'This Is a Test' for the Media," *USA Today,* November 14, 2017, https://www.usatoday.com/story/news/politics/2017/11/14/bob-woodward-trumps-presidency-this-test-media/863917001/.

181 *As he said to Larry O'Connor:* Josh Marshall, "Predatory, Aggressive and Childish," Talking Points Memo, November 2, 2017, http://talkingpointsmemo.com/edblog/predatory-aggressive-and-childish.

183 *In a January 2018 survey:* Mike Allen and Jonathan Swan, "Exclusive Poll: GOP Turns on FBI," Axios, February 3, 2018, https://www.axios.com/gop-turns-on-fbi-survey-78c4f486-8755-4c9e-be99-a1567bd3a625.html.

A late-2017 survey: Andrew Guess, Brendan Nyhan, and Jason Reifler, "'You're Fake News!' The 2017 Poynter Media Trust Survey," Poynter, November 29, 2017, https://poyntercdn.blob.core.windows.net/files/PoynterMediaTrustSurvey 2017.pdf.

184 *More worrying still:* Ibid.

185 *Instead, Shattuck said:* Jessica Shattuck, "I Loved My Grandmother. But She Was a Nazi," *New York Times*, March 24, 2017, https://www.nytimes.com/2017/03/24 /opinion/i-loved-my-grandmother-but-she-was-a-nazi.html.

187 *From Roosevelt to Reagan:* Richard E. Neustadt, *Presidential Power and the Modern Presidents* (New York: Simon & Schuster, 1991).

7. Our Common Fate

191 *By the 2010s:* Cas Mudde, "The 2012 Stein Rokkan Lecture: Three Decades of Populist Radical Right Parties in Western Europe. So What?'" *European Journal of Political Research* 52 (2013): 1–19.
     Rather, they tapped: Larry Bartels, "The 'Wave' of Right-Wing Populist Sentiment Is a Myth," *Washington Post*, June 21, 2017, https://www.washingtonpost.com /news/monkey-cage/wp/2017/06/21/the-wave-of-right-wing-populist-sentiment -is-a-myth/.

192 *As two scholars:* Liesbet Hooghe and Gary Marks, "Cleavage Theory Meets Europe's Crises: Lipset, Rokkan, and the Transnational Cleavage," *Journal of European Public Policy* 25, no. 1 (2017).

193 *In the process:* Bart Bonikowski, "Ethno-Nationalist Populism and the Mobilization of Collective Resentment," *British Journal of Sociology* 68 (2017): S1.
     It has made it: Sasha Polakow-Suransky, "White Nationalism Is Destroying the West," *New York Times*, October 12, 2017, https://www.nytimes.com/2017/10/12 /opinion/sunday/white-nationalism-threat-islam-america.html.

194 *GreenLeft Party tripled:* Jon Henley, "GreenLeft Proves to Be Big Winner in Dutch Election," *Guardian*, March 16, 2017.

195 *These findings mirror*: Karen Stenner offers evidence for a worldview divide in Europe using a somewhat different measure. Stenner, *The Authoritarian Dynamic* (New York: Cambridge University Press, 2005).

197 *Notably, this was:* Teresa Talò, "Public Attitudes to Immigration in the Aftermath of the Migration Crisis" (policy brief) Robert Schuman Centre for Advanced Studies, (September 2017), p. 2, http://cadmus.eui.eu/bitstream/handle /1814/48044/RSCAS_PB_2017_23.pdf?sequence=1&isAllowed=y.
     "the euro is our common fate": Quentin Peel, "German MPs Clash on Future of Eurozone," *Financial Times*, December 15, 2010.
     And at least another: United Nations High Commission on Refugees, "Syria Regional Refugee Response: Inter-agency Information Sharing Portal," March 30, 2017, http://data.unhcr.org/syrianrefugees/regional.php.

198 *Crucially, however:* Talò, "Public Attitudes to Immigration."
     It also drew: Von Paul Blickle et al., "The AfD Profits from Non-voters and Merkel

Defectors," *Die Zeit*, September 25, 2017, http://www.zeit.de/politik/deutschland
/2017-09/german-election-alternative-for-germany-angela-merkel.

199 *It is hard to imagine:* As remarkable as these results are, they may understate the
fixed/fluid gap among native-born Germans. Because the German Election Study
did not ask whether people were native-born or immigrant, these results include
both groups. Therefore, a fair number of fixed-worldview immigrants who presumably would be repelled by the AfD, much like African Americans in the United
States might be repulsed by Republicans despite having fixed worldviews, were
certainly included in the analysis. The relationship between worldview and voting
should be strongest, meanwhile, for the dominant societal group — in the German
case, native-born ethnic Germans. So there is good reason to think that the results
actually underestimate how disproportionately fixed-worldview Germans support
the AfD and fluid-worldview Germans support the Green Party.

200 *By railing against:* Talò, "Public Attitudes to Immigration."

201 *But the backlash against:* George Parker, "How David Cameron Lost His Battle for
Britain," *Financial Times*, December 18, 2016, https://www.ft.com/content
/3482b434-c37d-11e6–81c2-f57d90f6741a.

202 *But as the writer:* Ronald Brownstein, "Culture Is Replacing Class as the Key
Political Divide," *Atlantic Monthly*, June 30, 2016, https://www.theatlantic.com
/politics/archive/2016/06/britain-united-states/489410/.
Interviews with dozens: Justin Gest, *The New Minority: White Working-Class Politics
in an Age of Immigration and Inequality* (New York: Oxford University Press,
2016).

203 *Such complaints, about violent:* Ibid., pp. 59–61.
Indeed, the regions: "Hard Evidence: How Areas with Low Immigration Voted
Mainly for Brexit," Conversation, July 8, 2016, http://theconversation.com/hard
-evidence-how-areas-with-low-immigration-voted-mainly-for-brexit-62138.
In London itself: Brownstein, "Culture Is Replacing Class."
The demographics: David Goodhart, *The Road to Somewhere: The Populist Revolt
and the Future of Politics* (London: Hurst, 2017).

204 *The "anywheres" tend to value:* John Judis, "The Conflict Tearing Apart British
Politics: An Interview with David Goodhart," Talking Points Memo, June 22, 2017,
https://talkingpointsmemo.com/cafe/david-goodhart-on-the-conflict-tearing-apart
-british-and-american-politics.
Indeed, numerous analyses: Brownstein, "Culture Is Replacing Class."
Another poll of twelve thousand: Zack Beauchamp, "White Riot," Vox, September
19, 2016, https://www.vox.com/2016/9/19/12933072/far-right-white-riot-trump
-brexit.
And yet another reported: "Hard Evidence."
Those living in small towns: Will Jennings et al., *Cities and Towns: The 2017
General Election and the Social Divisions of Place* (London: New Economics
Foundation, October 2017), http://neweconomics.org/wp-content/uploads/2017/10/
FINAL-CITIES-AND-TOWNS.pdf.

205 *France's national ethos:* James Dennison and Teresa Taló, "Explaining Attitudes to Immigration in France" (working paper, European University Institute, Robert Schuman Centre for Advanced Studies, Migration Policy Centre, Florence, Italy, 2017), http://cadmus.eui.eu/bitstream/handle/1814/46245/RSCAS_2017_25 .pdf?sequence=1&isAllowed=y.

206 *When she first ran:* Rishi Iyengar, "Far Right Politicians Will Go on Trial for Comparing Muslims to Nazis," *Time,* September 23, 2015, http://time.com/4045803 /marine-le-pen-muslims-nazis-trial/.
One of the engineers: Michael Crowley, "The Man Who Wants to Unmake the West," *Politico,* March/April 2017, https://www.politico.com/magazine/story/2017/03 /trump-steve-bannon-destroy-eu-european-union-214889.
One observer noted: Sasha Polakow-Suransky, "Is Democracy in Europe Doomed?," *New York Review of Books,* October 16, 2017, http://www.nybooks.com/daily/2017 /10/16/is-democracy-in-europe-doomed/.

207 *And, again, the results demonstrate*: Thank you to Pavlos Vasilopoulos of Sciences Po who analyzed these data for us under a very short deadline. Thanks, too, to Martial Foucault, the director of the French Election Study, who allowed us to use these results even though the data were still officially embargoed at the time of our writing.

208 *Instead, 72 percent:* Another 28 percent of the fluid and 19 percent of the fixed said they neither agreed nor disagreed.
Only 19 percent: Similarly, 52 percent of the mixed said they agreed there were too many immigrants, twenty points less than the fixed and twenty-four points more than the fluid.

209 *That means the threat:* Bartels, "The 'Wave' of Right-Wing Populist Sentiment."
It established universal health care: Signild Vallgårda, Allan Krasnik, and Karsten Vrangbæk, *Health Care Systems in Transition: Denmark* (Copenhagen: European Observatory on Health Care Systems, 2001).
It has robust: Chris Weller, "These 10 Countries Have the Best Parental Leave Policies in the World," *Business Insider,* August 22, 2016, http://www.business insider.com/countries-with-best-parental-leave-2016-8.
The most popular: "Copenhageners Love Their Bikes," Denmark.com, http://denmark.dk/en/green-living/bicycle-culture/copenhageners-love-their-bikes/.
It did so in 1989: Pew Research Center, "Gay Marriage Around the World," August 8, 2017, http://www.pewforum.org/2017/08/08/gay-marriage-around-the -world-2013/.
A recent survey: "Denmark the 'Happiest Country' and Burundi 'the Least Happy,'" BBC News, March 16, 2016, http://www.bbc.com/news/world-europe-35824033.

210 *For example, the Danish:* Arwa Damon and Tim Hume, "Denmark Adopts Controversial Law to Seize Asylum Seekers' Assets," CNN.com, January 26, 2016, https://www.cnn.com/2016/01/26/europe/denmark-vote-jewelry-bill-migrants /index.html.
In an especially striking move: Rick Noack, "In an Effort to Limit Migrants'

Influence, a Danish City Wants Its Residents to Eat Pork," *Washington Post,*
January 20, 2016, https://www.washingtonpost.com/news/worldviews/wp
/2016/01/20/a-danish-city-wants-its-residents-to-eat-pork-to-defend-the
-nation/?utm_term=.6dbaf2d07da0.

Its founder, Pia Kjaersgaard: Rachael Cerrotti, "Sweden Was Among the Best
Countries for Immigrants. That's Changing," PRI.org, September 11, 2017, https://
www.pri.org
/stories/2017-09-11/sweden-was-among-best-countries-immigrants-thats-changing.

"If they want to turn Stockholm": Richard Milne, "Sweden Considers Closing the
Bridge to Denmark," *Financial Times,* December 3, 2015, https://www.ft.com
/content/b2a11dd2-99bd-11e5-bdda-9f13f99fa654.

One party leader: Caroline Mortimer, "'Religious Apartheid': Leading Danish
Politician Calls for Ban on Muslim Refugees," *Independent* (UK), July 29, 2016,
http://www.independent.co.uk/news/world/europe/denmark-muslim-refugees-ban
-islam-apartheid-asylum-seekers-migrants-a7161786.html.

211   *Investigators quickly discovered:* Andrew Higgins and Melissa Eddy, "Anger of
Suspect in Danish Killings Is Seen as Only Loosely Tied to Islam," *New York Times,*
February 16, 2015, https://www.nytimes.com/2015/02/17/world/europe/copenhagen
-denmark-attacks.html.

This anecdote might help: Caroline Mortimer, "A Third of Danish People Believe
the Country Is at War with Islam, Survey Says," *Independent* (UK), July 28, 2016,
http://www.independent.co.uk/news/world/europe/denmark-third-of-danish-people
-believe-war-with-islam-muslims-a7159941.html.

According to OECD data: "Foreign-Born Population," Organization for European
Cooperation and Development, https://data.oecd.org/migration/foreign-born
-population.htm. Accessed February 16, 2018.

212   *That being said, their demagogic appeals:* Mudde, "The 2012 Stein Rokkan
Lecture."

213   *And these parties:* Bartels, "The 'Wave' of Right-Wing Populist Sentiment."
The common thread: Mudde, "The 2012 Stein Rokkan Lecture."

Conclusion

215   *In a 2013 report:* Republican National Committee, "Growth and Opportunity
Project," March 2013, available at https://www.politico.com/story/2013/03/rnc
-report-growth-and-opportunity-088987.

217   *"Bull-horn politics":* "Trump and the Academy," *Economist,* September 1, 2016,
https://www.economist.com/news/united-states/21706341-political-science
-refashions-itself-deal-republican-nominee-trump-and. The term is from a quote
by Matthew MacWilliams.

219   *The distraction:* Nolan M. McCarty, Keith T. Poole, and Howard Rosenthal,
Polarized America: The Dance of Inequality and Unequal Riches (Cambridge, MA:
MIT Press, 2008).

the lowest levels of income and wealth inequality: Thomas Piketty, *Capital in the Twenty-First Century,* translated by Arthur Goldhammer (Cambridge, MA: Belknap Press of Harvard University Press, 2014).

220 *Especially alarming, the economists:* Anne Case and Angus Deaton, "Rising Midlife Morbidity and Mortality, US Whites," *Proceedings of the National Academy of Sciences* 112, no. 49 (2015): 15078–83.

That sense of grievance: Ross Douthat, "In Search of a Good Emperor," *New York Times,* April 5, 2017, https://www.nytimes.com/2017/04/05/opinion/in-search-of -a-good-emperor.html.

221 *In 2000:* These data come from Election Day exit polls tabulated by the Roper Center. "How Groups Voted," Roper Center for Public Opinion Research, https://ropercenter.cornell.edu/polls/us-elections/how-groups-voted/. Accessed April 12, 2018.

Whereas a third: Rebecca Ballhaus and Brody Mullins, "No Fortune 100 CEOs Back Republican Donald Trump," *Wall Street Journal,* September 23, 2016, https://www.wsj.com/articles/no-fortune-100-ceos-back-republican-donald-trump -1474671842.

222 *The resulting conflicts between climate haves and have-nots:* Our colleague, David Rohde, had the inspiration for this scenario.

INDEX

Numbers in italics refer to illustrations.